The 10-Point Test of a Great Small Town

1. **Screen test.** If it's love at first sight, score 1 point.

2. **Downtown test.** If the town center is well maintained and busy on a weekday, score 1 point. If the town is a county seat, add 1 bonus point.

3. **High school test.** Stop by for a visit. Ask the principal what makes the school exceptional. If you get a convincing answer, score 1 point. If there's a college in town, add 1 bonus point.

4. **Wal-Mart test.** A supermarket also will do. Shop for something. If you feel comfortable with other shoppers and are treated with courtesy, score 1 point.

5. **Population test.** If the population of the town is growing, score 1 point.

6. **Walk-in-the-park test.** If you can imagine using one or more of the public parks, score 1 point. If the town has a recreational center, a YMCA, or a Boys & Girls Club, score 1 bonus point.

7. **Hospital test.** If there's a hospital in town, score 1 point.

8. **Home-town bank test.** If there are at least three banking companies in town, score 1 point. If one or more of the banks is locally owned, add 1 bonus point each.

9. **Library test.** If the library has a good collection of books on tape and videos, and ample Internet access stations, score 1 point. Ask the reference librarian for the name of the best restaurant in town.

10. **Local restaurant test.** Have a meal at the restaurant locals say is best. If they're right, score 1 point.

Adding up the score: If the town scores 8 points or more, you may have found a very nice small town. If it scores less but you're smitten by the place, move there and make it better—that's how small towns work. For an interpretation of the 10-Point Test, please turn to pages 7–9.

Making Your Move to One of

America's Best Small Towns

Norm Crampton

M. Evans and Company, Inc.
New York

M. Evans and Company
216 East 49th Street
New York, New York 10017
www.mevans.com

Library of Congress Cataloging-in-Publication Data

Crampton, Norman.
    Making your move to one of America's best small towns / Norm Crampton.
      p.   cm.
    ISBN 0-87131-988-8
    1. Cities and towns—Ratings—United States. 2. Urban-rural migration—United States. I. Title: America's best small towns. II. Title
    HT123 .C6385 2002
    307.76′0973—dc21   2002029805

Printed in the United States of America

9 8 7 6 5 4 3 2 1

Contents

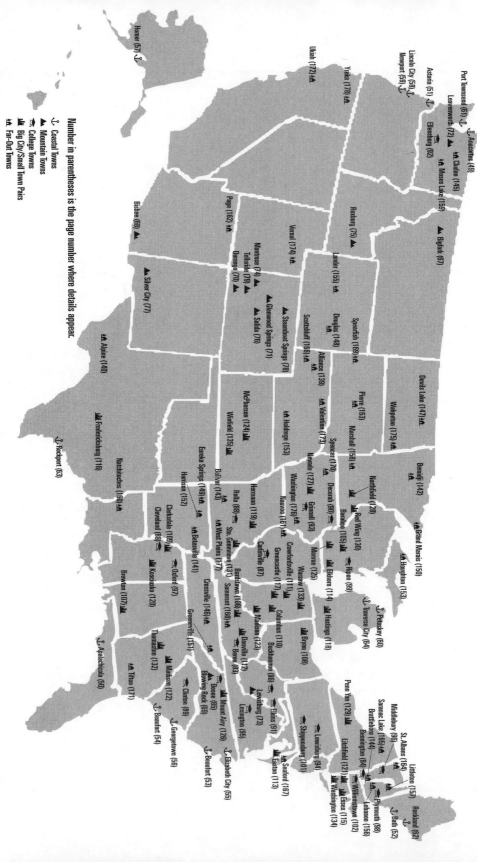

Number in parentheses is the page number where details appear.

⚓ Coastal Towns
▲ Mountain Towns
🎓 College Towns
🏙 Big City/Small Town Pairs
🏙 Far-Out Towns

Homer (57) ⚓

Lincoln City (58) ⚓🏙
Newport (59) ⚓🏙

Astoria (51) ⚓
Ukiah (172) 🏙

Port Townsend (61) ⚓
Leavenworth (72) ▲🏙
Yreka (178) 🏙
Ellensburg (92) ▲
⚓ Anacortes (49)
🏙 Chelan (145)
🏙 Moses Lake (159)

Bishee (68) ▲
Page (162) 🏙
Rexburg (75) ▲
▲ Bigfork (67)

Vernal (174) 🏙
Lander (155) 🏙
Douglas (148) 🏙
Spearfish (169) 🏙
Devils Lake (147) 🏙

Montrose (74) ▲
Telluride (79) ▲
Durango (70) ▲
▲ Steamboat Springs (78)
Scottsbluff (166) 🏙
Alliance (139) 🏙
Pierre (163) 🏙
Wahpeton (175) 🏙

▲ Silver City (77)
🏙 Glenwood Springs (71)
🏙 Salida (76)
McPherson (124) 🏙
Holdrege (153) 🏙
Valentine (173) 🏙

🏙 Alpine (140)
Winfield (135) 🏙
Marshall (158) 🏙
Bemidji (142) 🏙

🏙 Fredericksburg (116)
Eureka Springs (149) 🏙
Bolivar (143) 🏙
Spencer (170) 🏙
Neenah (127) 🏙
Decorah (99) 🏙
Northfield (128) 🏙
🏙 Grand Marais (150)

⚓ Rockport (63)
Harrison (152)
Rolla (88) 🏙
Washington (176) 🏙
Grinnell (93)
Baraboo (105) 🏙
Red Wing (130) 🏙
🏙 Houghton (153)

Natchitoches (160) 🏙
Clarksdale (109) 🏙
Cleveland (80) 🏙
Ste. Genevieve (137)
🏙 West Plains (177)
Hermann (119) 🏙
Nauvoo (161) 🏙
Monroe (125) 🏙
Elkhart (114) 🏙
Ripon (99) 🏙

Oxford (97) ⚓
Kosciusko (120) 🏙
Crossville (146) 🏙
Bardstown (106) 🏙
Crawfordsville (111) 🏙
Castleville (87)
Greencastle (117) 🏙
Wabasha (133) 🏙
Hastings (118) 🏙
⚓ Petoskey (60)
⚓ Traverse City (64)

Brewton (107) 🏙
Madison (122) 🏙
Somerset (168) 🏙
Danville (123) 🏙
Columbus (110) 🏙
Bryan (108) 🏙

Greenville (151) 🏙
Thomaston (132) 🏙
Greenville (115) 🏙
Buchannon (86) 🏙
Madison (123) 🏙

Madison (122) 🏙
Blowing Rock (69) 🏙
Berea (83) 🏙
Lewisburg (73)
Elkins (91) 🏙

Clinton (89) ⚓
Mount Airy (126) 🏙
Lexington (95)
Penn Yan (129) 🏙

Tifton (171) 🏙
⚓ Georgetown (56)
⚓ Beaufort (54)
⚓ Elizabeth City (55)
⚓ Beaufort (53)
⚓ Seaford (167)
🏙 Shippensburg (101)
Lewisburg (94) 🏙
Sanasac Lake (185) 🏙
Brattleboro (84) 🏙
Bennington (84) 🏙
Middlebury (96) 🏙
St. Albans (164) 🏙
Litchfield (121) 🏙
Easton (113) 🏙
Washington (134) 🏙
Williamstown (102) 🏙
Lebanon (156) 🏙
Plymouth (98) ⚓
Essex (115) ⚓
Bath (52) ⚓
Rockland (62) ⚓
Littleton (157) 🏙
🍎 Apalachicola (50)

Chapter 1:

Flying over Small Town USA

Why Streetwise City Kids Daydream about Small-Town Lifestyles

When I was growing up on the northwest side of Chicago, in Congressman Danny Rostenkowski's district, every summer they used to ship us by railroad out to a rural county for a few weeks of fresh air. The camp was only forty miles from downtown Chicago, but it might as well have been in the Belgian Congo. To us schoolkids in a working-class neighborhood decades before the Internet, everything that mattered in the world was contained in two places—the streets where we lived and the seasonal attractions that took us to selected other parts of the city. If we ever reflected on the possible pleasures of life elsewhere—and I don't think we ever did except for a twinge when they loaded us on the train for summer camp—most of us would have said that civilization ended at the city limits. Everyone knew there were no movie theaters, drug

stores, subways, crowds, Major League ballparks, St. Patty's Day parades, or Mafia hits out there, where the rail tracks bent over the horizon.

Which raises the question many years later: Why would anyone in his right mind choose to live anywhere but the city? Cities *are* civilization. Cities are symphony orchestras, bookstores, cathedrals, medical centers, public transportation, galleries, boutiques, neighborhood bars, pastrami on rye, ethnic variety, fabulous personalities, and everywhere crowds of people you've never seen before and may never see again. Cities are high speed, hard-hearted, demanding, and dangerous—endearing qualities if you have grown up as a city kid. "If you can make it here, you can make it anywhere," you tell yourself, taking pride in your urban upbringing.

At first glance, American small towns appear to be exactly the opposite. They are stoplights on the road to something better. They are sentimental Norman Rockwell paintings or dusty settings of sleepy stories or the locale of corny Christmas movies starring Jimmy Stewart. They are slower, safer, cheaper, and much less demanding than cities—definitely not the stuff that legends are made of.

Yet one day something may happen in your city environment and you begin to wonder whether you can trade some of your urban stock for a stake in a small town. Your company may offer you a managerial position in a factory in the boonies. Or a relative who's made a success of a small town enterprise may invite you to bring your special skills into the hinterlands and become a part owner. Or your offspring may enroll in a college in a small town, you start to spend time there, and the place grows on you. Or you hop off the urban treadmill, take early retirement, and start looking for a new home base that will help stretch your resources into, you hope, a gloriously golden old age, a boomer at peace.

Small town options can creep into your line of sight just like that, innocently and openly. You are bemused, and your friends are amused, when you speculate on the possibilities of relocation. Of course, you tell yourself out loud, there would be no permanent commitment to small town America, just a dalliance, an affair alfresco. You will not forsake the city but only burnish your urban patina—a city kid having a fling in Big Sky or the Panhandle or the Western Slope or deepest Dixie.

In my case, it was Dixie. I met and fell in love with a lady who had been reared in a small town in Mississippi. As a city-based married couple we began making pilgrimages into the Deep South for the usual and customary gatherings—holidays, triple-digit birthdays, funerals, things of that sort. As a

newcomer to the southern small-town scene, I was immediately taken prisoner by a large company of kissin' cousins—brothers, sisters, aunts, and uncles, an explosion of relationships that eclipsed anything I had ever known growing up in a small nuclear urban family. My southern family believes in frequent large gatherings for any reason or no reason, with plenty of food and drink and everyone crowded around huge tables. My in-laws are intelligent, articulate, good-natured, broadminded, well traveled, and totally opposite the popular notion of the small-town persona.

You can imagine the impression those southern trips made on me. Every time we drove back home to our city neighborhood I would raise the question: "What do you think: Could we live in a place like that?" I was intrigued with the thought, in part because it was so radically different. But some years passed as we reared a young family and developed our careers in the Chicago area.

In 1990, a job opportunity in Indiana gave us an option to move to a small town. My new office was on a university campus in a city of about 75,000, and we briefly considered living there until we tallied everything that was missing in this faux-urban intersection—there were none of the amenities of the world-class place we were leaving behind, none of the charm and intimacy of a much smaller place. So we decided that I would commute. We would make our home in a small town and I would make our living in the metropolitan area down the interstate highway. Not a bad idea: two totally separate places, one for the money, two for the—well, whatever came along. We selected, sight unseen, a small town that we knew only because friends had sent their kids to the classy little college located there. Our new home was Greencastle, population 7,000, the seat of Putnam County in west central Indiana.

I need to explain the difference between a small town and a suburb, and I'll go into this more later in the chapter. But you'll get the picture quickly if you remember the last time you flew on a clear night and glanced out the airplane window. You saw how cities and their suburban satellites glow in large clusters against the dark landscape. In parts of the United States, including most of the Atlantic Coast from Norfolk to Portland, around the Great Lakes from Milwaukee to Cleveland, and up the Pacific shore from San Diego to San Francisco, bright lights fill the night sky as far as you can see.

But flying over other parts of the nation on a cloudless night without a moon, especially southwest from the Appalachian Mountains, you look out the window and see mostly dark landscape, relieved here and there by little clusters of light where roads intersect. Some of these spots of light are the small settlements that I show you in this book. All of them are in rural counties, or what the Census Bureau calls in its reverse lingo, *nonurban* areas, meaning they are not within a county that is classified as part of a metropolitan area, like the four counties composing the Denver-Boulder-Greeley metro area (Adams, Arapahoe, Douglas, and Jefferson). This yellow tape that I'm wrapping around metro areas excludes from my definition of *small town* hundreds of lovely little places on the outskirts of cities, suburbs with names like Winnetka and Shaker Heights and Newton and Santa Barbara. Sorry, suburbanites—you may be justly proud of your community and culture, but it is tied much too closely to a big urban center for you to develop a distinctive small-town personality of your own.

How to Spot Where Urban-Suburban Ends and Rural–Small Town Begins

If you want to lease a jet and pack the family in for some night cruising in search of a neat small town, do it—and if there's room for a hitchhiker, please take me along! But you do not have to get airborne for this mission. Hop in the car and start driving into the countryside, in daylight. After you pass the last subdivision and clock at least twenty more miles through unoccupied territory—farmland, perhaps—you can raise your small town antenna and begin paying attention to the signals.

The small towns that I describe in this book have certain basic features that attract and retain residents. Common sense tells you what the essentials are: housing, jobs, stores, schools. You can make a longer list including parks, churches, and recreational and social services, and you'll find an inventory like that, with each town included, in the reference section, Chapter 6. But a small town with any future prospects needs just two things, and if it has them, the other necessities fall into place. The two essentials are:

- A high school
- A hospital

The high school and the hospital are like magnets—they keep people from flying off elsewhere for life's basic services. The high school is the more important of the two, because it's usually the largest gathering place in town and routinely during the school year attracts the largest crowds—for football and basketball games, track meets and other contests, stage plays and concerts, graduations and honors, and the dozens of other events that draw community residents together. The hospital or clinic is important for obvious reasons. Small-town residents know they have to go to an urban center for specialized medical care. But they want assurance that emergency and routine health care services are close by.

So as you begin to explore for small towns and come upon a high school, that's a good sign. If the school has the same name as the town, you're even hotter on the trail. And—what's that—a hospital! You begin to suspect that you are in a small town. To prove your hunch, drive to the center of town. You don't need a roadmap—any main road should lead you there. You are looking for an established and active commercial center. A town square? Yes, a town square. You've seen these places many times in the movies. There's a courthouse in the center of the square. It is a glorious four-story building of brick and stone, with a mansard roof and parapet wall and broad stairways leading up on all sides. The flag is flying. There is a war-surplus cannon planted in the grassy courthouse skirt and a monument to a native son who grew up here and achieved national prominence. And around the courthouse, on the streets forming the square, there are little shops and professional offices—a clothing store, a jeweler, a druggist with a soda fountain, a shoe store, an attorney, a café.

Reality check: If you've visited a number of small towns recently, you know that the picture I have just painted is more a nostalgic rec-ollection than an accurate portrait of the contemporary scene. A pretty little courthouse square with a buzz of shopping and socializing is the ideal, not the real, in many small towns. Big-box stores in strip malls on the edge of town have sucked the vital juices out of hundreds of towns, leaving only empty storefronts and marginal enterprises in the historic town center. When you come upon towns like that, keep driving, because what you see reveals a critical lack of vision, determination, and resources—qualities that small towns must continuously renew to survive.

Some small towns have figured out how to renew resources, and I show you what to look for later in this book, particularly in Chapters 5 and 10. Find these towns and put them on your list of prospects.

What if a town passes the first test—it has a high school and a hospital—but it doesn't have a traditional town square, only strip malls and mini–shopping centers. Are you in a small town? Probably not. More than likely you are in the outer fringe of urban sprawl, where shopping centers are the main landmarks and destinations, and local government is practically invisible compared to the elegant symbol of self-determination represented by the county courthouse.

How Trends in Employment and Telecommunications Are Improving Your Prospects for Success in a Small Town

In twentieth-century America, most people's jobs were located somewhere away from their homes. You went to another place to do your work because that's where you connected with your colleagues and tapped into the national communications system. Engineers, financial advisors, designers, writers and editors, producers, managers—just about everyone went to an office to get work done. That was still true to a large extent when I moved my family to rural Indiana in 1990. It was *possible* to move a city-based, office-based occupation into the outback, but you had to be very creative and full of the pioneer spirit to make it work. The big problem was how to send and receive large volumes of information between your remote address and the rest of the world. It is hard to imagine today, but the most reliable way to communicate back then was on a floppy disk or a piece of paper inside a Federal Express envelope for overnight delivery, assuming that you were not so far out in the country that second-day delivery was your only choice.

In the early years of the twenty-first century, time and space grow ever more compressed. Federal Express morphs into FedEx. Floppy disks gather dust as you blast-fax your message to an international audience in seconds, or pack e-mail attachments with megabytes of sensitive, encrypted data for instant delivery to a client in Timbuktu— make that Toledo. The speed-up in information processing and transmission means that *knowledge* workers can work practically anyplace, in theory at least. The companion development on the employment scene is the rise of the contractor-freelancer and the got-a-good-idea-and-gonna-run-with-it entrepreneur who can take his or her start-up enterprise practically anywhere he or she can find resources, primarily high-speed telecommunications and overnight freight service. If general community services also are available, so much the better. And if the overall cost of living is comparatively cheap, better still. You can see where this argument is going: Urban knowledge workers and entrepreneurs now have a much broader range of options when they are looking for a new home base. They can look outside the metro area and expect to find some small towns across the United States that provide all the essentials.

Overview of This Book

Moving from a city to a small town is an irrational act. I don't mean it's wrong, stupid, immoral, or a federal crime—just irrational, no matter how carefully you search for the right place and how carefully you plan the move. There comes a point in your quest when you have assembled all the data, made all the visits, talked with all the reliable sources, and nothing remains but to say yes, we're going, or no, we're not. All the due diligence you exercise up to this point is genuine science: You've got facts and reliable interpretations, plain for all to see. You've got a *case.*

The problem is, your evidence is bits and pieces, not a whole, and the whole will not come together until you are on the scene as a new arrival in your chosen small town. In other words, picking a small town is like choosing a mate: You meet, fall in love, and make a commitment based far more on faith than fact. Nothing wrong with that—we all do it in our relationships, and if we're lucky and work very hard, things work out. The purpose of this book is to help you reduce your dependence on luck and improve the odds that hard work will help you to succeed in your next home base, a small town.

My objective is to tell you what you need to know—before you go.

Examining Your Motives

What got you started on this crazy adventure? What aspect of city life is driving you nuts? Everyone can list a few quick reasons to move out of city center. Cost, crime, and congestion come to mind. But the key question to ask about your motives is, Do you have to move from an urban environment to make those problems go away? Will you only be trading one set of environmental problems for another when you move to a small town? Chapter 2 is designed to help you examine this equation. Chapter 3 considers the kinds of attitudes and outlooks that develop in small places simply because they are small. You'll want to solve for this *X* factor before moving.

Making the Search

Finding *the* small town can be exciting and, ultimately, very rewarding. The search can also be time-consuming, expensive, and in the worst case very disillusioning. No matter what, you can expect to drive down some dead-end roads as you explore the countryside looking for your special place. Chapter 4 helps you to get organized for this journey, adopt a realistic view, and include the significant other members of your household. Chapter 5 shows you where to look on the Internet for information about small towns, and how to plan trips to towns and set up interviews in advance so that you use your time well.

Making a Living

The cost of living is generally lower—sometimes much lower—in a small town compared with an urban area. Housing can be a terrific bargain. But unless you are independently wealthy, those piles of cash left over from the sale of your city place will run out one day and you'll have to generate a new stream of income. Chapter 7 helps you put together an initial budget in your adopted small town, Chapter 8 covers the housing prospects, and Chapter 9 looks at the job scene. If you are a knowledge worker and the Internet is your venue, you need to pay close attention to connection speeds. Digital subscriber lines (DSLs) are not as common in the country as in the city, as Chapter 9 points out.

Getting Accepted

Like it or not, you will be the object of some attention and a good bit of curiosity when you arrive in a small town. Newcomers stand out simply because the oldtimers know one another and you're *different*. But you can deal with this distinction if you know who runs the town and form a strategy for connecting with the power structure—becoming one of them. Chapters 10 and 11 give you ideas.

Getting Started

You want to find the absolute best small town in America. But you are impatient and don't have time to begin the search from zero. That's where Chapter 6 comes in. The center section of this book is a showcase of 120 small towns that various investigators, myself included, have studied and found to be good places with good prospects. If you don't know exactly what you are looking for in a small town, browse Chapter 6 and you'll get some leads.

Scoring a Town on the 10-Point Test

Screen test. Of course you want to move to a place that is a Norman Rockwell vision of small-town America, all fresh and friendly and full of sunlight and roses and pink-cheeked boys and girls and kindly shop-keepers and picket fences and tree-lined streets in summertime. Many small towns look exactly like that some of the time, and I hope you plan your visit for the right time. The look of the place is crucial and you should rely heavily on what your senses tell you upon first sight of a new community. Does it look like a stage-set (*Brigadoon*, not *High Noon*)? Are you smiling and saying, "Hey, look at that!" to your traveling companion as you drive down Main Street? Is it—romance? Well, if it is, that's great, because if there's any future prospect of moving there, you *should* feel some emotional attraction to a small town. On the other hand, the screen test is only the first part of a close examination of the community, and you may discover that the town is not quite what it appears to be at first glance. That's why the screen test comes first and why it gets only 1 point. If the town looks just as good after you have spent some time there, it's okay to fall in love.

Downtown test. The look and feel of downtown is crucial. You want to see few, if any,

empty storefronts, a decent amount of foot traffic, streets and sidewalks clean and in good repair. Downtown should have some flair, too—flags, banners, flowers. The advantage of being the county seat is the stream of official business that brings to the downtown courthouse, and the cluster of service establishments on the perimeter, including restaurants and coffee shops. In some small towns, the courthouse lawn is a stage for summer concerts.

High school test. If you have time to visit only one place as you evaluate a small town, go take a look at the high school and speak to some people there. For reasons both obvious and subtle, the high school is the heart and soul of a small town. More town residents—kids, teachers, staff, parents—come together every day at the high school than at any other local public place. Generally, the high school gymnasium or auditorium is the largest gathering space in town, not to mention bleacher seats at the football field (packed with cheering fans during the season).

But aside from the numbers and scale it represents, the high school also reflects community values—how much importance the community places on public education, measured in part by the condition and adequacy of the high school, by the scope of the curriculum, by the way students of different economic and ethnic heritage learn to study and play together, and by how well the school prepares young people to lead productive lives. It's impossible to evaluate all of that in one visit, but you can gain some impressions just by walking around inside and outside the school (make sure that you check in at the principal's office beforehand—schools are very security conscious).

See if you can spend a few minutes with the principal or a guidance counselor. Possible topics: What's the drop-out rate? Is there an alternative program for kids who can't handle the regular curriculum? What advanced-placement courses are offered? What are the composite scores on standard tests like the ACT or SAT?

If there's a college in town, ask what influence the college has on the high school. For example, can qualified high school seniors attend college classes for credit toward high school graduation? The presence of a local college can make a huge difference in the quality of the town high school if college faculty and staff send their offspring there and participate in high school governance.

Wal-Mart test. A decade ago, Wal-Mart was the small town bully. Sam Walton's scouts found an easy target, built their big box on the outskirts of town, and diverted consumer dollars out of the historic downtown shopping center. But much has changed. Small town merchants have learned how to cope with the big retailer from Bentonville; small town planners have learned how to rebuild downtown as a professional service, niche-retail, and government center. Today, many small towns consider it a badge of honor to have a Wal-Mart—independent outside verification that the community has a commercial future. So it's important to stop by Wal-Mart and see who's shopping. Go on a Friday afternoon or Saturday morning. You'll find a pretty good cross-section of the local population. Take a close look: These people may include your future neighbors. If there's no Wal-Mart in town, you can substitute another major discount store or a supermarket.

Population test. You can check the town's population over the Internet (at www.census.gov), but a more revealing way is to stop by the town government center during business hours and speak to the town clerk. Ask what the 1990 and 2000 census show for the town. Ideally, you will see slow, steady growth, indicating that the town remains attractive. But in either case, growth or decline, ask the town official for an interpretation. Why are people moving in? Where are they coming from? If the town is losing population, how come?

Walk-in-the-park test. You should find a substantial public park on one of the main roads through town. Check it out for facilities and maintenance. Everyone needs easy access to good recreational options—and especially young kids and teens. The best small towns have raised enough community support and money to establish a YMCA, a Boys & Girls Club, or a locally sponsored recreation center, which may be a cooperative program between the parks department and the high school.

Hospital test. Easy access to emergency care is the main idea. A small-town hospital also should have a relationship with—and air transportation to—larger institutions offering specialized care.

Home-town bank test. The town economy has to be attractive enough to support at least a few banks; and because of consolidation in the banking industry, most of them will be branches of regional banks. But if the town has one or more locally owned banks, consider it a plus—a rough indicator of the presence of locally controlled investment capital, which every town needs to help its residents and business enterprises to realize their aspirations.

Library test. Of course libraries have books and magazines. The better small-town libraries also have an active reference desk, an inviting children's section, a business reference room, and lots of electronic media, including audio books, CDs, videos, and Internet access stations. You might ask whether the library has installed filters on its Web-browsing system to block access to certain kinds of content. That's a controversial topic in some communities.

Local restaurant test. To quote the Romans, *de gustibus non est disputandum:* This is not an argument about taste. You go for goose liver pâté and I go for grits—no problem. But it may be a problem if the small-town eatery that everyone regards as a five-star establishment gets no stars in your book.

Chapter 2:

Looking at Your Motives for Moving to a Small Town

Taking Inventory

A thoroughly urban and very urbane couple named Wanda Urbanska and Frank Levering moved from their home in Los Angeles to Frank's birthplace, Mount Airy, North Carolina, in 1986, shortly after Frank's father had suffered a heart attack and could no longer manage the family orchard business. Friends in L.A. admired their loyalty to kith and kin and the Levering cherry orchard but also thought that Frank, a screenwriter, and Wanda, a business reporter at the Los Angeles *Herald Examiner*, were nuts. How could this city couple reconstruct anything resembling a sophisticated life in the foothills of the Blue Ridge Mountains? Your minds will turn to mush, a writer friend counseled Wanda.

Surprise, surprise—it didn't turn out that way. Frank and Wanda rescued the orchard and expanded it into the largest pick-your-own cherry operation in the South. And they continued to write, producing dozens of magazine articles and four books, including *Moving to a Small Town*. They became community leaders in Mount Airy, which an older generation of TV viewers know best as Andy Griffith's hometown and the inspiration for "Mayberry," the TV-prototype American small town and setting of Griffith's long-running show.

People move from cities to small towns for all kinds of reasons, including going back home to help family members in need. I don't know how much small-town migration is prompted by family situations—the Census Bureau doesn't track motives. But I would guess that the family factor accounts for a significant proportion of urban-rural traffic simply because tens of millions of Americans living in metro areas have small-town roots.

Russ Cochran is an example. He grew up in West Plains, Missouri, left the remote Missouri town for his higher education, got a Ph.D. in physics, and eventually became chair of the physics department at Drake University, in Des Moines. But outside the world of classroom physics he was an avid collector of comic books, and the hobby led him into a sideline venture: republishing the old titles like *Tales from the Crypt*, *Weird Science*, and *Mad*. Soon, the publishing business rekindled his long dream of returning to his home town, for the practical reason that it gave him a livelihood. "There are not too many things you can do in West Plains, Missouri, with a Ph.D. in physics," he once told me. The printing business was a natural, however, for the small town location, and his kids could run free there, under the watchful eye of two sets of grandparents and a multitude of other family and friends.

But what if you have no family connections to a rural area? What if your mother is a third-generation Clevelander and your father traces his clan to Quebec City? You have always lived in an urban area and so have your forebears. You are completely urban. What could you possibly find interesting about small-town life? Actually, quite a few things, and most are quality-of-life issues. Here's what pops into mind:

- More space
- Cleaner air
- More quiet
- Less traffic
- Less concern about personal safety—the crime factor
- More courtesy and civility
- Reduced cost of living
- Better environment for children
- More opportunity for community involvement
- Better control of your life

Some battle-scarred city dwellers will happily trade that whole list for the excitement that only a city can deliver 24-7, and I'll respond to their arguments later in this chapter. But if you are willing to accept the items on the list as tangible, they amount to a pretty strong enticement, I think. More

space? You can calculate it precisely in the additional square feet of your small-town dwelling compared to your city place. More courtesy and civility? You can count how often strangers say hello or at least look you in the eye and smile. The difference in the cost of living is easy: Just compare your city and small-town bank balances. Better air? Take a sample. Less traffic? Count cars.

Taking Control

The last item on the list—gaining better control of your life—is the most important quality you will discover in a small town, I think. It's also the hardest to measure. Control is primarily a feeling, like a deep sigh of relief, but it is a giant step removed from hard data. That's why you must be careful when you're calculating *control*. You can take actual readings on the tangible benefits of small-town life, such as fewer cars and cleaner air, and come to a grand conclusion that you have better control of things in your new environment. You can even put some spin on your research by weighting all the factors and calculating a bottom-line number, sort of a "control quotient." But that's not realistic, because your various measurements are merely snapshots of moments in the life of a community, and conditions do change. How many pleasant little valleys have seen the clean air fouled by too many wood-burning stoves? How many attractive seacoast towns have seen gridlock develop on Main Street?

If control is not a summary of the environment but something you can positively *feel* in your new, small-town hometown, what explains it? I believe it is your knowledge, based on living there awhile, that if you want to change your town—make it prettier, quieter, safer, friendlier—you can do it. *Control* is the potential for change if you care to exercise it. You may never exercise it, but you know that you can, and that's reassuring. I talk more about this in Chapter 11.

Your sense of control in a small town is the opposite of that urban sense of frustration expressed in the aphorism, "You can't fight city hall." Actually, as a kid growing up in the city I never completely believed that you couldn't fight city hall, because my household was full of professional social workers who were always itching for a fight. At least they talked a lot about reform. Meanwhile, we all knew that hundreds of civil servants were on the job everyday keeping a lid on anything really outrageous happening in our city environment. We didn't have to worry much about a sense of controlling the local environment because layers of bureaucracy were doing a fine job. We didn't have to fight city hall if we voted the right guys in, at least that was my youthful understanding of the way things worked.

Things are totally different in a small town. Everything is scaled down. The total payroll of town employees may be no more than a dozen people, and some are your friends. You know the mayor and you always stop and chat when you see her in the supermarket. Her number is in the phone book and she answers the telephone herself. If something's happening in town that you think is misguided, you can talk about it with the mayor without making an appointment. Access is very easy.

Action may not be easy, however, because most towns have limited resources—fewer people to do the work, smaller budgets and contingency funds. These may look like defi-

ciencies when you evaluate a particular small town, and you may conclude that such a place has no future. My advice: Guard against a hasty judgment. Look beyond the numbers at the potential. Try to determine how receptive the town is to the enthusiasm and talents that newcomers bring with them. If you are reading between the lines, you get my point: One of the immense pleasures of living in a small town is making a contribution to the quality of life—by volunteering leadership, labor, or whatever special skill you bring to the community. The pleasure becomes intense when you and your neighbors can look back at your town and say, "We made it better." That's what I mean by control. It comes at a price, but the price for individuals is much more affordable in a small town than in a city.

So when you get serious about moving to a small town, make time to go meet the mayor or village president. This will give you a quick reading on how interested the town is in attracting new residents and how imaginative the chief executive is in solving community problems with the help of resident volunteers. I talk more about this in Chapter 5.

Personal Safety

Small towners like to brag that they always leave the key in the car ignition and never lock the front door. And many are telling the truth! You do feel safer in a small town, and the feeling is based on some simple distinctions compared to city life. Obviously, fewer people drive aimlessly through the streets of a small town simply because small towns are off the main line. If your car is unfamiliar or your license plate shows that you are away from home, small town residents do notice and remember, not particularly out of fear but just curiosity. Small towns are natural "Neighborhood Watch" zones, without the warning signs. That's a big deterrent to crime by outsiders.

The big deterrent concerning insiders, meaning local residents, is that everybody knows you in a small town. Some people call this the curse of small-town life: the fact that someone calls you by name or recognizes you practically everywhere you go. There's no escape. It's a fishbowl existence—and a great crime stopper. So if you're dumb enough to mug a neighbor or stick up the local convenience store or drive off in someone else's car without permission, your future choices are to leave town permanently or surrender peacefully. It won't take long for the cops to come and arrest you—they already know where you live.

The fishbowl life of a small town is not teenage-cool, either. But parents of teens love it. One mother of two young teens who moved the family from a major eastern city to a midwestern town recalled that the kids didn't catch on at first. "It took them awhile to understand that everybody knew what they were doing all the time, which I count a tremendous plus," she told me. "Things go wrong, of course, but never in secret, at least not for very long. People find out. It gets back home. There's not this anonymity you have in the city."

So far as kids' safety is concerned, she added, anonymity is enemy number one. I agree with her. But I also regret the passing of a time when kids could be anonymous and safe in cities. I think of my own mother, who gave me the run of a big city from a very early age and years before cell phones. "Be sure to carry some identification on you," she always reminded me. She did not explain that this was so they could tag my toe with the right address if I got run over by a truck, but I understood.

If your kids forget to carry ID in a small town and they get into trouble, someone will care. A mother in a Rocky Mountain town recalled the day she got a call at the office. Her daughter was out bicycle riding, it had rained, and the streets were slick. "She fell and knocked herself out," Molly D. said. "Somebody picked her up and took her to the hospital and then called us. That's the type of concern you have in a small town."

Courtesy and Civility

How do you measure courtesy? Probably the simplest gauge is recognizing another person with a smile, a nod, or a greeting. Good morning! Hiya! Howdy! How y'all? If you have grown up in a city, greetings like that in public from strangers, for no apparent reason, only put you on guard. Going on semi-high alert, you check your valuables and think, "What's he up to?" If you move to a small town, you must be prepared for relentless acts of courtesy. Small towns reek with courtesy.

Jean J. remembered what it was like moving from a city to a small Iowa town to staff a state employment office. When she stopped by the post office that first day on the job, total strangers said hello. "This was foreign to me," Jean said. "I came from a community where waving and speaking just did not happen." Dan M. had worked for six years in New York City before moving to a southern Illinois town as a trailing spouse.

When another New Yorker came out to see how things were going for these ex-pats, "He walked around the town square and became really paranoid," Dan recalled. "Why is everyone smiling at me?!" the visitor from Manhattan demanded to know.

Actually, it's what the old-timers don't know that prompts some small-town courtesy—a friendly curiosity that may seem intrusive. Dan remarked, "People ask you questions that if it were anyplace else you'd say, 'None of your damn business.'" Like, What church do you attend? and Why didn't I see you at the town meeting?

An antiques dealer in a Virginia town put a different slant on small-town courtesy. You are not anonymous in a small town, he pointed out. Therefore, you cannot exercise the city option of being rude, hostile, aggressive, or pushy toward another person, because you are surely going to meet that person again, probably quite soon. "You're kind of on your good behavior," he said.

Being Totally Honest: Do You Have to Move to Satisfy Your Needs?

So what's your hurry about moving to a small town? Haven't you had these daydreams before, and haven't they faded, and haven't you then smiled, a bit wiser about yourself? If it's different this time, why is that? If you believe you have figured everything out, I think you must consider the downside risk of all of those upside potentials of small-town life that I listed earlier in this chapter:

There's more room in a small town because there are fewer people.
You may like the anonymity and unpredictability of crowds.

The air is cleaner and quieter in a small town because there's less traffic and industry.
You may be addicted to the urban buzz.

There's less concern about personal safety in a small town because muggers and robbers figure the territory isn't worth the trip.
Well—what does *that* do to your self-esteem out in the boonies?!

Small towners are more courteous and civil because they are expected to be.
You may be happier being yourself.

It costs less to live in a small town in part because personal consumption generally is lower.
If consumption is important to your self-image, you may be uncomfortable living where it's on display.

Kids who do well in small towns make good use of limited community resources.
You may want them to grow up where resources are plentiful.

It's easy to become involved in the life of a small town because there's a constant need for community volunteers.
The only way to escape this compulsory draft is to hide—or stay in the city.

If you are unfazed by this list of small-town horrors; if you are saying yes, yes, I want it all right now, I still think you need to spend some time trying to find happiness in the city, because you cannot begin to imagine all that is suddenly missing or very far away when you move to a small town. I go into this more in Chapter 3, but permit me to list only ten things you will rarely if ever find in a small town:

1. Fresh fish all year round.
2. Ethnic diversity.
3. Major league anything.
4. Shopping malls.
5. Foreign films.
6. Restaurants where nobody knows you.
7. Gay bars.
8. Home delivery of a national newspaper.
9. Starbucks.
10. Awesome architecture.

I could go on *(wine merchants who know what's in the bottle, foreign car dealers, public transportation, blockbuster bookstores, etc.).* But you are still denying reality and persisting in this small-town quest, so I will speak more plainly.

Being Totally Honest about Small Towns: No Utopias but Lots of Very Nice Places

All civilization can be divided into three parts: cities, suburbs, and small towns. I recognize that some little pockets of life are left out of that accounting, like hamlets at crossroads and isolated settlements halfway up the mountain, but for the most part that's the picture. Before you reverence this trinity, however, I will reduce it to two parts only: cities and small towns. I'm skeptical about suburbs as civilized centers in their own

right because they are dependencies. Like sucklings attached to the mother sow, suburbs draw all their vitality from the cities that produced them. To disclose fully, I have lived in suburbs a total of thirty years. Many suburbs are pleasant, well-scrubbed places. They are highly dependable and predictable, and there is nothing wrong with any of those qualities except that suburbs can be awfully boring, too. You have to leave town to be somewhere. Take Los Angeles away from Santa Monica and you have a town without players. Pluck New York from New Rochelle and all you've got is a railroad to New Jersey, after you change trains.

Small towns are not suburbs, not by my definition. Small towns may have relationships with cities (Grinnell is 60 miles east of Des Moines; some residents of Alpine drive 223 miles to El Paso to shop). But small towns have their own reason for being that is independent of nearby cities. Towns provide jobs of many kinds—factory jobs; retail store and service-industry jobs; school teaching, farm, and local government jobs. Every workday, people stream into small towns to go to work. In that regard, small towns are like cities: They provide a livelihood. Small towns are also home base for people who make a living elsewhere, including cities within daily commuting distance (Chapter 6 contains a section listing those places, titled Big City/Small Town Pairs).

Even if you happily give up many elements of city culture and accept the peculiar personalities of small towns, don't expect to find a utopia in a small town. All of them have problems. That's normal. The real measure of a community is how quickly and honestly it senses a problem and how ably it responds.

House Calls

I love hardware stores. I can happily spend hours inspecting bins of plumbing fittings and electrical wiring parts or considering the purchase of a new, must-have tool of some sort.

Hardware stores love me back. I use the word broadly—this is agape, not eros. I can always count on a cheery greeting from the checkout clerk when I breeze in, which is generally several times over any weekend and sometimes frantically late on Sunday afternoon if I'm halfway through a project and need one more thingamajig to finish it off.

Randy, the hardware store owner, is a good friend. He married into the business founded by his father-in-law, Jim, who helps out during the week and spends winters in Florida. Randy is an astute small-town businessman with a worldly perspective, and that's an exciting combination when you are standing among the nuts and bolts. We talk about stuff—local issues, national events, and often the ingredients of success when you are an independent, home-grown, small-town business just down the street from Wal-Mart.

All of which is preamble to this little story. It was January and the town was frozen solid under a layer of snow and ice that had built up over several weeks. People had cancelled New Year's Eve plans because the weather was so bad. On Epiphany, a warm front rolled in and the rain began, light at first but heavier as the day wore on. I hate this kind of weather, because my old cellar walls let a lot of groundwater seep in. It's bad even in summer, when the ground is a sponge, but awful things can happen in winter when the earth is frozen and rainfall seeks someplace to pond. I depend on the sump pump to keep ahead of the deluge. I checked the pump late on that January night and it was cycling every minute. If we didn't lose power, we'd be okay, I thought. And I went to bed.

About 3 A.M. I awoke, listened for the hum of the pump—listened—and heard nothing. On full alert, I flew out of bed and down the stairs, opened the cellar door, turned on the light, and gasped—the cellar was flooding. I could see the water level would soon extinguish the pilot light on the water heater, and who knows what it would do to my ancient furnace. Back upstairs, I grabbed the phone book. Sump pump dead, gotta call Randy! His last name is Jones, and the first Jones I call is—the wrong Jones! Yet, without protest at being aroused by a wrong number at 3:10 A.M., the woman on the other end says, "You must want Randy," and even gives me his number.

"Meet me at the store in ten minutes," Randy says. We rendezvous at the darkened store, he unlocks, flicks on a light, grabs a new pump off the shelf, and sends me on my way. "We'll take care of the paperwork tomorrow," he says.

When someone rescues you like this, you think of it as a singular event, a milepost in the history of human kindness. I have recalled that night to Randy several times, and the last time he seemed to draw a blank, then said, "Oh, sure, I remember—that was quite a night!" Evidently my call was not the first plea for help in the middle of the night, or the last. Randy added something about taking care of people in a small town, and changed the topic.

Chapter 3:
Looking at Small-Towners

Searching for Rural Sophisticates

Sophistication is a city thing. Culture, knowledge, complexity, subtlety—small towns may have a sprinkling, but great urban centers are the wellspring. Think of Athens, Rome, Paris, New York. If that's the case, why waste your time searching for sophisticates in the countryside? Small towns aren't exactly hotbeds of urbanity!

Still, anyone moving from a city to a small town without prior exposure needs to know that there really are sophisticates out there, more than you might imagine. The bad news is that most of them are not in the usual places. No smoke-filled coffee houses à la Europe. No neighborhood bars à la Chicago. No salons as in Boston and San Francisco. You're pretty much on your own when you go looking for rural sophisticates—mass media offers little direction or insight, preferring to repeat the old stereotypes of a

backcountry full of cheerful but shallow country folk happily scratching a living from the land, pledging allegiance to God and country, and otherwise just surviving their mortality.

Writing in *Harper's*, Tom Bissell says Hollywood's illusionists like to cast small towns as "myth-fogged" places. That's apt—fog blotting the details and leaving it to your imagination, or to someone else's storyline. The thing about small-town stories is that so many are set in the past, thematically if not chronologically, revealing selected truths about human nature. Some make lasting impressions. Think of Sherwood Anderson's *Winesburg, Ohio*, or Edgar Lee Masters's *Spoon River Anthology*, or Thornton Wilder's *Our Town*, or Sinclair Lewis's *Main Street*. All of them present archetypes of human nature in small town settings.

A few small-town stories concern the fantastic. *Back to the Future* is an outstanding movie example—crackpot scientist crafts a time machine out of homespun virtue. But there are few stories in popular media that show small-town characters saying important things about serious contemporary issues. Oh, it happens now and then, and with stunning impact. Think of *To Kill a Mockingbird* or *Inherit the Wind*.

But for the most part, contemporary mass media does not ask small-towners for penetrating insights into contemporary affairs. For that sort of thing, you go to a sophisticated urbanite. Not that small-towners don't have exactly the same insights. No question, some do. The problem is their address. Small-towners, as brought to life by the illusionists, are not sufficiently disillusioned, a prerequisite of being invited to an urban symposium.

But back to those closeted rural sophisticates. They keep their leading edges tucked safely in the scabbard, I think, because sophisticates do not go to the country to be sophisticated. They go in quest of more elusive things, putting peace, quiet, and comfort ahead of sparkling conversation and rapier wit on the list of daily essentials. Sublimating your innate sophistication is a defensive attitude, in part because small towns sniff out people putting on airs. When you live in the country, it's acceptable to be intelligent, learned, and wise, and known for those qualities, but it is not acceptable to be sophisticated—no offense—simply because that quality is out of place.

Small-town writers Wanda Urbanska and Frank Levering state this proposition well in *Moving to a Small Town*. "Small towners are sensitive to anything that smacks of condescension or superiority," they write. "Some may fear that because they haven't seen the world as you presumably have, or because they've never tested their wings in a big-city job market, that they're somehow

out of your league. These are feelings you'll want to dispel if you want to establish a comfort zone."

And what are you likely to find in your personal, small town "comfort zone"? You can find clues on almost every page of a small-town newspaper, where the important events of the day, the week, and the passing years include milestones like, "Couple Mark 65 Years," the headline under a very large photograph of a handsome pair—he, a retired professor of chemistry; she, a homemaker. "Everyone is welcome to attend the reception," the story says. "No invitations will be sent. Cards are welcome but gifts should be omitted." I did not check to see how many people attended but guess that this general invitation prompted a good turnout of longtime friends. It's difficult to imagine such an informal—unsophisticated—social routine in a city.

Measuring Socioeconomic Diversity in the Hinterlands

If you want your kids to grow up with some understanding of economic class differences in America, a small town is a very good place to rear them. Compared to suburbs, for example, small-town neighborhoods present a much wider mix of household income. "The people living on my street are not all at one financial level," a resident of a town in the upper Midwest once told me. "I think my friends on this street are a lot more cosmopolitan than those who live in the suburbs of Chicago."

I think she meant wise to the vicissitudes. When the Cramptons moved from an upper-middle-class suburb of Chicago to a small town in west central Indiana, our sixth-grade son quickly learned that not everyone in America drives an SUV and shops at the mall. Some drive pickup trucks and shop at Wal-Mart. (For protective coloration, we bought a shiny black pickup truck when we arrived in the country, but we did our major shopping at the nearest mall, about forty-five miles away.)

Street by street and block by block, small towns are more democratic, small *d*, than other American communities. You can say this is the triumph of the common man or you can say it's just a matter of scale: The whole town may be no larger than a city neighborhood, so there is less space available for creating class divisions. Of course, small towns do have those divisions. In many, a railroad track still marks the dividing line between upper and lower. In some, a new subdivision creates a homogeneous economic zone. In the South, and to some degree in any town with an African-American population, race continues to draw neighborhood boundaries. In an Iowa community, a local employer creates a neighborhood of Mexican immigrants—factory workers—out of a cluster of mobile homes on the edge of town. That happens in many places: Small towns do segregate Blacks and Hispanics exactly the way that cities do.

But there's no denying the variety of socioeconomic circumstance. Take my block, for example. I live next to a college campus, introducing a touch of student transience to the mix, but there's a huge range of household situations on the block having no connection at all with campus life. None of the single-family dwellings was built later than the 1930s or so; the oldest home on the

block, a charming little brick bungalow, dates to the 1860s. The most stunning structure is a Victorian built in the 1880s and very nicely restored by a recent owner.

Then there are the other places—nondescript, two-story wood-frame buildings in various states of repair. One across the street from me appears to be abandoned. We had a waving acquaintance with the young family living there, then they just disappeared, and sometime later a legal-sounding notice was taped on a front window, something about "Asset Recovery." I wish that someone would paint the place.

Two doors down is a house owned by a faculty member. He used to live there but has since moved to another town and converted his old house into two apartments. They're both vacant right now. Three doors farther down is a large white-painted frame building that I suspect was a single-family dwelling when it was built but long ago morphed into four or five rental units. The door to the mail lobby hangs open most of the time. At the end of the block there's a trim and well-maintained two-unit apartment house for households that qualify for rent subsidies. The educational range on my block is just as wide as the housing stock, beginning with high school dropouts and terminating with Ph.D.'s.

In small towns, you don't find many trophy houses sitting atop landscaped hillsides. You *do* find a huge variety of housing and family income among close neighbors. (For details on the housing stock, see Chapter 8.) It's all quite democratic, or at least it can be, depending on good will among men and women—and the success of the annual street festival and garage sale. I enjoy living in a place like this, because it reminds me of the city neighborhood where I grew up, a mélange of incomes and education. You don't find that mixture in most suburbs, and I think that leaves a lot of suburban kids without much knowledge of how the rest of the country lives. I doubt that our son yet considers the family move from suburb to small town a net gain: no grade school kid appreciates being uprooted. But I do know that his old suburban pals who came to visit frequently in the years immediately after our move got a kick out of viewing this strange culture plopped down in the middle of cornfields.

Sorting out Race and Religion in a Small Town

Items:

• You don't find many synagogues in small towns. Among the 120 towns listed in the center section of this book, 23 report a Jewish congregation in town.

• Other denominations are represented even less: Christian Scientist, 15 instances; Unitarian-Universalist, 12; Eastern Orthodox, 7; Quaker, 5; Buddhist, 2; Islamic, 2.

As regular listeners to *A Prairie Home Companion* will attest, small towns are not divinely diverse. Garrison Keillor's hometown of Lake Wobegone may be fictional but the setting he creates in the upper Midwest is not, with a Lutheran church anchoring one end of religious life and a Roman Catholic parish holding down the other, plus a few other mainline Protestant denominations thrown in for full gospel measure. In other parts of the country the big players may be the Baptists, Methodists, or Congregationalists.

Concerning race, outside of the South and the Southwest, you won't find many Blacks or Hispanics in small towns, although the Spanish-speaking population is increasing in many rural communities in the Midwest and Northeast.

What's the point of counting racial and religious representation in small towns? It is simply to measure in a general way two of the ingredients of a diverse community. I think that diversity is good; it makes life interesting and can lead to better understanding among people from different origins. In a previous book about small towns I searched for places that came close to reflecting the same proportions of ethnic diversity as the nation at large. Based on the 1990 census, I was looking for towns that were roughly 84 percent non-Hispanic White, 13 percent Black, and 2 percent Asian/Pacific Islanders. I didn't find any—didn't even come close. (I didn't try to compare the representation of various religious denominations, small town vs. city, because there are even more variables than with race.)

What I did find, as you have guessed already, is that northern small towns are virtually all White and southern towns have an extraordinarily large Black population. The little table below, compiled from Census Bureau findings, shows the White, Black, and Asian/Pacific Islander population of two northern towns and two southern towns and gives you the general picture. The closest any of the four places comes to the national mix is Littleton, New Hampshire, with a population of 1.1 percent Asian/Pacific Islanders.

Town	Whites	Blacks	Asians
Marshall, Minn. (Lyon County)	99.0 %	0.3%	0.5%
Littleton, N.H. (Grafton County)	98.0%	0.5%	1.1%
Kosciusko, Miss. (Attala County)	60.0%	39.5%	0.3%
Brewton, Ala. (Escambia County)	69.0%	28.0%	0.2%

How does the racial composition of a small town affect personal attitudes of residents concerning racial matters in the rest of the world? I don't really know, but I think it's important to ask that question of residents in northern towns who have had practically no experience living with non-Whites or any other racial minority as neighbors. Among people who have grown up in such a small-town setting, what you find more than anything else is simply indifference. Lacking direct experience living, working, and worshipping among people of diverse origins and beliefs, small-towners do not dwell much on ethnic differences.

Curiously, this lack of exposure may make such communities ripe planting grounds for organizations with ultra-extreme agendas, like the Ku Klux Klan, which has recently demonstrated, or threatened to, in several towns in my home state, for example. The question is not what the Klan is up to, which surely must be to win sympathy and support. The question is why the Klan targets a particular small town. What does the Klan see happening there—or not happening there—that makes the place look like a good setting for a rally? Is it a matter of the small scale, making the local establishment easier to get your arms around, or, in the case of the KKK, easier to cover with a white sheet? The message for anyone concerned about religious tolerance in a small town is to spend some time talking with local professionals, such as ministers and mental health professionals, to determine how the wind is blowing. It can be pretty scary to witness a mean streak ripping through a small country settlement.

But that doesn't happen often. What you see far more frequently was well described by the college president in an Appalachian town. Thinking about the sizable Black population in his town, he told me, "There is more of a security net or safety net in a small town than in a major city. The poor who are here still need more help than they are getting. [But] the churches seem a little more sensitive to the problem than they do in a large city. There is no insulation from the need. You go to school with these people. You see them on the streets."

Spotting Who's Missing on the Small-Town Scene

Who's missing from the small-town scene? That's easy: young, college-educated people, particularly singles and couples without kids. There are not enough good jobs for this cohort in small towns; neither is there anything like the social life that a city offers. Young, unattached college graduates who have grown up in a small town probably have a lifelong sentimental attachment to the place. But they have little reason to come back home except for holidays and high school class reunions. The permanent residents recognize this, and regret it. "A lot of our kids—we educate them and export them," an Iowa farmer told me. Some hometown kids do come back eventually, perhaps to join the family business, perhaps to launch a business of their own in a familiar setting, perhaps to retire.

The exceptions are young marrieds with kids, urban refugees who choose a small town for the lifestyle but commute to jobs elsewhere, and the young people who have grown up in town, entered the local workforce after high school graduation, married, and settled down to raise a family.

No matter your age, if you want a snapshot of who your neighbors will be in a small town, I suggest parking for an hour or two on Friday afternoon or Saturday morning near the entrance to a local supermarket or discount store, like Wal-Mart. Watch who's shopping. Note the variety of age groups. Are you seeing younger women with kids? Older couples? People alone? How are people dressed? How many in business attire? How many in overalls? Do people greet one another? How many are smoking? How many are overweight? You decide what criteria are important. Probably the key question is whether you see enough people who *look* interesting, people like you who could become your friends in your new hometown.

Robert James Waller, author of *The Bridges of Madison County*, once told me how he checked out Alpine, Texas, while he was considering buying a ranch outside of town. He shopped in the local stores to see how he would be treated—a stranger just stopping in to pick up a few supplies. What he found was a rare blend, he said, "the best of the Old West and the Old South— extremely civil, very polite, very circumspect." And he declared Alpine "one of the last bastions of civility and politeness."

May you find the same in another small town one day.

Calculating the Odds That You'll Fit In

An author acquaintance of mine who writes about practical things, such as moving your household from one place to another, points out a frequently overlooked benefit of relocating. Packing up all your stuff and going from A to B gives you an opportunity, he says, to *rethink* things. In fact, he says you can rethink *everything*. That's fairly encompassing—rethinking more than just your employment or the scenery or neighborhood or relationships. I'm glad he calls it an opportunity, not a prerequisite. You are not *required* to rethink anything when you move from an urban place to a small town. I think you will, however.

Moving from an urban place to a small town can expose the core of your soul—not a self-examination but a sort of community exercise in which you are Exhibit A, and the examiners are your neighbors and friends, people whom you may grow very fond of over the years. This intense interest in *you* has little to do with your fascinating personality but is more about the simple fact that there aren't many other distractions. In any given month there can't be more than a handful of newcomers in most small towns, perhaps even fewer. So your arrival is something of an event and you are the object of much attention. You are fair game for curiosity, of course, but also much more. Over time, as you build relationships, the community compiles a dossier on you. I intend no sinister accent on the *d* word. It's quite a democratic process because everyone at one time or another is both an examiner and the examined.

The short of it is, you become a known quantity in a small town. People keep an eye on you and test you for consistency. You can be vain or cocky or short-tempered and people will accept you as authentic. But pretense is unacceptable, because honesty is the fundamental value. If you can be happy in those circumstances and everything else checks out okay, you may just fit in.

God and Country

If you are passionate about keeping church and state separate, a small town will test your resolve: The Bible Belt runs straight down Main Street. I remember how startled I was one spring weekend to see a banner strung across my main street inviting everyone to the Youth for Christ rally at the public high school. Hey, wait a minute—you can't use a public building as a church, can you? Out in the country, the answer is yes, of course you can, and God bless you! School prayer may be debated elsewhere, but in most small towns the question is when, not if.

As a reporter at a small-town newspaper, I have covered the periodic gathering of students for prayer around the high school flagpole. I have also covered the county commissioners' meetings, where the agenda begins with an impromptu prayer by the board president, concluding, "In Jesus name I pray, Amen." I wish I could bring some old ACLU friends to one of these public meetings.

As a card-carrying Episcopalian, I worry about the rights of unbelievers and other-believers. That's the issue out in nonurban territory, where small minorities of any kind can feel suddenly quite uncomfortable in the midst of a very strong majority belief and practice—Protestant Christianity, with some tempering by Roman Catholics. I don't for a minute doubt the sincerity or good will of members of the established, largely fundamental Christian church, but I regret that my small-town neighbors who practice in other ways have to frequently look the other way when the Establishment unfurls its banners across Main Street. If you're in the minority, you have little choice.

Recently, in another town that I visit occasionally, county officials approved a request to post the Ten Commandments on the courthouse lawn. But when a local civil rights group threatened to sue, county officials decided they could not afford a defense, no matter how righteous the cause, and the Decalogue was taken away. Practically the next morning, a local real estate agent made available free copies of the Ten Commandments for residents to display on their front lawn, like a political poster, and hundreds of households did so. I guess you'd have to call that a victory for freee speech.

Chapter 4:

Deciding What Matters Most

Understanding Key Differences Between Cities and Small Towns

When you lift the veil of romance and peer at the true nature of a small town, what you see, after you set aside obvious things like reduced cost of living and enhanced sense of personal security, are differences in two fundamentals: *time* and *space*. I think you can account for everything important under those two headings, though it may take you awhile to run the equations. The concepts of small-town time and space are like onions—you can peel away layer after layer until you reach the place where you say, yes, this is how time and space are different for me in a small town compared to a city. It's a different experience for everyone, and it begins with your prior experience.

Growing up in a city, my personal space was fairly limited. Our apartments were small, the lot our house sat on was small. The street was totally occupied by houses or apartment build-

ings. Subways, streetcars, and buses provided little physical space in addition to what I occupied with my body and belongings. We jostled our way through department-store shoppers, and we squeezed around restaurant tables.

But I didn't think of this as crowded space. I was surrounded by a sort of no-fly zone that was off-limits to other city residents, and they were protected by the same kind of shield, making it possible for all of us to get along rather well in close quarters, lost in our thoughts and avoiding eye contact. The only intrusion was personal hygiene. Few people bothered with deodorant back then, and bad breath was rampant—downwind of you, if you were lucky. But that's just the way things were. I remember Mother reporting that certain of my grade-school classmates were sown into their long underwear from December to April. It was an old-country thing and normal for the neighborhood.

City space, though quite limited if you calculated it in square feet, actually was all that you needed to feel comfortable. As a kid, I never thought about it that way, but I don't remember ever feeling uncomfortable for lack of space.

City time was a different sort of proposition. The conventional wisdom then as now was that you never had enough time in the city, and you had daily proof in the rush hour, twice a day. I didn't disagree—anyone could see people rushing down the street toward the bus stop. Anyone with a number of stops to make—bakery, shoe repair, post office, bank—had to allow extra time to touch all those bases. It took time to move from place to place, and it took time to do your business at each stop. But if you picked up your clipboard and stopwatch and analyzed how this city time was actually used, you saw that much of it was spent waiting—standing in line, stuck in traffic, waiting for the train, waiting for someone to wait on you. In fact, there is plenty of personal time in the city, though much of it is absorbed by the urban environment.

Exactly the same thing happens in a small town—plenty of time but much of it controlled by the *environment*. What's different is the definition of environment. Obviously there are no traffic jams in small towns (except when they block Main Street for the County Fair Parade), and you will spend little time standing in line or waiting for a sales clerk (unless Wal-Mart has a 5 A.M. sale the day after Thanksgiving). In a small town, the environment is not air quality; it is your network of personal relationships—the many people you know and meet whenever you leave your home. You cannot ignore these people. You must say hello and stop to chat. Sometimes that's a chore or a trial—you really do need to be going about your business.

But most of the time these regular chance encounters are pure pleasure, a reaffirmation of brotherhood, right there in plain sight on the post office steps or in the supermarket aisle.

I think that women value this side of small-town life more than men do. A stronger bonding instinct, maybe? A higher priority placed on personal relationships? But I also know from personal experience how surprisingly pleasant it can be for two no-nonsense, agenda-driven guys—friends or acquaintances—to encounter each other in a small town and stop to talk for a bit. That doesn't happen every day in the city.

Another way to compare city time and small-town time is to think about child rearing. Bringing up kids in the city may mean devoting a big chunk of the day to transporting them from one activity center to another, arranging car pools, coordinating schedules, and attending other parental responsibilities. Not to mention time spent worrying about whether your kids are safe out there in the impersonal city landscape.

By contrast, child rearing in a small town takes both less and more time:

- It takes *less* time because the kids are known by name or family connection, sometimes even by home address. Because other residents of the community know who your kids are and where they belong, the community supplies an informal but effective supervisory and security system, relieving parents of total responsibility—maybe the better word is *sharing* the total responsibility with parents, relieving some of Mom and Dad's concern because other people of goodwill are part of the child-rearing system.

- On the other hand, child rearing in a small town can take *more* time than in a city environment, because parents feel more obligated to volunteer their services in children's programs, at school, at church, on the ball field, wherever. Exactly the same thing happens in a city, of course. The big difference in a small town is that the list of available volunteers is shorter and your name pops to the top of the list more often.

But what about small town *space?* How does it compare to city space? Earlier I said that my personal space in the old city neighborhood was fairly limited by the built environment—small living quarters, crowded city streets and public accommodations. But I never felt I had too little space for self-expression, because everyone respected everyone else's space, small as it was. Now you are jumping ahead and guessing where this argument is heading: toward the surprising conclusion that small towns appear to offer more space per capita but actually do not. And that's exactly my point.

Two forces are at work here. First is the friendship factor. Because you have more friends and acquaintances per square meter in a small town than in a city, you encounter more of them in your daily routine, and each one happily invades your personal space, as you do theirs. So there goes your buffer zone!

The other factor is the matter of physical space. Viewed from the city, the small town appears to be part of a vast wilderness of space, a spot of light in the center of a huge unoccupied area. You begin to hum, "Oh, Give Me Land, Lotsa Land, Under Starry Skies Above," and you think of the town the same way: a spacious getaway for a harried urban-

ite. In fact, you may experience a strong sense of confinement in a small town—because you will quickly know the whole place, every street and landmark, every school, church, and store. You can almost span the place with arms stretched wide. And once you know every street and landmark, the illusion of space goes poof!

City space appears larger than life because so much of it is unexplored and mysterious. Small-town space feels much smaller than it appears because you know every inch of it. I think that explains why some city types feel confined in the country.

Listing What You're Willing to Trade for a Small Town Lifestyle

This part is easy: List everything that you consider the normal, everyday conveniences, pleasures, or essentials of city life. My list includes:

> Five-star restaurants (I'll settle for three)
> Pastrami on rye
> Upscale shopping
> Newsstands
> Bakeries
> Bright lights
> Skylines
> Broadway shows
> Foreign films
> Specialists in everything
> Experts in everything
> Museums
> Galleries
> Roar of the crowd
> Celebrities

Scoundrels
Public transportation
Sense of excitement
Sense of danger (a wee bit)

That's not everything. City life offers a satisfying sense of having arrived and proven yourself that rarely is duplicated elsewhere, unless you are an urban cowboy who finally discovers a home on the range. I remember how deeply satisfying it was to work as a newspaper reporter in a big city, measuring my skill against the legends of the past, some of them still on the beat.

Cities offer companionship of all kinds, if you want it. Cities offer privacy, if you want it, no questions asked. Don't forget, if you want to be alone, the possibilities are much better in an urban placed packed with people than in a rural place where you are expected to acknowledge the presence of others. I come back to that point in Chapter 11.

My list of city essentials is a stacked deck. Small towns have no way of matching my list except for a few odd moments of excitement and danger, but those are rare. To be fair, I should list the aspects of city life that I can give up in a minute, and you should, too:

Dirt
Noise
Crime
Rudeness
Cost
Graffiti
Corruption
Hassle (undefined)

There may be others but those are the biggies. City people complain about those things. But they don't move because of them. They are proud of hassle, noise, dirt, graffiti, and bad behavior because ignoring them proves your identity as an urbanite. Corruption and crime prove there's something of value to the place. Want to make a Bostonian swell with pride? Mention the Brinks heist or the Strangler. In Chicago, quote a tabloid headline from Prohibition, like "Gangland Guns Roar Again" and they'll accuse you of unbridled boosterism.

Seeing If You Can Combine the Best of City and Small Town

You're a happy small-town resident but you miss the city lights. What to do? I think the only practical solution is to plan regular trips to the city to indulge your tastes. We've done that ever since moving to our small town a decade ago, and it works well. Monthly trips to attend a concert, the theater, a favorite restaurant, or to go shopping can provide a pleasurable contrast to wholesome small-town life. Don't believe any small-towner who tells you, "This town has everything you'll ever need." For some residents that may be true, but I guarantee they won't be in your circle of friends.

Some small towns offer city-style attractions: orchestras, amateur theater, visiting celebrity speakers. (Some college towns do an extraordinary job of this and invite town residents at little or no cost; for leads to college towns, see the special section of Chapter 6.) But for the most part, unless the town attracts steady tourist traffic from the city, city-style cultural attractions are practically nonexistent. Ditto for city-style restaurant food. That should come as no surprise. In any case, you are not moving from the city for city-style reasons. You are moving for the small-town lifestyle. Just be sure to follow my advice below.

Taking Care to Include All Members of Your Group in the Decision

Nobody moves on a whim, not even nomads. Something motivates you; if you're a nomad, it's hunger. In America the propellant is likely to be a new job or a new love or your health. Generally, you move to solve a problem or consummate a deal. Your decision to move from a city to a small town likewise is prompted by your desire to solve a problem, real or perceived. The problem may be one of those awful city characteristics I listed earlier in this chapter.

If you're moving alone, the decision is yours alone, though you'll probably run the idea past friends and relatives. But if your move to a small town involves other people—spouse, kids, other relatives—all of them should participate in the general discussion leading up to the move and possibly in the final decision itself. You may want to have a family conference, or several conferences, to discuss the move and let everyone speak his or her mind.

Who makes the final decision? Do you have a show of hands, one-man-one-vote, toddlers and teenagers included? If your motive to move is some irrefutable factor like essential employment or the care of an elderly parent, voting is irrelevant because the decision has already been made and your main task is to sell the idea as best you can, throwing in some incentives if you need to. But if moving to a small town truly is optional, that's where full discussion and debate come into play, with flipchart lists of the pros and cons. You'll want to do extensive field research, too. Chapter 5 covers that topic.

The Road Home

You have to journey through a stretch of unoccupied space to reach a small town. Your road may bisect a mountain valley or run through a forest or along a seacoast. My road home is a two-lane blacktop angling twenty miles across two counties, the link between my street and the Interstate. This is midwestern farm country—corn and soybeans grown in great abundance—and I mark the seasons by what's happening in the fields, from the winter stubble of crops long gone, into the fresh turn of soil at planting time, through the bloom of green rows in May and June, to the simmer of August and brown withering of leaves in September, waiting for harvest.

My road twists and turns but mostly runs flat. The highest point rises only forty feet or so above surrounding terrain, but that's enough for me to survey my domain—thousands of orderly acres of row crops standing at attention. Cell phone towers stake the horizon.

The rules of the road change from month to month. In January, when I can see for miles, the occasional STOP signs are optional if there's no traffic. In August, when much of the route is a green tunnel of corn stalks, I do not blow through those intersections with the abandonment of winter.

I don't know anyone along the road, but I do know something about their routines. A school bus driver lives at one house. She parks Big Yellow in a special spot next to the house, August through May. Downwind from her, a hog farmer scents the air sour-sweet. Ranch houses are the preferred architectural style, and concrete bric-a-brac ornament the front yards— geese, deer, cherubs. The lettering on pickup trucks tells you who lives where. There's a plumber at one place, a heating-cooling guy, and some other tradesmen. A long-haul driver bunks at another house, I figure, spotting the big tractor parked there on some weekdays. At one tidy dwelling close to the road, a poster planted in the front yard declares a dependable, Middle Western sentiment: "Get US Out! of the United Nations."

There's a point on every approach to a small town where you catch first sight of the settlement, perhaps at a curve or a hill or the other side of a clump of trees, or at night when you see the lights of a factory on the outskirts. At Christmastime in my town, they string lights from the top of the courthouse and you can see them from seven miles away on a clear night.

Nearing my hometown, I drive past the tree farm, the county fairgrounds, the new Wal-Mart, the auto dealers, the high school, and fast-food alley. There's the hardware store, the supermarket, and the ice cream shop. Then the street becomes residential, including the undertaker, who has the biggest and neatest house on the block. I drive through Courthouse Square and past St. Paul's, down to the gas station and my corner. Three blocks to the right, take a left, and I'm home.

Small towns all have pretty much the same parts, so you know what to expect when you journey from one to another, and that makes a town familiar and pleasant even to a newcomer. But the unique arrangement of parts also makes each place unlike anyplace else on earth and, to the residents, enchanting. It always feels good to come home.

Chapter 5:

Due Diligence—Spending Some Time in Small Towns

Using the Internet to Launch Your Search

Name a small town, any small town. Type the name into your favorite Internet search engine and press "Enter." Eight out of ten times you will land on a page containing at least a bit of useful information about the town, if nothing more than the telephone area code. Companies that produce classified telephone directories have not wasted any time selling ads to motels and local tourist attractions all across the nation, and they have keyed the information into Internet sites. You can practically throw a dart at the map blindfolded and land on a town that's listed in one database or another.

Most of what you find initially may be bare bones and heavily slanted toward the interests of local retail and service establishments. But you may also get lucky and strike a mother lode of really good stuff, including town history and government, names and telephone numbers of local officials, school information, calendars of events, and even bulletin boards.

To show you that the Internet approach really works, I have just closed my eyes and dropped a dart from five feet onto a map of the United States. It has landed by chance at the southwestern corner of Nebraska, near the town of Ogallala. Now I turn on Yahoo! and type in "Ogallala Nebraska" (notice there's no comma and I spell everything out) and press enter. And here's what comes up on the monitor:

1. **Ogallala Chamber of Commerce**
   http://www.ci.**ogallala**.ne.us/
   More sites about: **Nebraska > Ogallala** > Chambers of Commerce

2. **Western Insurors of Nebraska**
   http://www.winins.com
   More sites about: **Nebraska > Ogallala** > Shopping > Insurance

3. **Ogallala Middle School**
   http://www.esu16.k12.ne.us/~ckay/warrior.html
   More sites about: **Nebraska > Ogallala** > Public Middle Schools

4. **Ogallala Homes, Inc.** - manufactured homes.
   http://www.**ogallalahomes**.com/
   More sites about: **Nebraska > Ogallala** > Prefabricated Houses

Figure 5-1: What you see when you search the Internet for "Ogallala Nebraska."

The search produces four Web site matches, including two that look promising: the Ogalalla Chamber of Commerce and the Ogalalla Middle School. Probing further, I find a main page (Figure 5-2) with links to data on city government, schools, businesses, and community development. I discover that Ogalalla is known as "The Cowboy Capital of Nebraska" and that the current temperature is 23 degrees above zero with a windchill of 11 (okay, it's December!).

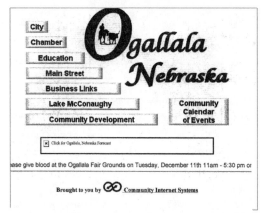

Figure 5–2: A simple but effective main page for a remote Nebraska town.

For a come-what-may, stab-in-the-dark test of Internet resources on small towns, little Ogalalla (population 5,000) produces an example of very good community-marketing. Some towns go much further, providing extraordinary detail about local organizations. Northfield, Minnesota, for example—one of the towns listed in this book and a place I know from interviews and a visit—yields twenty Web page matches when I type in the town name and go streaking down the Net. After skipping past a few "Sponsor Matches" for local hotels, here are some of the Web pages that come up for inspection:

- *Northfield News*, weekly online edition

- Northfield Chamber of Commerce

- City of Northfield

- Northfield Citizens Online ("working to create an electronic commons in Northfield")

- Northfield Cross Country (high school sports)

- Northfield Public Schools

- Country Inn of Northfield

- Northfield High School's GSA (gay-straight alliance, a student group)

- Cantus, Minnesota-based men's vocal ensemble

- League of Women Voters

- Ecofeminism, a St. Olaf Honor House (at a local college)

- Prairie Creek Community School

- St. Peter's Lutheran Church

There are others with a more commercial twist, but you can sort them out quickly. Intrigued by "Northfield Citizens Online," I click on the page, scroll around among topics, and select one that's hot in Northfield and many other towns—the debate over whether a big-box retailer should be permitted to build a megastore on the outskirts of Northfield and possibly reduce retail traffic in the historic downtown. Take a look at this bit of dialogue:

Griff Wigley - 09:43am Dec 8, 2001 CDT
Web Cafe mgr, forum moderator, host of Gov't and Bridge Square

Use this topic to discuss the prospect of Cub Foods opening a grocery stor
Target, and the prospects of Petricka's relocating there.
Griff Wigley - 09:46am Dec 8, 2001 CDT (#1 of 13)
Web Cafe mgr, forum moderator, host of Gov't and Bridge Square

There've been a few postings in other places here in the Cafe about this iss
them over here.

ChrisR - 10:39am Dec 5, 2001 CDT (#2 of 13)
Chris Robbins, Nature & Environment Host

Grocery stores moving

What do you think about the proposed Cub Food store next to Target? The
say the proposed size is already too small only 2 years later. Should Petricl
there to run the Cub, leaving the County Market to be redeveloped into sor
Should the County Market stay downtown but expand? Can grocery stores
forever? People used to walk a few blocks down the street for a carton of n
they walk the equivalent of a few blocks inside the store!

Griff Wigley - 02:03pm Dec 5, 2001 CDT (#3 of 13)
Web Cafe mgr, forum moderator, host of Gov't and Bridge Square

Chris, I'd like to see CM stay downtown... expansion there would be fine v
biased, tho... it's only 3 short blocks from my house.

My worry is what would become of that building if Petricka's relocates out
wiped out a big chunk of low to middle income housing when it moved the
very devisive process. I can't imagine what type of business could move in
would be complementary to downtown and the neighborhood.

Figure 5–3: Residents of Northfield, Minnesota, talking online about the pros and cons of letting a big national retailer come to town. (Some of the dialogue is lost, but you can get the gist.) Many small towns wrestle with this issue.

Contacting Local Residents

Some of your best advance information about a town will come from local residents who do not have a particular axe to grind or cause to promote—people who have nothing to sell you other than their credibility as experienced observers of the community. But who are these people and how do you connect with them? If you have scouted the town on the Internet, you may have found the telephone numbers of a few key local institutions, such as the public library and town newspaper. That's what you need to start this part of the town-search process. I call it "Dialing for Details."

During a decade of research on small towns, I have found this technique to be very effective. When I want to get acquainted with a town, I first call someone visible and accessible such as:

- The reference desk person at the public library

- The editor of the local newspaper

- The town clerk (at town hall)

- The director of community economic development

Of course, when I call I have a very specific mission: to interview someone for a book I'm writing about small towns. But you don't have to be an author for this approach to work. In fact, you will probably have better luck calling simply as a curious, sophisticated person from afar. Are you skeptical about this naïve approach? Are you smelling snake oil? All I can tell you is that I have never been refused help on hundreds of telephone inquiries to small towns. If you are courteous and honest, small towners will help you. So, what do you say on the phone? Your conversation can begin like this, for example:

Hello, my name is _____ and I'm calling from _____. I wonder if you can help me learn more about (name of town). I have an interest in visiting and possibly relocating to town and would like to talk to someone who has recently arrived. Can you suggest anyone that I might call for a chat?

Notice that I narrowed the zone of interest to "someone who has recently arrived." You can set any criteria you want, within reason. You may not get very far if you ask to speak with "a mother of two adopted children from the Far East" or "a former Boston brain surgeon," though both types could be fascinating. You may want to set broader criteria, like "a family with school-age children" or "a retired couple." I used the example of the new arrivals simply as a broad match with your own circumstances. You can tailor it a bit by saying "someone who has recently arrived from a big city."

However you develop this conversation, be prepared to talk freely about your own situation—how you heard of the town in the first place, why you're thinking about moving, what you do for a living, where you are in life, personal stuff like that. The more you open up about yourself, the more likely you are to receive useful references (and telephone numbers!).

But why use the phone? you're thinking. Why not use the Internet? My experience is that the Internet is very good for initial backgrounding on a town—the kind of search-and-download tactics that I illustrate earlier in this chapter—and for follow-up with your primary sources of information, but it's not effective at all in connecting with those primary sources in the first place. Your message to a stranger at an e-mail address is just part of the junk that gets swept out of the In-box every morning and night.

It may be that your first telephone contact in a small town—the reference librarian, the editor, the chamber of commerce director, the economic development person, or someone like that—will have the time and inclination to talk with you at length. If so, great!

Make the most of it. I have learned much of value from members of the small town "establishment." But the most important information I receive from these professionals is the names, phone numbers, and "introductions," so to speak, to informed and articulate residents who are a step or two removed from an official position but are known to have a fairly balanced view of community affairs. Someone with a reputation as an effective community volunteer can be a very good source of information. And when you place your call you can say something like, "Eric, the editor at the paper, gave me your name." References like that are effective conversation starters, I've found.

Writing Your Checklist of Key Small-Town Qualities

If there's a core principle to this book, I think it must be *plan ahead*. Unless you have a personal manager to do your bidding, scouting, and vetting, you and all the significant other members of your group can expect to have dozens of questions about any small town that looks interesting enough to live in more or less permanently. You may not be able to answer many of the questions until you actually get there, but that shouldn't stop you from framing your expectations. So, think of yourselves as "The Framers," writing the "Constitution" of the new place you will call home. Make it lofty—you are describing heaven on earth, or something close.

Much of what you list can be described as *infrastructure*. I don't mean streets and sewers—let's assume that all the utilities are in place. I'm thinking about the social infrastructure, including schools, recreational facilities, places of worship, health care, and the like. For example, look at Chapter 6, where towns are listed, and you will see details at each listing about what the town offers, including number of beds in the local hospital and number and size of public parks, to name just two indicators of quality of life in a small town. If you have any difficulty getting started on your personal list, check out the town details in Chapter 6.

But wait: What if your move to a small town is driven by someone *else's* agenda, like an employer or a member of your extended family? In a case like that, you are thinking, it's pointless to tick off the must-have qualities you want in your new home town. What difference does it make—you're moving no matter what!

My advice: Write the list anyway. You can slosh around in fatalism if you want to, but once you arrive in your new community, you will have an irresistible urge (I confidently predict) to jump right in and *improve* the place. Maxim: All small towns need improvement, all the time. The reason is, they have limited resources—ready cash—and unlimited lists of things that need to be done, like attracting more employers, making the place prettier, or connecting the town neighborhoods more effectively. I know that from more than a decade living in a small town and serving on long-range planning groups.

Listing the Pros and Cons

When a group of forty or so local residents, all volunteers, gathered in my small town to dust off and update the long-term plan for the community, the first thing we did was a warm-up exercise. We listed the big news stories that we might imagine seeing in the town newspaper five years or ten years hence, both the good stuff and the bad. On the positive side, we thought we'd like to read about:

- A boom for small businesses
- An outstanding educational event (unspecified)
- A thriving downtown
- Thriving major industries providing high-benefit/high-wage jobs
- An integrated network of social service organizations
- More parks and green spaces, connected by trails and pathways

That list reads like a small-town Bill of Rights, I think. We had no illusions, however, and identified the kinds of disappointing news we might read in the newspaper sometime in the future—reflecting current concerns, of course:

- For lack of a bypass road, too many trucks rumbling through Courthouse Square
- Town utilities continuing to degrade
- Historic homes neglected and torn down
- Businesses closed
- Agricultural land pushed out of the way by subdivision sprawl
- More strip malls on the edge of town, dragging business away from the historic town center

You don't have to be a long-time resident to evaluate a town for any of those problems— just have a look around. To investigate subtler matters, however, like the quality of the high school, the extent of recreational facilities, or the political climate, you'll have to spend more time on the premises.

Planning a Trip

If the town you are planning to visit has a bed-and-breakfast establishment, plan to stay there. Actually, a B&B is a pretty good test both of the town and your comfort level with small-town society. On the town side, the presence of one or more B&Bs tells you that people find a reason to visit the town, and that's a good sign. On the personal side, your comfort level staying in a B&B may give you a rough reading on your comfort level living in a small town, because the bed-and-breakfast environment encourages personal interaction both with the B&B proprietor and with other guests, and that's the sort of thing that happens spontaneously in a small town. At a B&B, you have the opportunity to talk with at least one local innkeeper, and if you're lucky, she or he will be an acute observer of human affairs and willing to share. But if the thought of interaction with another human before high noon is simply revolting, maybe this part of the scouting should be someone else's job, while you reconsider your life options.

The second part of your plan is the agenda for your visit. You may want to plan the trip to coincide with a festival or other local event, and you can begin to get some ideas by running an Internet search. Figure 5-4 shows the calendar of events for one month in Bigfork, Montana, for example.

There are pros and cons to planning a trip to a small town during an annual celebration. On the pro side, it may be a lot of fun;

April 2001

Bigfork Art and Cultural Center Anual Art Auction and Dinner
April 7th
Benefit for the bigfork Art and Cultural Center
837-6927

Masters Pro Am (two man best ball)
April 7th
Eagle Bend Golf Course
837-7312

Easter Sunday Buffet
April 15
Check with Bigfork's fine restaurants for more information.

"Clean The Fork"
April 28
Joint Civic Organizations clean-up Bigfork
837-5888

"Done To Death" - Bigfork Community Players
April 20, 21, 22 and 27,28,29
Bigfork Center for the Performing Arts
837-5286

Taste of Bigfork
April 29th
2PM-6PM

Figure 5–4: April events in Bigfork, Montana, range from an art auction to a clean-up campaign. The calendar came from the Internet.

if it's not—well, that tells you something about the town or yourself. On the con side, you are seeing the place under unusual circumstances. It's like those memories of going over the river and through the woods to Grandma's place for Thanksgiving. The old lady may be the soul of hospitality one day a year but a complete mess the other 364.

If you have spoken with any town residents by telephone before your trip, see if you can arrange to meet them while you are in town. Small towners like to receive visitors. Arranging to meet a local resident for a cup of coffee can make you feel instantly at home.

Interpreting and Weighing What You Hear and See

Let's face it: Moving to a small town is a crapshoot. Your happiness there depends a lot on luck—the people who become your friends, the success of your employment, the happiness of other members of your household once they get there and begin living a routine, daily life. None of those factors (and the dozens of others you could list) can be guaranteed in advance, no matter how much advance work you do. Does this large chance factor mean you can ditch the scouting and methodical measuring and comparing of towns? Not at all! Doing your homework on a small town won't guarantee that you find heaven on earth, but it will help you avoid places that are sheer hell.

All moves are risky. In fact, moving ranks right up there with serious illness or loss of employment on the list of bad things that can happen to good people. So why are you even considering moving when you could stay put and stay safe, or safer, at least? The answer, I think, is that you have a sense of adventure and confidence in your ability to make things turn out okay. And the other members of your tribe feel the same way. Therefore, the key question to ask about all the information you've gathered and impressions you have formed about a small town is very simple: Shall we give this place a try?

If that sounds like a subjective conclusion to an objective process of selection—well, that's about the best you can expect. But if you have paid close attention to what you have seen and heard during the investigation phase, your intuition will serve you better. For example:

- How quickly and enthusiastically do people in official positions in town respond to inquiries from outsiders? If you have school-age kids, are school officials accessible, helpful, and forthright?

- What's the level of civility and courtesy in town? Remember, you can get a quick reading on that by walking around, shopping, and just keeping your eyes open. (For example, what sort of response do you get when you, a stranger in town, smile at someone you pass on the street?)

In short, everything you learn about a place is distilled to a single feeling, and that's what governs your decision, go or no go. That's how I would do it, anyway.

Chapter 6:

Zeroing in on Your Small Town: 120 of America's Best

Taking a Look at the Prospects

This chapter is designed to get you on your way. It's a sampler of 120 small towns all across the United States, places that I have researched and believe to represent some of the most attractive small-town living situations for 2002 and beyond.

The towns are organized into five categories:

- Coastal Towns—If you sail, fish, ski, or just like being near the water, these places may catch your fancy.
- Mountain Towns—Can't live without sight of the mountains? One of these towns may be picture-perfect.
- College Towns—A college or university is in each one of these towns, adding a cultural component and guaranteeing you'll see young people on the streets.

- Big City/Small Town Pairs—A special collection of small towns near big cities—for people who want to stay in touch with an urban environment.
- Far-Out Towns—You don't mind driving a few miles to get to your "little house on the prairie." Some of these places are remote, but far-out is a better descriptor.

Interpreting Town Data

Each town listed in this chapter is described by a standard set of data, mostly numbers and lists, with references for you to use in conducting further research on your own. Data are presented in the same format for each town. To help you extract the most value from the data, I show you the format on the next page and add some notes for your guidance.

Small Town, USA 55555

Population: 0,000 (+00%) The figure in parentheses is the change in population between the 1990 and 2000 federal censuses. Growth rate is important. Ideally, a town will grow at a steady rate that does not exhaust local resources or change the character of the place. Towns can lose a bit of the population base without ill effect. But any decline in population is always worth investigating.

Banks: Two points: The first should be obvious, that the number of banks is a rough indicator of the volume of banking business and some measure of general economic vitality. The second point is local ownership. The data line labeled "Banks" tells you first the total number of banking companies represented in town; and, second, the number of those banks that are branches of banks headquartered out of town, including regional and national banks. It's a good sign for a small town to have one or more locally owned banks—good because that tells you there is investment capital available locally, and because local ownership should help bank officers to focus better on local needs.

Hospital: If the hospital is not in town (rare in these listings), consider how long it will take to get to the emergency room.

Location: Ask yourself these questions about the distance from the town to an urban center: How will those miles affect your cost of transportation? Will you need to buy another vehicle? How will your budget for gasoline and maintenance be affected? How will those miles influence the number of visitors who come calling from other places—people you really want to see now and then?

Geography/Climate: Weather data give you some understanding of the climate. But you have to be on the scene to feel it in your bones. The same goes for geography.

Five Largest Employers: The job scene tells you a lot about the socioeconomic mix of a town. If the largest payrolls are factories, you may have a significant group of youngish residents and a pretty good source of tax revenue and retail business—and school kids! If the largest employer is a casino, you may have steady jobs at the gambling emporium plus a large influx of tourists. If the big payroll is a hospital, the town may be attractive to older folks. So, consider the implications of local employment. And check out your hunches.

High School: In Chapter 1, I describe the high school as the irreplaceable essential of every small town. No high school, no small town, at least by my definition. This entry tells you more about the school. You can compare the enrollment to other schools you are familiar with as well as the graduation rate and the percentage of graduates who go to college. When you note the various numbers, base your comparisons on these national statistics:

- 63% of high school graduates go to college.
- Average scores on the SAT reported in 2001: math, 514; verbal, 506. Total, 1020.
- Composite score on the ACT reported in 2000: 20.1.

Also, pay attention to the proportion of students taking either test compared to the number eligible to take the test. A higher proportion of students tested yields a more representative sample for the school as a whole.

Housing: Housing is a big bargain in small towns compared to cities. In fact, you may not believe the prices quoted in town listings for a "3BR 2BA" house. And well you should be skeptical! I believe that you can find decent housing within the price range quoted, but you may be accustomed to something more upscale than "decent." Small towns have neighborhoods, just like cities. Some neighborhoods cost more, some cost less. So, think "small-town middle class" when you interpret housing costs quoted here. The fuel that people use to heat their homes is indicated so that you can make comparisons with fuel costs you are familiar with.

Telecommunications: Look for towns where the telephone company offers DSL (digital subscriber line) service, or where you can make your Internet connection through cable-TV service. Most but not all towns offer one or the other.

Sales, Income Taxes: These are self-explanatory. But in low-tax states, ask around to discover if there are any other taxes that you may not be familiar with. Indiana counties, for example, charge a hefty annual excise tax for automobile licenses. For quick information on standard consumer taxes, call a CPA in the state or the office of a tax preparer like H&R Block.

Cost of Living: The items selected as a sample of local costs—movie ticket, doctor's appointment, plumber service, baby-sitting, dry cleaning, dinner out—are a grab bag of familiar services to give you some comparison numbers.

Community Infrastructure & Amenities: The items listed here need no introduction, but the ones I consider most important are a program to train future community leaders; some kind of program for kids, which could be offered through YMCA/YWCA, Boys & Girls Club, 4H, or a community recreation center; and a shelter for people in emergency home situations. A community that has the resources to provide all of these is soundly based.

United Way
Community foundation (Assets $_____)
Community leadership training program
Main Street
National Historic District
YMCA/YWCA
Boys Club/Girls Club
4-H
Bed-and-breakfast
Community recreational center
Motion picture theater
Public library
Public parks: No. ___, total acres _____
Public swimming pool
Airport
Country club
Golf course, __ holes
Emergency home shelter

Religious Denominations: If a church home is important to you and your denomination is not represented in a town that's otherwise appealing, check to see if your church is represented in a nearby town. The denominations represented in this book are listed below.

AME (African Methodist Episcopal)	Evangelical
	Four Square
Apostolic	Friends
Assemblies of God	Full Gospel
Baha'i	Independent
Baptist	Interdenominational
Buddhist	Jehovah's Witnesses
Catholic	Jewish congregation
Charismatic	Lutheran
Christian	Lutheran (ELCA)
Christian Science	Lutheran (Missouri)
Church of Christ	Mennonite
Church of God	Methodist
Church of Jesus Christ of Latter-Day Saints	Nondenominational
	Pentecostal
Church of the Nazarene	Presbyterian
Community	Presbyterian USA
Congregational	Seventh Day Adventist
Disciples of Christ	United Church of Christ
Eastern Orthodox	United Methodist
Episcopal	Wesleyan

Newspaper: If you get serious about a town, subscribe for a few months to the local newspaper. Letters to the editor may give you a feel for what's on people's minds.

Annual Festivals and Events: Only the highlights are listed. For a detailed calendar, contact the chamber of commerce (see below).

Further Information: Before telephoning or writing, try the town Web site, which may be run by the chamber of commerce or the town government. Some sites are better than others. A comprehensive, easy-to-use site tells you more than just town facts: It's a principal indicator of the value the town places on attracting visitors, businesses, and residents. One of the best I've seen is the Web site of Port Townsend, Washington. Take a look: www.porttownsendwa.com.

My Picks: The Top Ten

In my previous books about small towns, I introduced a method for ranking towns— No. 1, No. 2, No. 3, and so on. This has been a hugely popular feature among the upper-ranked towns and a challenge for many of the others that did not place as well. In this book, except for expressing my personal preferences about a limited number of towns (as you'll see in a moment), there are no rankings. I've concluded that it's impossible to rank small towns fairly. Too many qualities of town life simply can't be measured objectively. How do you score the overall social climate of a place? How do you score it for beauty? One person's Shangri-la is another person's Swampsville.

But we all have our opinions, don't we? And we love to share them! So I'm listing below the ten places among the 120 listed in this book that I consider the Top Ten among America's small towns, for reasons briefly explained here (you can find more in the listings later in the chapter). Incidentally, other researchers on the small-town scene also support one or more of these picks. Those experts are the National Trust for Historic Preservation; John Villani, author of *The 100 Best Small Art Towns in America;* and the editors of National Geographic's *Guide to Small Town Escapes.*

Berea, Kentucky
Columbus, Indiana
Fredericksburg, Texas
Litchfield, Connecticut
Madison, Georgia
Newport, Oregon
Oxford, Mississippi
Petoskey, Michigan
Port Townsend, Washington
Red Wing, Minnesota

Berea, the town, reflects the unique character of Berea, the college, founded in opposition to "sectarianism, slaveholding, caste, and every other wrong institution or practice." That was quite a position to take in Kentucky in 1855. The liberal tradition remains strong in Berea today and makes a nice blend with the traditional crafts practiced by a large number of local artists and craftsmen. Berea College is the largest employer in town, and its presence is a major influence on a high-quality public school system. See page 83.

Columbus, at 38,000 population, stretches the definition of "small town." But you forget the headcount on Main Street, which has the look and feel of a comfortable county seat in the Midwest, which Columbus is. But that's not all. Columbus is recognized nationally for public and private buildings designed by I. M. Pei, Eliel Saarinen, and Cesar Pelli, among other celebrated architects, and public art by Henry Moore. The town's principal employer and long-time benefactor, Cummins Engine Company, gets most of the credit. See page 110.

Fredericksburg tallied its assets in the mid-1970s and found: one dead president, LBJ, whose ranch was nearby; one dead admiral, Chester W. Nimitz, a native son; and one very large granite outcropping on the landscape. Not much else was going on. Flash forward. Fredericksburg today is a year-round destination for visitors attracted by upscale restaurants, galleries, and shops. Some residents commute to jobs in Austin and San Antonio. The Hill Country town has one of the best public school systems in Texas. See page 116.

Litchfield is often compared to Williamsburg, Virginia. Residents of the Connecticut town quickly observe that Litchfield is the real thing, not a re-creation. Incorporated in 1719, Litchfield was a crossroads in Colonial New England, a resting point for Founding Fathers on the road between New York and Boston. Besides the pleasures of a very pretty and well-stocked town—boutiques, eateries, antique shops, art galleries—Litchfield today offers its residents some of the best elementary and secondary schools in the nation. See page 121.

Madison is where the cotton planters of Morgan County built their homes in the early part of the nineteenth century. And it must have been some place. A Georgia history described Madison as the "most cultured and aristocratic town on the stagecoach route from Charleston to New Orleans." Madison today is very much the same place: a picture-perfect southern town that appreciates good quality and good taste and welcomes visitors who want to sample those delights, strolling under the shade trees along Main Street. See page 122.

Newport, once mainly dependent on fishing and forestry, broadened its economic base beginning in the 1980s by adding tourism and the arts to its attractions—not hard to do considering the spectacular Oregon Coast, though not everyone can tolerate the sturm und drang of oceanfront life. Two local institutions that thrive in the setting are the Oregon Coast Aquarium and Hatfield Marine Science Center. The latter draws Ph.D. residents into Newport. Kite flying and surf casting are favorite pastimes at the beach. See page 59.

Oxford is where William Faulkner lived and wrote, and it's where John Grisham began his writing career. Faulkner often took the air around Courthouse Square. Grisham and other contemporary authors often stop by to say hello at Square Books, the celebrated bookstore downtown. The permanent residents of Oxford are roughly equal in number to the student body at the University of Mississippi—Ole Miss—the major cultural influence in town. It's an agreeable mix, especially on football weekends. See page 97.

Petoskey, the name, is a corruption of a Native American word meaning "rising sun." The sunsets aren't too bad, either. Summer visitors from Detroit, Chicago, and other parts of the Midwest first put Petoskey on the map. Ernest Hemingway, who is reported to have spent twenty-two summers in Petoskey, pronounced it "priceless." Cottagers, skiers, and sightseers are an important economic prop to the town on Little Traverse Bay of Lake Michigan. Some clever folks have figured out how to live in Petoskey year-round. See page 60.

Port Townsend, once the busiest seaport on the West Coast, is a showcase of Victorian architecture, fully restored and forever protected in historic districts. The town hums with the normal activity of an 8,500-population community and is popular with retirees and second-home households. The romance of an old sailing town is part of the draw, as is Port Townsend's fortunate location in the rain shadow of the Olympic Mountains. It doesn't rain nearly as much as in nearby Seattle, and the weather's always mild. See page 61.

Red Wing has a long history of public-private partnerships, built upon strong industry, skilled labor, and a large number of very generous people—entrepreneurs interested in plowing profits back into community improvements, like restoring old buildings to life. The result is a stunning town center of well-preserved nineteenth century architecture and pleasant public parks. Sheldon Theatre, built in 1904, was America's first municipally funded performing arts center. Many Twin Cities workers call Red Wing home. See page 130.

Coastal Towns

Anacortes, WA 98221

Population: 14,557 (+28%)
Banks: 8 banks, including 2 branch banks.
Hospital: Island Hospital, 43 beds.

Location: On Fidalgo Island, across Deception Pass from Whidbey Island, in Puget Sound, 72 miles north of Seattle, 89 miles south of Vancouver, British Columbia.

Geography/Climate: Scenic seacoast island bounded on three sides by Puget Sound, mainland connection to the San Juan Islands. Temperate marine climate, usually cool, seldom extremely hot or very cold. January averages: low 33, high 46. Trace to 3 inches snow, frequent light rain, but location in the "rain shadow" of the Olympic Mountains keeps annual precipitation to about 25 inches, 10 inches less than Seattle. July averages: low 50, high 73. Warm, dry summers. Residents say they don't need air conditioning—or screens, apparently: no mosquitoes.

Five Largest Employers: Puget Sound Refining Co., 355 employees; Tesoro Northwest Co., 307; Anacortes School District, 250; Dakota Creek Industries, 225; Island Health Northwest, 200 (plus 224 part-time).

High School: Anacortes High School enrolls 1,000 students in grades 9–12. Graduation rate, 87%. 65% of graduates enroll in college/university. Composite ACT score, 24.5.

Housing: 3BR, 2BA house in good condition averages $239,000. Real estate tax, 1% of market value. Natural gas available. Residents also heat with electricity. Skagit River provides municipal water supply.

Telecommunications: Verizon—no DSL service. AT&T Broadband and Northland offer Internet connection via cable.

Sales, Income Taxes: 7.8% retail sales tax, groceries exempt; no state income tax.

Cost of living: Movie ticket, $7; doctor appointment, routine, $98; plumber per hour, $65; baby-sitting, per hour, $5; dry cleaning, men's suit, $9; dinner for 4, local restaurant, $65.

Community Infrastructure & Amenities:

United Way	Public library
Main Street member	Public parks: 14, totaling
Boys Club/Girls Club	2,420 acres
4-H	Public swimming pool
Bed-and-breakfast	Airport
Community recreational	Golf course
center	
Movie theater	

Religious Denominations

Apostolic	Four Square
Assemblies of God	Jehovah's Witnesses
Baptist	Jewish
Catholic	Congregation
Christian	Lutheran
Church of Christ	Methodist
Church of God	Nondenominational
Church of Jesus Christ Of	Pentecostal
Latter-Day Saints	Presbyterian
Episcopal	

Newspaper: *Anacortes American*, P.O. Box 39, Anacortes, WA 98221. 360-293-3122. goanacortes.com. Jack Darnton, editor. Published weekly. 6-month subscription, $29.

Annual festivals and events: May, Waterfront Festival; August, Arts Festival.

Further information: Anacortes Visitor Information Center, 819 Commercial Ave., Anacortes, WA 98221. 360-293-7911. anacortes@sos.net

Apalachicola, FL 32320

Population: 2,834 (+9%)
Banks: 3 banks, including 1 branch.
Hospital: George E. Weems Memorial Hospital, 25 beds.

Location: 65 miles southwest of Tallahassee, 60 miles southeast of Panama City, on the Florida Gulf Coast.

Geography/Climate: Shallow bays, spectacular white beaches, and dunes with elevations ranging from a few feet above sea level to almost 100 feet inland. Subtropical climate, reporting cooler summer temperatures than downstate and generally pleasant winters. Mediterranean-type weather good for citrus trees and vegetables. January temperatures range from low-30s at night to near 65 midday; July temperatures range from upper 60s to 90s. Year-round averages, 6 days below 32 degrees, 37 days above 90, humidity 73%. Precipitation 65 inches; snow, a trace. Precipitation on 66 days, thunderstorms on 68 days on average.

Five Largest Employers: Franklin County, 200 employees; George E. Weems Memorial Hospital, 80; Leavins Seafood, 60; Gulf Side TGA, 56; Lynn's Quality Seafood, 32.

High School: Apalachicola High School enrolls 360 students in grades 7–12, graduates 58%, sends 45% to college/university. Recent composite ACT score, 20.

Housing: 3BR 2BA house in good condition sells for $150,000 on average, but housing ranges up to $500,000. Annual real estate tax on average house, $2,975. Most people heat with electricity.

Telecommunications: DSL service "soon," town officials report.

Sales, Income Taxes: 6% retail sales tax, food exempt. No state income tax.

Cost of Living: Doctor appointment, routine, $57; plumber per hour, $50; baby sitting, per hour, $4–6; dry cleaning, men's suit, $7; dinner for 4, local restaurant, $150.

Community Infrastructure & Amenities:

United Way	Bed-and-breakfast
Main Street	Public library
National Historic	Public parks: 2
District	Airport

Religious Denominations:

Assemblies of God
Baptist
Catholic
Church of God
Church of Jesus Christ of
 Latter-Day Saints
Episcopal
Holiness Church of
 Living God
Jehovah's Witnesses
Pentecostal
United Methodist

Newspaper: *Apalachicola Times*, 82 Market Street, Apalachicola, FL 32320. 850-653-8868. apalachtimes.com. Published weekly. John F. Lee, editor. 3-month subscription by mail, $6.50. Tallahassee and Panama City dailies also sold in town.

Annual Festivals and Events: March, St. George Island Chili Cookoff; April, Historic Apalachicola Antique & Classic Boat Show; May, Annual Spring Tour of Historic Homes; November, Annual Florida Seafood Festival.

Further Information: Apalachicola Bay Chamber of Commerce, 99 Market St., Apalachicola, FL 32320. 850-653-9419. chamber@digitalexp.com

Astoria, OR 97103

Population: 9,813 (–2.5%)
Banks: 5 banks, including 4 branch banks.
Hospital: Columbia Memorial Hospital, 45 beds.

Location: 96 miles west of Portland, at the north-western corner of Oregon, where the Columbia River pours into the Pacific Ocean.

Geography/Climate: Pacific air moderates the overall climate, and ocean breezes preserve air quality. Moderate year-round temperatures. Rainy winters, pleasant summers, long growing season. Average summer temperatures range from 60s by the water to 80s inland. Winter daytime average, 50 degrees, dropping to lower 40s at night. Often cloudy, averaging 200+ cloudy days, 75 or so part-ly cloudy, 70 or so clear. Summer and fall are best bets for sunshine.

Five Largest Employers: United States Coast Guard, 386 persons; Columbia Memorial Hospital, 240; Management Training Corporation, 186; Clatsop Care Centers, 90; Red Lion Inn, 80.

High School: Astoria High School enrolls 750 stu-dents in grades 9–12, graduates 82%, sends 65% to college-university. Recent composite SAT for 52% of eligible students taking test, 1,083.

Housing: 3 BR 2BA house in good condition sells for $145,000 to $165,000. Real estate taxes on such a house, $2,600. Bear Creek Watershed supplies the municipal water system. Most people heat with natural gas.

Telecommunications: Charter Communications provides Internet connection via cable at 500 Kbps.

Sales, Income Taxes: No retail sales tax in Oregon. State income tax is scaled 5% to 9%.

Cost of Living: Movie ticket, $7; doctor appoint-ment, routine, $80; plumber per hour, $110; baby-sitting, per hour, $4; dry cleaning, men's suit, $12.50; dinner for 4, local restaurant, $80.

Community Infrastructure & Amenities:

United Way
Community leadership
  training program
Main Street
National Historic District
4-H
Bed-and-breakfast
Community
  recreational center
Motion picture theater
Public library

Public parks: 30 parks,
  totaling 90 acres
Public swimming pool
Country club
Golf course, 18 holes
Emergency home shelter

Religious Denominations:

Baptist
Catholic
Church of Jesus Christ of
  Latter-Day Saints
Church of the Nazarene
Episcopal
Lutheran
Lutheran (Missouri)
Methodist

Nondenominational
Presbyterian

Newspaper: *Daily Astorian*, 949 Exchange Street, Astoria, OR 97103. 503-325-3211. dailyastorian.com. Steve Forrester, editor. 3-month subscription by mail, $39. *New York Times, Wall Street Journal* also sold in town.

Annual Festivals and Events: February, Fisher Poets Gathering; April, Crab and Seafood Festival; June, Scandinavian Mid-Summer Festival; October, Great Columbia Crossing Bridge 10K Run, Silver Salmon Celebration. Astoria is the oldest American town west of the Rockies.

Further Information: Astoria-Warrenton Area Chamber of Commerce, 111 W. Marine Drive, Astoria, OR 97103. 503-325-6311. awacc@seasurf.com

Bath, ME 04530

Population: 9,266 (–8%)

Banks: 6 banks, 4 of which are branches.

Hospital: Midcoast Hospital in Brunswick (10 miles), 120 beds.

Location: One-third of the way up the Maine coast, on the Kennebec River, 35 miles northeast of Portland, 109 miles southwest of Bangor

Geography/Climate: Elevation 70 feet. Surrounding area is rolling farmland, forests, islands, peninsulas, bays, and beaches. Moderate climate influenced by proximity to the Atlantic Ocean, about 18 miles southeast. Winter temperatures range from zero to 40; summer from 50 to 85. Average rainfall, 40 inches; snowfall, 75. Very pleasant summers; brilliant falls when foliage becomes red, orange, and gold.

Five Largest Employers: Bath Iron Works, shipyard, 12,000 employees during peak employment; U.S. Navy at Brunswick, 4,500; L.L. Bean in Freeport and Brunswick, 5,000; Midcoast Hospital, Brunswick, 600; Bath Public Schools, 400.

High School: Morse High School enrolls 819 students in grades 9–12. Approximately 50% of graduates enroll in college/university. Recent composite SAT scores: verbal, 413; math 460.

Housing: 3BR 2BA house in good condition sells for about $100,000. Most people heat with oil.

Telecommunications: Verizon offers DSL service; Susquehanna Communications provides Internet access on the cable system.

Sales, Income Taxes: Retail sales tax, 5%. State income tax scaled 3% to 9%.

Cost of Living: Movie ticket, $8; doctor appointment, routine, $40; plumber per hour, $40; baby sitting, per hour, $6; dry cleaning, men's suit, $15; dinner for 4, local restaurant, $45.

Community Infrastructure & Amenities:

United Way
Community leadership training program
National historic district
Bed-and-breakfast
Community recreational center/YMCA
Public library
Public parks (2)
Public swimming pool
Country club
Golf course, 18 holes

Religious Denominations:

Apostolic
Assemblies of God
Baptist
Catholic
Christian
Church of Christ
Church of Jesus Christ of Latter-Day Saints
Church of the Nazarene
Episcopal
Evangelical
Four Square
Jewish Congregation
Methodist
Pentecostal
Presbyterian
Salvation Army
Seventh Day Adventist
United Church of Christ
United Methodist

Newspaper: *Times Record*, P.O. Box 10, Brunswick, ME 04011. 207-729-3311. timesrecord.com. Published daily. *New York Times*, *Wall Street Journal*, *Portland Press Herald* also sold in town.

Annual Festivals and Events: July 4, Bath Heritage Days.

Further Information: Chamber of Commerce of the Bath/Brunswick Region, 45 Front Street, Bath, ME 04530. 207-443-9751. chamber@midcoast-maine.com

Beaufort, NC 28516

Population: 12,098 (+17%)

Banks: 5, all branches of out-of-town banks.

Hospital: Carteret General Hospital in Morehead City (7 miles), 117 beds.

Location: 145 miles southeast of Raleigh, 90 miles northeast of Wilmington, at the southern end of the Outer Banks on the Atlantic coast.

Geography/Climate: Mild winters, warm summers, glorious spring and fall seasons, and all seasons influenced by the humid ocean air. Winter air masses from the northwest do reach this far but lose much of their punch at the Atlantic. Annual precipitation, 54 inches; snowfall, a trace. Seasonally, 45 days at freezing or below; 43 days at 90 or above; humidity, 74%. January daily temperatures from low 30s to low 50s; July, from upper 60s to upper 80s.

Five Largest Employers: Carteret County, 353 employees; Atlantic Veneer Corporation, 325; Duke University Marine Laboratory, 100; Beaufort Fisheries, 75; Clawson's Restaurant, 70.

High School: East Carteret High School enrolls 650 students in grades 9–12, graduates 99%, sends 84% to college/university. Composite SAT for 70% of eligible students taking test, 1000.

Housing: 3BR 2BA house, outside the Historic District, $175,000 to $180,000, with real estate tax of about $1,400 a year; inside the Historic District, $250,000 to $1 million. An architectural showplace, Beaufort (pronounced BO-furt) has more than a hundred well-preserved houses in Greek Revival, federal, and Victorian style. Most are heated/cooled with electricity or LP gas.

Telecommunications: Sprint provides DSL service. Time-Warner provides Internet connection by cable.

Sales, Income Taxes: Retail sales tax, 6.5%. State income tax, 6% to 7.75%.

Cost of Living: Doctor appointment, routine, $40–$70; plumber per hour, $25–$50; baby-sitting per hour, $5; dry cleaning, men's suit, $6.50; dinner for 4, local restaurant, $70+.

Community Infrastructure & Amenities:

Community leadership training program	Boys Club/Girls Club
	Public library
National Historic District	Public parks: 4
Bed-and-breakfasts (many)	Airport

Religious Denominations

AME	Lutheran (ELCA)
Baptist	Mennonite
Christian	Methodist
Church of Christ	Nondenominational
Church of Jesus Christ of Latter-Day Saints	Pentecostal
Disciples of Christ	Presbyterian
Episcopal	Seventh Day Adventist
Independent	United Church of Christ
Jehovah's Witnesses	United Methodist

Newspaper: *Carteret News Times*, P.O. Box 1679, Morehead City, NC 28557. 252-726-7081. www.carteretnewstimes.com. Published Wednesday, Friday, Sunday. Walter Phillips, editor. 3-month subscription by mail, $13. *New York Times, Wall Street Journal, USA Today*, and major North Carolina dailies also sold in town.

Annual Festivals and Events: last weekend April, Music Festival; first weekend May, Wooden Boat Show; Arts & Crafts Coalition Shows, Memorial Day weekend, 4th of July weekend, Labor Day weekend; last full weekend June, Old Homes & Gardens Tour; Sunday before Thanksgiving, Community Thanksgiving Feast; two weekends December, Christmas Walk. The discovery of Blackbeard's ship, *Queen Anne's Revenge*, in the Beaufort Inlet has received wide attention.

Further Information: Beaufort Historical Association, P.O. Box 363, Beaufort, NC 28516. 800-575-7483. bha@bmd.clis.com

Beaufort, SC 29901

Population: 9,516 (+ 6%)
Banks: 19 banks including 8 branches.
Hospital: Beaufort Memorial Hospital, 200 beds.

Location: 67 miles southwest of Charleston, 38 miles northeast of Savannah, Georgia, just up from Hilton Head, on the Atlantic Ocean.

Geography/Climate: The town is an island in a county of 64 major islands and hundreds of smaller ones, in the Georgia low country, elevation 21 feet. Maritime, nearly subtropical climate. Mild winters; hot, humid summers. Average growing season 293 days. Average temperatures—January: high, 59; low, 38; July: high, 89; low, 71. Possible sunshine averages 63% year-round; April and May are sunniest. Average rainfall, 50 inches.

Five Largest Employers: Beaufort County School District, 2,055; Beaufort Memorial Hospital, 958; Beaufort County, 955; Super Wal-Mart, 550; U.S. Marine Corps Air Station, 505.

High School: Beaufort High School enrolls 1,511 students in grades 9–12, graduates 94%, sends 85% to college/university. Recent composite score on SAT for 100% of eligible students taking test, 957.

Housing: 3BR 2BA house in good condition sells in range of $125,000 to $200,000 depending on views. Taxes, $1,200–$2,000. Most people heat with electricity.

Telecommunications: DSL service available through Sprint and Hargray at 516 Kbps.

Sales, Income Taxes: Retail sales tax, 5%. State income tax ranges from 3% to 7%.

Cost of living: Movie ticket, $5.50; doctor appointment, routine, $35; plumber per hour, $45; baby sitting, per hour, $5; dry cleaning, men's suit, $9; dinner for 4, local restaurant, $75.

Community Infrastructure & Amenities:

United Way	Bed-and-breakfast
Community foundation	Community recreational center
Community leadership training program	Movie theater
Main Street member	Public library
National Historic District	Public parks: 13
YMCA/YWCA	Public swimming pool
Boys Club/Girls Club	Airport
	Country club
	Golf course

Religious Denominations:

AME	Episcopal
Apostolic	Evangelical
Assemblies of God	Full Gospel
Baptist	Jehovah's Witnesses
Catholic	Jewish Congregation
Christian	Lutheran (ELCA)
Church of Christ	Methodist
Church of God	Presbyterian
Church of Jesus Christ Of Latter-Day Saints	Seventh Day Adventist
Church of the Nazarene	United Church of Christ
Community	United Methodist

Newspaper: *Beaufort Gazette*, 843-524-3183. beaufortgazette.com. Published daily. James Cato, editor. 3-month mail subscription, $42. *New York Times*, *Wall Street Journal* also sold in town.

Annual festivals and events: March, Spring Tour of Homes, Gallery Walk; April, A Taste of Beaufort; May, Gullah Festival; July, Town of Port Royal July 4th Celebration and Water Festival; October, Shrimp Festival; December, Port Royal Christmas Tree Lighting Ceremony.

Further information: Greater Beaufort Chamber of Commerce, 1106 Carteret St., Beaufort, SC 29901. 843-986-5400. chamber@islc.net

Elizabeth City, NC 27909

Population: 17,218 (+17%)
Banks: 12 banks, including 6 branch banks.
Hospital: Albemarle Hospital, 182 beds.

Location: 160 miles northeast of Raleigh, 60 miles south of Norfolk, Virginia, off Albemarle Sound in coastal North Carolina.

Geography/Climate: Situated at the narrows of the Pasquotank River, 12 nautical miles up from Albemarle Sound. Elevation 8 feet. Low, level land with Great Dismal Swamp to the north. Common track of hurricanes and tropical storms passes south of the area, continental storm system passes to the north, favoring Elizabeth City with pleasant springs and falls, mild winters. January temperatures range from 32 low to 49 high. July, 70 low to 87 high. Summers are warm, humid, long, with average 30 days at 90 or above. Annual average rainfall, 40 inches; snowfall, 5 inches.

Five Largest Employers: Elizabeth City-Pasquotank County Schools, 825 employees; Albemarle Hospital, 816; United States Coast Guard, 950 including 500 military; Elizabeth City State University, 415; City of Elizabeth City, 256.

High School: Northeastern High School enrolls 850 students in grades 9–12, graduates 95%, sends 51% to college/university. Recent composite SAT for 73% of eligible students taking test, 916.

Housing: 3BR 2BA house in good condition sells for average $98,000, though some properties range up to $225,000. Average annual real estate tax, $1,445. Residents heat with oil, LP gas, electricity.

Telecommunications: Sprint provides DSL service. Adelphia provides Internet connection via cable.

Sales, Income Taxes: Retail sales tax, 6.5%. State income tax scaled 6% to 7.7%.

Cost of Living: Movie ticket, $4; doctor appointment, routine, $50; plumber per hour, $40–45; baby-sitting, per hour, $5; dry cleaning, men's suit, $10; dinner for 4, local restaurant, $40.

Community Infrastructure & Amenities:
United Way
Community foundation
Main Street
National Historic District
Boys Club/Girls Club
4-H
Bed-and-breakfast
Community recreational center
Motion picture theater
Public library
Public parks, 6 parks totaling 15 acres
Public swimming pool
Airport
Country club
Golf course, 9 holes par 3
Emergency home shelter (women and children only)

Religious Denominations
AME
Apostolic
Assemblies of God
Baptist
Catholic
Charismatic
Christian
Church of Christ
Church of God
Church of Jesus Christ of Latter-Day Saints
Church of the Nazarene
Community
Disciples of Christ
Episcopal
Evangelical
Full Gospel
Holiness
Independent
Interdenominational
Jehovah's Witnesses
Lutheran
Mennonite
Methodist
Nazarene
Nondenominational
Pentecostal
Presbyterian
Presbyterian USA
Seventh Day Adventist
United Church of Christ
United Methodist
Wesleyan

Newspaper: *Daily Advance*, P.O. Box 588, Elizabeth City, NC 27907. 252-335-0841. dailyadvance.com. Published daily. Mike Goodman, editor. 3-month subscription by mail, $31.50.

Annual Festivals and Events: May, Albemarle Potato Festival; June, Juneteenth Celebration; July, River City Bull Bash, bull riding competition; September, Moth Boat Regatta; October, Albemarle Craftsmen's Fair.

Further Information: Elizabeth City Area Chamber of Commerce, 502 E. Ehringhaus Street, Elizabeth City, NC 27909. 252-335-4365.

Georgetown, SC 29442

Population: 8,950 (–6%)

Banks: 8, including 3 branch banks.

Hospital: Georgetown Memorial Hospital, 142 beds.

Location: 35 miles south of Myrtle Beach, 60 miles north of Charleston, 8 miles inland from the Atlantic Ocean, on U.S. Highway 17 in the Low Country.

Geography/Climate: Coastal flatlands ranging from sea level to about 20 feet elevation. 70% of county land area used for cultivation of predominantly softwood trees. Temperate climate, modified by the ocean. Mild winters; warm, windy, often stormy springs; long, hot, humid summers; very nice but short falls, with much sun and pleasant temperatures. Averages for January: low, 36; high, 59. July: low, 70; high, 89. Annual rainfall, 50 inches. Trace of snow.

Five Largest Employers: Georgetown County School District, 1,850; International Paper Company, 1,400; Georgetown Steel Corporation, 750; Georgetown Memorial Hospital, 600; County of Georgetown, 420.

High School: Georgetown High School enrolls 1,080 students in grades 9–12, graduates 40%, sends 60% of graduates to college/university.

Housing: 3BR 2BA house sells for about $150,000, pays real estate tax of about $1,200. Most households heat with electricity.

Telecommunications: Verizon offers DSL service. Time Warner offers Internet connection via cable.

Sales, Income Taxes: Retail sales tax, 5%. State income tax scaled 2% to 7%.

Cost of Living: Doctor appointment, routine, $30; plumber per hour, $55; baby-sitting per hour, $5; dry cleaning, men's suit, $6.60; dinner for 4, local restaurant, $100.

Community Infrastructure & Amenities:

United Way
Community leadership training program
Main Street
National Historic District
4-H
Bed-and-breakfast
Community recreational center
Public Library
Public parks: 8, totaling about 40 acres
Airport
Country club
Golf courses: 11 in the area
Emergency home shelter

Religious Denominations:

AME
Apostolic
Assemblies of God
Baptist
Catholic
Christian
Church of Christ
Church of God
Church of Jesus Christ of Latter-Day Saints
Church of the Nazarene
Eastern Orthodox
Episcopal
Evangelical
Friends
Full Gospel
Independent
Jehovah's Witnesses
Lutheran
Methodist
Nondenominational
Pentecostal
Presbyterian
Salvation Army
United Methodist

Newspaper: *Georgetown Times*, 615 Front Street, Georgetown, SC 29440. 843-546-4148. www.gtown-times.com. Published three times a week. 6-month subscription by mail, $16.

Annual Festivals and Events: June, Annual Harbor Walk Festival and Boat Race; October, Annual Georgetown Wooden Boat Exhibit and Boat Building Contest.

Further Information: Visitor Service Director, 1001 Front Street, Georgetown, SC 29440. 843-546-8436.

Homer, AK 99603

Population: 3,946 (+8%)
Banks: 2, both branches of out-of-town banks.
Hospital: South Peninsula Hospital, 45 beds.

Location: Off the Gulf of Alaska, 225 miles south-west of Anchorage, near the end of the Kenai Peninsula and adjacent to Kachemak State Park & Wilderness Park.

Geography/Climate: Remarkably tolerable weather for so far north, with the Gulf of Alaska providing warmth and moisture and the Alaska Range blocking the worst onslaughts of cold from the Pole. January average low temperature, 16 degrees; high 28. July: 40 degrees low, 60 high. Annual rainfall, 25 inches; snowfall, 58 inches. May is the sunniest month.

Five Largest Employers: South Peninsula Hospital, 227 employees; Kenia Peninsula School District, 154; City of Homer, 99; Lands End Resort, 71; Safeway supermarket, 71.

High School: Homer High School enrolls 508 students in grades 9–12, graduates 95% (including students enrolled in the alternative high school, currently 50), sends 70%–80% of graduates to college/university. Composite ACT for 80% of eligible students taking test, 23.2. Composite SAT for same percentage, 1100.

Housing: 3BR 2BA house in good condition sells in the range of $120,000 to $180,000 depending on the view and pays about $1,020 to $1,530 in real estate tax. Most people heat with propane gas or oil.

Telecommunications: Alaska Communication Service (ACS) provides DSL service.

Sales, Income Taxes: 5.5% retail sales tax, grocery food exempt. No state income tax.

Cost of Living: Movie ticket, $6; doctor appointment, routine, $75; plumber per hour, $65; baby-sitting per hour, $5–$6; dry cleaning, women's slacks, $3.50; dinner for 4, local restaurant, $56–$60.

Community Infrastructure & Amenities:

United Way	Public parks: 4 within the
Community foundation	city, 3 very large parks
Boys Club/Girls Club	nearby
4-H	Public swimming pool
Bed-and-breakfast (120	Airport
establishments)	Golf course, 18 holes
Community recreational	Emergency home shelter
center	
Motion picture theater	
Public library	

Religious Denominations:

Assemblies of God	Friends
Baha'i	Independent
Baptist	Jehovah's Witnesses
Catholic	Lutheran
Christian	Methodist
Church of Christ	Nondenominational
Church of Jesus Christ of	Presbyterian
Latter-Day Saints	Salvation Army
Church of the Nazarene	Seventh Day Adventist
Covenant	Shekinah
Eastern Orthodox	Unitarian
Episcopal	United Methodist

Newspaper: *Homer News*, 3482 Landings Street, Homer, AK 99603. 907-235-7767. homeralaska.com. Published weekly, Thursday. Gary Thomas, editor. *Homer Tribune*, 601 E. Pioneer Avenue, Suite 109, Homer, AK 99603. 907-235-3714. visithomeralaska.com. Published weekly, Tuesday. June Pascall, editor. *Anchorage Daily News* also sold in town.

Annual Festivals and Events: early February, Homer Winter Carnival; March, King Salmon Tournament; April, Sea-to-Ski Triathlon; early May, Kachemak Bay Shorebird Festival; May through Labor Day, Halibut Derby; August, Summer String Festival; Octoberfest; December, Nutcracker performance; New Year's Eve, "Edible Arts" Exhibition and Feast.

Further Information: Homer Chamber of Commerce, P.O. Box 541, Homer, AK 99603. 907-235-7740. home@xyz.net

Lincoln City, OR 97367

Population: 7,437 (+26%)
Banks: 7 branch banks.
Hospital: Samaritan North Lincoln Hospital, 37 beds.

Location: 88 miles southwest of Portland, 122 miles northwest of Eugene, on the central Oregon coast.

Geography/Climate: 7 miles of sandy Pacific shoreline, backed up by the Coast Ranges. 12 miles east of Lincoln City, Scott Mountain peaks at 3,128 feet. Marine climate, controlled by warm, moist ocean air. Moderate year-round temperatures. Average summer temperatures range from breezy 60–70 degrees at ocean front to 80–90 degrees a few miles inland. Winter daytime average, 50 degrees, dropping to upper-30s at night. Light winter rains mixed with sunny days, occasional winter storms. Annual rainfall, 72 inches; snowfall, trace. Coastal winds preserve excellent air quality.

Five Largest Employers: Chinook Winds Casino, 800 employees; Samaritan North Lincoln Hospital, 328; Westin Salishan Resort, 200; Inn at Spanish Head, 118; Lincoln City Government, 100.

High School: Taft High School enrolls 653 students in grades 9–12.

Housing: 3BR 2BA house in good condition, $135,000 to $160,000. Households heat with electricity and natural gas.

Telecommunications: Charter Communications provides Internet connection via cable.

Sales, Income Taxes: No retail sales tax. State income tax scaled 5% to 9%.

Cost of Living: Movie ticket, $7.25; doctor appointment, routine, $52; plumber per hour, $68.50; babysitting (10-hour day), infant, $24.40; preschool, $20.50; dry cleaning, men's suit, $8.95; dinner for 4, local restaurant, no alcohol or dessert, $63.80.

Community Infrastructure & Amenities:

Bed-and-breakfast
Community recreational center
Motion picture theater
Public library
Public parks: 14, totaling 97 acres, plus 216 acres of undeveloped land
Public swimming pool
Golf course, 18 holes

Religious Denominations:

Assemblies of God
Baptist
Catholic
Christian
Church of Jesus Christ of Latter-Day Saints
Church of the Nazarene
Congregational
Episcopal
Evangelical
Four Square
Jehovah's Witnesses
Lutheran
Nondenominational
Presbyterian
Presbyterian USA
Seventh Day Adventist

Newspaper: *The News Guard*, 930 SE Hwy 101, Lincoln City, OR 97367. 541-994-2178. www.thenewsguard.com. Published weekly, Gail Kimberling, editor. 3-month subscription by mail, $7.50. *Wall Street Journal*, *USA Today*, and Oregon metro dailies also sold in town.

Annual Festivals and Events: August, Sand Castle Building Competition; September, Fall Kite Festival; October, Glass Float Ball.

Further Information: Lincoln City Chamber of Commerce, 4039 NW Logan Blvd., Lincoln City, OR 97367. 541-994-3070. lcchamber@harborside.com

Newport, OR 97365

Population: 9,532 (+13%)
Banks: 8 branch banks.
Hospital: Pacific Communities Hospital, 48 beds.

Location: 133 miles southwest of Portland, 93 miles northwest of Eugene, on the central Oregon coast.

Geography/Climate: Situated just west of the Coast Ranges at Yaquina Bay. Moderate coastal climate with mild winters, cool summers. December–March period can be dreary as Pacific Ocean moisture turns to clouds and rain onshore. January averages: high, 50; low, 39. July: high, 64; low, 51. August through October is sunniest stretch. Annual rainfall, 63 inches. Rare snowfall melts fast.

Five Largest Employers: Lincoln County School District, 282; Pacific Communities Health District, 267; Oregon State University/Hatfield Marine Science Center, 265; Depoe Bay Fish Company, 150; Lincoln County, 127.

High School: Newport High School enrolls 695 students in grades 9–12, graduates 94%, sends 40% of graduates to college/university. Composite SAT score for 30% of eligible students taking test, 1094.

Housing: 3BR 2BA house sells in range of $112,000 to $129,000, pays real estate tax of $2,000 to $2,300. Most people heat with electricity.

Telecommunications: Qwest planning to offer DSL service "sometime in 2002." Charter Communications offers Internet connection via cable.

Sales, Income Taxes: No retail sales tax. State income tax scaled 5% to 9%.

Cost of Living: Movie ticket, $7.25; doctor appointment, routine, $73; plumber per hour, $60; baby-sitting per hour, $2.50; dry cleaning, men's suit, $8.95; dinner for 4, local restaurant, $65.

Community Infrastructure & Amenities:

United Way	Community recreational
Community foundation	center
(Assets $700,000)	Motion picture theater
Community leadership	Public library
training program	Public parks: 29 state
Main Street	parks in area
National Historic District	Public swimming pool
YMCA/YWCA	Airport
Boys Club/Girls Club	Golf course, 9 holes
4-H	Emergency home shelter
Bed-and-breakfast	

Religious Denominations:

Apostolic	Four Square
Assemblies of God	Jehovah's Witnesses
Baptist	Lutheran
Catholic	Lutheran (ELCA)
Christian	Methodist
Church of Christ	Pentecostal
Church of Jesus Christ	Presbyterian
of Latter-Day Saints	Presbyterian USA
Church of the Nazarene	Seventh Day Adventist
Episcopal	
Evangelical	

Newspaper: *Newport News-Times*, 831 NE Avery, Newport, OR 97365. 541-265-8571. www.newport-newstimes.com. Published twice weekly, Leslie O'Donnell, editor. 3-month subscription by mail, $13. *Wall Street Journal, USA Today* also sold in town.

Annual Festivals and Events: February, Seafood and Wine Festival; March, Home and Garden Show; April, Newport Swing Choir Festival (high school choir competition); June, Newport Marathon, Gem & Mineral Show; September, Rhythms By the Bay Festival, Stories by the Sea Festival; November, Oyster Cloister; December, Whale Watching Week.

Further Information: Newport Chamber of Commerce, 555 SW Coast Highway, Newport, OR 97365. 541-265-8801. chamber@newportnet.com

Petoskey, MI 49770

Population: 6,080 (+0.3%)
Banks: 13, including 6 branch banks.
Hospital: Northern Michigan Hospital, 228 beds.

Location: 37 miles below the Straits of Mackinac, 260 miles northwest of Detroit, in the northwest corner of the Lower Peninsula of Michigan.

Geography/Climate: Scenic Lake Michigan shore town on Little Traverse Bay. Forested rolling hills. Snowbelt location brings average 121 inches a year, 32 inches of rain. January average temperatures range from 15 to 28 degrees; July, 59 to 76. Long winters, mild summers, colorful falls.

Five Largest Employers: Northern Michigan Hospital, 1,250 employees; Boyne USA Resorts, ski and golf resort, 600; Continental Structural Plastics, 250; Petoskey Plastics, 162; H&D, Inc.

High School: Petoskey High School enrolls 1,088 students in grades 9–12, graduates 96.4%, sends 66% of students to college/university. Composite ACT for 72% of eligible students taking test, 23.6.

Housing: 3BR 2BA house in good condition sold for average $195,500 in 2001. Real estate tax on such a house with homestead exemption, $4,078. Most people heat with natural gas.

Telecommunications: Charter Communications offers Internet connection via cable.

Sales, Income Taxes: Retail sales tax, 6%. State income tax, flat 4.1%.

Cost of Living: Movie ticket, $6.50; doctor appointment, routine, $50; plumber per hour, $65; baby-sitting per hour, $3–$6; dry cleaning, men's suit, $9; dinner for 4, local restaurant, $60.

Community Infrastructure & Amenities

United Way	Public library
Community foundation (Assets $7 million)	Public parks, 24 parks, totaling 1,200 acres
Community leadership training program	Public swimming pool: planned part of new community college
Main Street	
National Historic District	Airport
Boys Club/Girls Club	Country club
4-H	Golf courses: 2 18-hole courses in town; 20 courses in area
Bed-and-breakfast	
Community recreational center	Emergency home shelter
Motion picture theater	

Religious Denominations

Assemblies of God	Jewish Congregation
Baptist	Lutheran
Catholic	Lutheran (ELCA)
Christian	Mennonite
Christian Science	Methodist
Church of Christ	Missionary
Church of God	Nondenominational
Church of Jesus Christ of Latter-Day Saints	Pentecostal
Church of the Nazarene	Presbyterian
Episcopal	Salvation Army
Independent	Seventh Day Adventist
Interdenominational	United Church of Christ
Jehovah's Witnesses	United Methodist

Newspaper: *Petoskey News-Review*, 319 State Street, Petoskey, MI 49770. 231-347-2544. www.petoskeynews.com. Published daily, Ken Winter, editor. 3-month subscription by mail, $52.50. *New York Times, Wall Street Journal, Detroit Free Press* also sold in town.

Annual Festivals and Events: February, Winter Festival at Winter Sports Park; June, Gallery Walk (food, wine, art); July, Art in the Park (fine art show), sidewalk sales, concerts; December, Christmas Holiday Open House.

Further Information: Petoskey Regional Chamber of Commerce, 401 E. Mitchell St., Petoskey, MI 49770. 231-439-9124. chamber@petoskey.com

Port Townsend, WA 98368

Population: 8,334 (+19%)
Banks: 7, including one locally owned.
Hospital: Jefferson General Hospital, 31 regular beds, 6 ICU beds.

Location: 55 miles northwest of Seattle by ferry, on the northeast corner of the Olympic Peninsula at the entrance to Puget Sound.

Geography/Climate: Marine mild climate. Pacific air stream produces a mild but damp winter and mildly warm, sunny summer. January average temperatures range from 35 to 44 degrees; July, 50 to 71. About 20 inches of rain, mainly from November through March. Up to 5 inches of snow, but none some years.

Five Largest Employers: Port Townsend Paper Corporation, 375 employees; Jefferson County Government, 273; Jefferson General Hospital, 217; Port Townsend School District, 173; Safeway supermarket, 135.

High School: Port Townsend High School enrolls 616 students in grades 9–12, graduates 92%, sends 55% to college/university. Composite ACT for 7% of students taking test, 22.

Housing: 3BR 2BA house in town, $239,000 to $425,000 depending on views. Most people heat with electricity.

Telecommunications: Millennium cable provides broadband Internet connection to subscribers in a limited section of town.

Sales, Income Taxes: Retail sales tax, 7.9%. No state income tax.

Cost of Living: Movie ticket, $6.50; doctor appointment, routine, $50–60; plumber per hour, $90; baby sitting per hour, $6.50; dry cleaning, men's suit, $4.95; dinner for 4, local restaurant, $60+.

Community Infrastructure & Amenities:

United Way
Community foundation
Main Street
National Historic Districts (2)
YMCA/YWCA
Boys Club/Girls Club
4-H
Bed-and-breakfasts (17)
Community recreational center
Motion picture theaters (3)
Public library
Public parks: 3 within city limits, vast recreational area in Olympic National Forest nearby
Public swimming pool
Airport
Golf course, 9 holes
Emergency home shelters (2)

Religious Denominations:

Apostolic
Assemblies of God
Baptist
Catholic
Christian Science
Church of Christ
Church of God
Church of Jesus Christ of Latter-Day Saints
Church of the Nazarene
Community Congregational
Disciples of Christ
Eastern Orthodox
Episcopal
Evangelical
Four Square
Friends
Full Gospel
Independent
Interdenominational
Jehovah's Witnesses
Jewish congregation
Lutheran
Mennonite
Methodist
Nondenominational
Pentecostal
Presbyterian
Presbyterian USA
Seventh Day Adventist
Unitarian
United Church of Christ
United Methodist
Unity
Zen

Newspaper: *Jefferson County Leader*, P.O. Box 552, Port Townsend, WA 98368. 360-385-2900. Published weekly. 6-month subscription by mail, $28. *New York Times*, *Wall Street Journal* also sold in town.

Annual Festivals and Events: February, Chamber Music Festival, Shipwrights' Regatta, Arctic Open Gold Tourney; March, Kitemakers' Conference, Taste of Port Townsend; April, Port to Port Regatta; May, Rhododendron Festival; June, Olympic Music Festival, American Fiddle Tunes Workshop; July, JeffCo Airport Fly-In, Jazz Port Townsend; August, Chamber Music Workshop; September, Wooden Boat Festival; October, Art in Port Townsend, Mushroom Show; November, Fall Arts & Crafts Fair; mid-December, Christmas Bazaar.

Further Information: Port Townsend Visitor Center, 2437 E. Sims Way, Port Townsend, WA 98368. 360-385-2722. 888-365-6978. ptguide.com

Rockland, ME 04841

Population: 7,609 (5%)

Banks: 10, including 8 branch banks.

Hospital: Penobscot Bay Medical Center, located in Rockport (3 miles), 120 beds.

Location: 81 miles northeast of Portland, 63 miles southwest of Bangor, on a well-protected Atlantic Ocean harbor at the mouth of Penobscot Bay.

Geography/Climate: Rocky New England sea-coast. Winters can be long and severe but are tempered by the ocean. Average 160 days at freezing or below. Up to 70 inches of snow, but it doesn't last long. Extremely pleasant summers with only 5 days on average into the 90s. Sunny, pleasant falls.

Five Largest Employers: Samoset Resort, 260–400 employees; MBNA New England, 400; Nautica apparel distribution center, 320; Fisher Engineering, 160; Carrier Publications, 150.

High School: Rockland District High School enrolls 600 students in grades 9–12, graduates 95%, sends 70% to college/university. Composite SAT for 60% of senior class taking test (93 students): math, 504; verbal, 511. Composite ACT for 12% of seniors taking test (18 students): 22.1.

Housing: 3BR 2BA house in good condition sells for $110,000 to $120,000, pays about $2,100 in real estate tax. Most people heat with oil.

Telecommunications: Adelphia provides Internet connection via cable.

Sales, Income Taxes: Retail sales tax, 5.5%. State income tax scaled 2% to 8.5%.

Cost of Living: Movie ticket, $7; doctor appointment, routine, $45; plumber per hour, $40–$45; baby-sitting per hour, $6–8; dry cleaning, men's suit, $8–$9; dinner for 4, local restaurant, $80.

Community Infrastructure & Amenities:

Main Street	Motion picture theater
National Historic District	Public library
Boys Club/Girls Club	Public parks, 7 parks
4-H	totaling 19 acres
Bed-and-breakfast	Golf course, 18 holes
Community recreational	Emergency home shelter
center	

Religious Denominations:

Baptist
Catholic
Christian
Church of God
Church of Jesus Christ of
  Latter-Day Saints
Church of the Nazarene
Congregational
Episcopal
Jewish Congregation
Methodist
Pentecostal
Salvation Army
Unitarian Universalist

Newspaper: *Courier-Gazette*, P.O. Box 249, Rockland, ME 04841. 207-594-4401. www.courierpub.com. Published three times a week, Michael McGuire, editor. Out-of-state monthly subscription by mail, $14. *New York Times*, *Wall Street Journal*, *Boston Globe*, *Boston Herald* also sold in town.

Annual Festivals and Events: July, North Atlantic Blues Festival, Friendship Sloop Days (homecoming and regatta with sloop races, demonstrations); early August, Maine Lobster Festival in the "Lobster Capital of the World"; October, Festival of Scarecrows; Thanksgiving–Christmas, Festival of Lights.

Further Information: Rockland-Thomaston Chamber of Commerce, P.O. Box 508, Rockland, ME 04841. 207-596-0376. rtacc@midcoast.com

Rockport, TX 78382

Population: 7,385 (+55%)
Banks: 5 branch banks.
Hospital: North Bay Hospital at Aransas Pass (9 miles), 45 beds.

Location: 30 miles northeast of Corpus Christi, 147 miles southeast of San Antonio, at Aransas Bay of the Gulf of Mexico.

Geography/Climate: Harbor town on a peninsula and Key Allegro, with miles of sandy beaches and coastal prairie inland. Weather influenced by the subtropical northeast Gulf Coast and semiarid Texas desert to the west and southwest. Tropical storms in the June–November period contribute most of the 30 inches of rain per year. Mild winters with only 7 days below freezing—long growing season: mid-February to mid-December. Long, hot summer with daily highs from the upper 80s to lower 90s. Seasonally, 107 days at 90 degrees or above. Sea breezes cool the nights to mid-70s. But humidity remains high, averaging 76%.

Five Largest Employers: Aransas County Independent School District, 465 employees; Production Services Group, 150; Wal-Mart, 150; State of Texas, 132; H-E-B supermarket, 130.

High School: Rockport-Fulton High School enrolls 1,053 students in grades 9–12, graduates 97%, sends 70% of graduates to college/university. SAT composite score for 56% of eligible students taking test, 972.

Housing: 3BR 2BA house at low end of the market sells for $75,000 and pays about $1,600 in real estate tax. But properties run as high as $500,000 in the more desirable waterfront locations. Most people heat with natural gas or electricity.

Telecommunications: Southwestern Bell Telephone provides DSL service.

Sales, Income Taxes: Retail sales tax, 8.25%. No state income tax.

Cost of Living: Movie ticket, $5.75; doctor appointment, routine, $35; plumber per hour, $45; baby-sitting per hour, $5; dry cleaning, men's suit, $8; dinner for 4, local restaurant, $50.

Community Infrastructure & Amenities:

United Way	Public parks
Community foundation	Public swimming pool
Community leadership	Airport
training program	Country club
YMCA/YWCA	Golf courses (2), 9 and 18
4-H	holes
Bed-and-breakfast	
Motion picture theater	
Public library	

Religious Denominations:

Assemblies of God
Baptist
Catholic
Church of Christ
Church of God
Church of Jesus Christ of
  Latter-Day Saints
Episcopal
Jehovah's Witnesses
Lutheran
Lutheran (ELCA)
Pentecostal
Presbyterian
Seventh Day Adventist
United Methodist

Newspaper: *Rockport Pilot*, 1002 Wharf Street, Rockport, TX 78382. 361-729-9900. www.rockport-pilot.com. Published twice weekly; Mike Probst, editor. *New York Times*, *Wall Street Journal*, numerous Texas dailies sold in town.

Annual Festivals and Events: Mid-October through March, bird watching at one of the nation's best birding spots; March, Fulton Oysterfest; September, Hummer/Bird Celebration, viewing ruby-throated hummingbirds and other species; October, Rockport Seafair, seafood, music, arts and crafts.

Further Information: Rockport-Fulton Area Chamber of Commerce, 404 Broadway, Rockport, TX 78382. 361-729-6445. chamber@dbstech.com.

Traverse City, MI 49684

Population: 14,532 (–4%)

Banks: 10 banks, including 3 locally owned.

Hospital: Munson Medical Center, 368 beds.

Location: 257 miles northwest of Detroit, on Grand Traverse Bay of Lake Michigan.

Geography/Climate: Scenic snowbelt town located on a spectacular bay and surrounded by hills and small lakes. Popular skiing destination: average 120 inches of snow a year, 32 inches of rain. January average daily temperature range from 15 low to 28 high; July, 59 low to 76 high. Long winters, mild summers, colorful falls.

Five Largest Employers: Munson Medical Center, 3,389 employees; Traverse City Public Schools, 2,100; Lear Corp., 829; Grand Traverse Resort & Spa, 650-1,000; Sara Lee Bakery, 675.

High School: Traverse City Central and Traverse City West high schools enroll total 2,902 students in grades 10–12, graduate 98.4%, send 74.7% to college/university. Composite ACT for 65% of eligible students taking test, 22.4.

Housing: 3BR 2BA house sells for $167,000, pays $1,800 in real estate tax. Most people heat with natural gas or LP gas.

Telecommunications: Ameritech provides DSL service.

Sales, Income Taxes: Retail sales tax, 6%. State income tax, 4.4%.

Cost of Living: Movie ticket, $7.50; doctor appointment, routine, $56; plumber per hour, $63; baby-sitting per hour, $5; dry cleaning, men's suit, $9.30; dinner for 4, local restaurant, $100.

Community Infrastructure & Amenities:

United Way
Community foundation
Community leadership training program
Main Street
YMCA/YWCA
Boys Club/Girls Club
4-H
Bed-and-breakfast
Community recreational center
Motion picture theater
Public library

Public parks: 32 parks, totaling 302 acres, plus a quiet area of 1,275 acres
Public swimming pool
Airport
Country club
Golf course
Emergency home shelter

Religious Denominations:

Apostolic
Assemblies of God
Baptist
Catholic
Christian
Christian Scientist
Church of Christ
Church of God
Church of the Nazarene
Episcopal
Evangelical
Four Square
Friends
Full Gospel
Independent
Jehovah's Witnesses
Jewish Congregations (2)
  Reform
  Independent
Lutheran

Lutheran (ELCA)
Lutheran (Missouri)
Mennonite
Methodist
Nondenominational
Presbyterian USA
Reformed
Salvation Army
Seventh Day Adventist
United Church of Christ
United Methodist
Wesleyan

Newspaper: *Traverse City Record Eagle*, 121 W. Front Street, Traverse City, MI 49684. 231-946-2000. www.record-eagle.com. Published daily. 13-week subscription, $44.90.

Annual Festivals and Events: January and February, Wine, ski, B&B weekends; May, Blossom Days; August, Bluegrass Festival, Jazz at Sunset; October, Vintage Car Show.

Further Information: Traverse City Convention & Visitors Bureau, 101 W. Grandview Parkway, Traverse City, MI 49684. tccvb@traverse.com

Mountain Towns

Bigfork, MT 59911

Population: 1,421 (+315%)
Banks: 3, including one locally owned.
Hospital: Kalispell Regional Medical Center (15 miles), 110 beds.

Location: 101 miles north of Missoula, 62 miles south of the British Columbia border, at the northeast corner of Flathead Lake in northwestern Montana.

Geography/Climate: Situated on a bay where the Swan River runs into Flathead Lake, the largest natural freshwater lake west of the Mississippi. Elevation 2,900 feet. Given its far northern location, Bigfork has a relatively mild climate, influenced by both Pacific Coast and continental weather patterns. Range of 7,500-foot mountains to the northeast blocks the worst of cold Alberta air in winter. January average temperatures range from 11 degrees to 27 degrees above zero; July, 48 degrees low to 82 high. Moderately dry summer and fall, moderately wet winter and spring. Annual rainfall, 20 inches; snowfall, 49 inches

Largest Employers: Marina Cay Resort & Conference Center; Lakeview Care Center; Flathead Bank of Bigfork; Sliter's Hardware.

High School: Bigfork High School enrolls 367 students in grades 9–12, graduates 97%, sends 50% of graduates to 4-year college, 20% to 2-year, 10% to technical school. Composite SAT: 575 verbal, 509 math. ACT, 23.5.

Housing: 3BR 2BA house sells for about $200,000, pays about $2,100 real estate tax. Most households heat with natural gas or electricity.

Telecommunications: Century Tel provides DSL service.

Sales, Income Taxes: No retail sales tax. State income tax scaled 2% to 11%.

Cost of Living: Doctor appointment, routine, $60; plumber per hour, $40; baby-sitting per hour, $7; dry cleaning, men's suit, $10; dinner for 4, local restaurant, $60.

Community Infrastructure & Amenities:
Bed-and-breakfast
Public library
Public parks: 3, totaling 20 acres
Golf course, 27 holes

Religious Denominations:
Baptist
Catholic
Church of Jesus Christ of Latter-Day Saints
Episcopal
Jehovah's Witnesses
Lutheran
Methodist

Newspaper: *Bigfork Eagle*, P.O. Box 406, Bigfork, MT 59911. 406-837-5131. bigforkeagle.com. Published weekly; Laurie Dillard, editor. 3-month subscription, $6.

Annual Festivals and Events: June, Whitewater Festival, kayak races; August, Festival of the Arts.

Further Information: Bigfork Area Chamber of Commerce, P.O. Box 237, Bigfork, MT 59911. 406-837-5888. bigfork.org.

Bisbee, AZ 85603

Population: 6,090 (–3%)
Banks: 3, including 1 branch.
Hospital: Copper Queen Community Hospital, 49 beds.

Location: 100 miles southeast of Tucson, 35 miles east of Sierra Vista, 4 miles from the Mexican border, in extreme southeastern Arizona.

Geography/Climate: 5,300-foot-high canyon town in the Mule Mountains. Dry, sunny climate most of the year. January averages: low, 34; high, 57. Snow, sleet, hail totaling 4.5 inches. July averages: low, 64; high 89. Bisbee is usually 15 to 20 degrees cooler than Phoenix or Tucson. 16 inches of rain a year, most likely in monsoons during July and August.

Five Largest Employers: Cochise County, 1,001 employees; Bisbee Unified School District, 176; City of Bisbee, 150; Copper Queen Community Hospital, 140; Copper Queen Hotel, 73.

High School: Bisbee High School enrolls 400 students in grades 9–12, graduates 75% to 85%, sends 30%–40% to college/university. Composite ACT score for 20% of eligible students taking test, 19.

Housing: 3BR 2BA house in good condition sells in range of $65,000 to $80,000, pays 1% to 2% of market value in real estate tax.

Telecommunications: Qwest provides digital connections at 256 Kbps.

Sales, Income Taxes: Retail sales tax, 8.6%. State income tax ranges 10% to 34% of federal tax liability.

Cost of Living: Doctor appointment, routine, $50; plumber per visit, $45; baby-sitting per hour, $2; dinner for 4, local restaurant, $60.

Community Infrastructure & Amenities:
Main Street
National Historic District
Boys Club/Girls Club
Bed-and-breakfast
Community recreational center
Public library
Public parks: 7 parks total 5 acres
Public swimming pool
Airport
Golf course, 18 holes
Emergency home shelter

Religious Denominations:
Assemblies of God
Baptist
Catholic
Church of Christ
Church of Jesus Christ of Latter-Day Saints
Church of the Nazarene
Community
Episcopal
Jehovah's Witnesses
Lutheran
Lutheran (ELCA)
Lutheran (Missouri)
Methodist
Nondenominational
Presbyterian USA
Science of Mind Center
Seventh Day Adventist

Newspaper: *Bisbee Observer*, 7 Bisbee Road, Bisbee, AZ 85603. 520-432-7254. Published weekly. 3-month subscription, $29.40.

Annual Festivals and Events: 4th of July Weekend, Mining History Celebration (hardrock drilling contest, mucking contest, etc.); Labor Day Weekend, Brewery Gulch Daze (historical celebration).

Further Information: Bisbee Chamber of Commerce, P.O. Box BA, Bisbee, AZ 85603. bisbeearizona.com

Blowing Rock, NC 28605

Population: 1,334 (−11%)
Banks: 2 branch banks.
Hospital: Blowing Rock Hospital & Extended Care, 100 beds.

Location: 90 miles west of Winston-Salem, in a hardwood forest of the Blue Ridge Mountains.

Geography/Climate: Mountain setting, elevation 3000+ feet, just northeast of Grandfather Mountain, elevation 5,964 feet. Crisp mountain air; 38 inches of snow and 56 inches of rain on average. January daily temperature range, 24 to 40 degrees average; July, 55 to 77 degrees.

Five Largest Employers: Chetola Resort, 160 employees; Blowing Rock Hospital, 107; Town of Blowing Rock, 55; Appalachian Ski Mountain (seasonal), 300; Tweetsie Railroad (seasonal), 250.

High School: Watauga High School enrolls 1,519 students in grades 9–12, graduates 98%, sends 85% to college/university. Composite SAT for 65% of eligible students taking test, 1054. ACT, 22.3

Housing: 3BR 2BA house, $300,000 to $350,000. Real estate taxes on such a house, $1,800 to $3,000. Most people heat with oil.

Telecommunications: Bell South provides DSL service.

Sales, Income Taxes: Retail sales tax, 6%. State income tax, scaled 6% to 7.75%.

Cost of Living: Doctor appointment, routine, $60; plumber per hour, $50; baby-sitting per hour, $6; dry cleaning, men's suit, $10; dinner for 4, local restaurant, $140.

Community Infrastructure & Amenities:
Community foundation
Bed-and-breakfast
Community recreational center
Public library
Country club
Golf course, 18 holes

Religious Denominations:
Baptist
Catholic
Church of God
Episcopal
Lutheran
Methodist
Presbyterian

Newspaper: *Blowing Rocket*, P.O. Box 126, Blowing Rock, NC 28605. 828-295-7522. Published weekly; Jerry Burns, editor. 3-month subscription, $12. *Wall Street Journal* also sold in town.

Annual Festivals and Events: May through October, Art in the Park juried art and craft shows; late July through early August, Blowing Rock Charity Horse Show; Saturday after Thanksgiving, Christmas Parade.

Further Information: Blowing Rock Chamber of Commerce, P.O. Box 406, Blowing Rock, NC 28605. 828-295-7851. info@blowingrock.com

Durango, CO 81302

Population: 14,796 (+16%)
Banks: 6 banks, 3 locally owned.
Hospital: Mercy Medical Center, 110 beds.

Location: 332 miles southwest of Denver, 214 miles northwest of Santa Fe, in extreme southwestern Colorado near the Four Corners junction with New Mexico, Arizona, Utah.

Geography/Climate: Elevation 6,512 feet in the Animas River Valley. To the north, San Juan Mountain peaks rise to about 10,400 feet. Desert land to the south and west. Generally dry and sunny with four seasons. January lows average 20; highs, 39. July highs average 88; lows, 64. Snowfall averages 69 inches in town, 300-plus inches at Purgatory-Durango Ski Resort, 25 miles north. Average annual rainfall, 19 inches.

Five Largest Employers: Southern Ute Indian Tribe, 935 employees; Mercy Medical Center, 820; Fort Lewis College, 684; Public School District, 619; Wal-Mart, 400.

High School: Durango High School enrolls 1,493 students in grades 9–12, graduates 83%, sends 77% to college/university. Composite score on recent ACT for 100% of students eligible for test, 21.

Housing: 3BR 2BA house in good condition, $200,000–$240,000. Taxes on such a house, $700–$800. Most people heat with natural gas. Town water supply from reservoir.

Telecommunications: U.S. West.

Sales, Income Taxes: 7.5% retail sales tax; 4.75% state income tax.

Cost of living: Movie ticket, $7; doctor appointment, routine, $50–$115; plumber per hour, $62.50; baby-sitting, per hour, $6; dry cleaning, men's suit, $9.90; dinner for 4, local restaurant, $80.

Community Infrastructure & Amenities:

United Way	Public library
Community leadership training program	Public parks: 17 parks, totaling 506 acres
Main Street member	Public swimming pool
National Historic District	Airport
4-H	Golf courses, 54 holes
Bed-and-breakfast	Emergency home shelter
Community recreational center	
Movie theater	

Religious Denominations:

Assemblies of God	Innerlight
Baha'i	Jehovah's Witnesses
Baptist	Jewish Congregation
Buddhist	King James Bible
Catholic	Lutheran
Christian	Methodist
Christian Science	Nondenominational
Church of Christ	Presbyterian
Church of Jesus Christ of Latter-Day Saints	Seventh Day Adventist
	Unitarian Universalist
Church of the Nazarene	United Methodist
Episcopal	Unity
Evangelical	Unity in Spirit
Four Square	
Friends	
Humanist	

Newspaper: *Durango Herald*, P.O. Drawer A, Durango, CO 81302. 800-530-8318. durangoherald.com. Published daily. Morley Ballantine, editor. 3-month subscription by mail, $65. *Wall Street Journal*, *USA Today*, Sunday *New York Times* also sold in town.

Annual festivals and events: February, Snowdown (winter festival); April, Durango Bluegrass Meltdown; May, Iron Horse Bicycle Classic; June, Animas River Days (kayak rodeo and other river events); September, Four Corners Motorcycle Rally; October, Durango Cowboy Poetry Gathering.

Further information: Durango Area Chamber Resort Association, P.O. Box 2587, Durango, CO 81301. 970-247-0312 or 800-525-8855. info@durango.org

Glenwood Springs, CO 81601

Population: 7,736 (+18%)
Banks: 6 branch banks.
Hospital: Valley View Hospital, 80 beds.

Location: 159 miles west of Denver, 91 miles east of Grand Junction, on the western slope of the Rocky Mountains.

Geography/Climate: Elevation 5,746 feet. A valley town located at the junction of the Roaring Fork and Colorado rivers. Winter low temperatures around 20 degrees, highs to 40. Cold snap of 10 days or so below zero. Snowfall from early December typically covers the ground until March, averaging 57 inches for the season. Spring daytime highs into the 60–70 range. Summer days, mid-80s with hot spell to mid-90s, cooling to 50s at night. Low humidity. Average annual precipitation, 17 inches.

Five Largest Employers: RE1 School District, 650 employees; RE2 School District, 320; Garfield County, 320; Valley View Hospital, 318; Hot Springs Lodge & Pool, 225.

High School: Glenwood Springs High School enrolls 739 students in grades 9-12. Graduation rate, 84%. 55% of graduates enroll in 4-year college, 25% in 2-year. Composite score on ACT for all junior-year students, 22.6.

Housing: 3BR, 2BA house sells in the $280,000 to $300,000 range. Natural gas and electricity used about equally as heating fuel.

Telecommunications: Qwest provides DSL service to residences, and dial-up 56 Kbps connection speed. AT&T Broadband provides cable.

Sales, Income Taxes: Retail sales, 3.45%. State income tax, flat rate 2.9%.

Community Infrastructure & Amenities:

United Way	Movie theater
Community leadership training program	Public library
	Public parks
Main Street member	Public swimming pool
National Historic District	Airport
Boys Club/Girls Club	Country club
4-H	Golf courses: (2) 9-hole
Bed-and-breakfast	
Community recreational center	

Religious Denominations

Assemblies of God	Church of the Nazarene
Baha'i	Episcopal
Baptist	Four Square
Catholic	Jehovah's Witnesses
Christian	Lutheran
Christian Science	Mennonite
Church of Christ	Methodist
Church of Jesus Christ Of Latter-Day Saints	Presbyterian
	Seventh Day Adventist
Church of Scientology	

Newspaper: *Glenwood Springs Post Independent*, P.O. Box 550, Glenwood Springs, CO 81601. www.postindependent.com. 970-945-8515. Published daily. 6-month subscription by mail, $26. Heather McGregor, editor. Other papers available daily in town: *New York Times, Wall Street Journal, Denver Post, Rocky Mountain News, USA Today.*

Cost of living: Movie ticket, $6.75; doctor appointment, routine, $70; plumber per hour, $67; baby-sitting, per hour, $7; dry cleaning, men's suit, $9; dinner for 4, local restaurant, $55.

Annual festivals and events: February, Ski Spree; June, Strawberry Days, a 100-year-old annual celebration; June–July, Summer of Jazz; summer, Latino Festival; September, Fall Arts Festival; November, Arts & Crafts Shows; December, Winter Fest.

Further information: Glenwood Springs Chamber Resort Association, 1102 Grand Avenue, Glenwood Springs, CO 81601. info@glenwoodchamber.com

Leavenworth, WA 98826

Population: 2,260 (+48%)
Banks: 3, including one locally owned.
Hospital: Cascade Medical Center, 7 beds.

Location: 128 miles east of Seattle in a river valley of the Wenatchee Mountains in central Washington.

Geography/Climate: Alpine village at 1,200 feet elevation but surrounded by forested mountains rising to 8,000-9,000 feet. January average temperature, 14 low, 32 high; July, 50 low, 85 high. Average annual snowfall near 100 inches; rainfall, about 20 inches. June through September it is warm and dry; cross-country skiing excellent November into March.

Five Largest Employers: U.S. Forest Service, 371 full-time equivalent employees; Cascade School District, 244; Winton Mill, lumber, 86; Cascade Medical, 72; City of Leavenworth, 48.

High School: Cascade High School enrolls 561 students in grades 9–12, graduates 97%; sends 31% to 2-year college, 32% to 4-year college, 16% to technical school, 7% to the military, 14% to other employment. Composite ACT for 25% of eligible students taking test, 23.3. Composite SAT for 42% of eligible students taking test: verbal 541, math 551.

Housing: 3BR 2BA house sells in the range of $130,000 to $150,000, pays about $1,000 in real estate tax. Most people heat with electricity.

Telecommunications: Verizon provides DSL service.

Sales, Income Taxes: Retail sales tax, 8%. No state income tax.

Cost of Living: Movie ticket, $4.50; doctor appointment, routine, $42; plumber per hour, $60; baby-sitting per hour, $8; dinner for 4, local restaurant, $45.

Community Infrastructure & Amenities:
Boys Club/Girls Club
4-H
Bed-and-breakfast
Motion picture theater
Public library
Public parks: Vast recreational area in the Wenatchee National Forest
Public swimming pool
Golf course, 18 holes

Religious Denominations:
Assemblies of God
Baptist
Catholic
Christian
Church of Christ
Church of God
Church of Jesus Christ of Latter-Day Saints
Church of the Nazarene
Evangelical
Lutheran
Methodist
Seventh Day Adventist
United Methodist

Newspaper: *Leavenworth Echo*, P.O. Box 39, Leavenworth, WA 98826. 509-548-5286. leavenworthecho.com. Published weekly; Bill Forhan, editor. 6-month subscription, $11. *New York Times*, *Wall Street Journal*, *Seattle Times*, *Seattle Post-Intelligencer* also sold in town.

Annual Festivals and Events: January, Bavarian Ice Fest; February, Fasching (Mardi Gras); May, Maifest; June, German Accordion Celebration; July 4, Kinderfest, celebrating children; September, Wenatchee River Salmon Fest; end September, early October, Washington State Autumn Leaf Festival; mid-October, Oktoberfest; late November, Chriskindlmarkt (European Outdoor Market); Christmas Lighting Festival.

Further Information: Leavenworth Chamber of Commerce, P.O. Box 327, Leavenworth, WA 98826. 509-548-5807. info@leavenworth.org

Lewisburg, WV 24901

Population: 3,624 (+0.7%)
Banks: 3, all branches of banks headquartered elsewhere.
Hospital: Greenbrier Valley Medical Center, 122 beds.

Location: 115 miles southeast of Charleston, 250 miles southwest of Washington, D.C., in the Allegheny Mountains of West Virginia.

Geography/Climate: Mountain valley town with the Allegheny Range to the northeast. January average temperatures range from 17 to 38 degrees; July, 59 to 82. Average annual precipitation, 39 inches.

Five Largest Employers: The Greenbrier, conference center and resort, 1,265 employees; Greenbrier County Board of Education, 898; Greenbrier Valley Medical Center, 390; Wal-Mart, 351; ABB Automation, 245.

High School: Greenbrier East High School enrolls 350 students in grades 9–12, graduates 98%, sends 57% to college/university. Composite ACT, 20.5.

Housing: 3BR 2BA house, $115,000 to $119,000. Real estate tax, $1,200. Most people heat with natural gas.

Telecommunications: Charter Communication provides broadband connection via cable.

Sales, Income Taxes: Retail sales tax, 6%. State income tax, scaled 3% to 6.5%.

Cost of Living: Movie ticket, $6.50; doctor appointment, routine, $60; plumber per hour, $45; baby-sitting per hour, $8 for up to 4 hours; dry cleaning, men's suit, $7.50; dinner for 4, local restaurant, $60.

Community Infrastructure & Amenities:
United Way
Community leadership training program
National Historic District
YMCA/YWCA
4-H
Bed-and-breakfast
Motion picture theater
Public library
Public parks: 3
Airport
Country club
Golf course, 18 holes
Emergency home shelter

Religious Denominations:
Baptist
Catholic
Christian
Church of Christ
Church of God
Church of the Nazarene
Episcopal
Independent
Interdenominational
Jehovah's Witnesses
Methodist
Nondenominational
Pentecostal
Presbyterian
Seventh Day Adventist
United Methodist

Newspaper: *West Virginia Daily News*, 200 S. Court Street, Lewisburg, WV 24901. 304-645-1206. Published daily; Frank Spicer, editor. *Mountain Messenger*, P.O. Box 429, Lewisburg, WV 24901. 304-647-5724. mountainmessenger.com. Published weekly; Carol Hall, editor. $15 a year.

Annual Festivals and Events: second weekend June every other year, Greenbrier Valley Home & Garden Tour; summer, Greenbrier Valley Festival of the Arts; second Saturday October, T.O.O.T. (Taste of Our Towns).

Further Information: Greenbrier County Convention & Visitors Bureau, 111 N. Jefferson Street, Lewisburg, WV 24901. 304-645-1000, 800-833-2068. wvepostcards.com/lewisburg, greenbrierwv.com

Montrose, CO 81401

Population: 12,344 (+39%)
Banks: 13 banks, including 3 branch banks.
Hospital: Montrose Memorial Hospital, 75 beds.

Location: 260 miles southwest of Denver on the western slope of the Continental Divide.

Geography/Climate: Elevation 5,820 feet. Situated in center of Uncompahgre Valley; 14,000-foot San Juan Mountains to the south, 10,000-foot Uncompahgre Plateau to the West, Grand Mesa to the north, Black Canyon National Park to the east. Surrounding high mountains buffer harsh weather, lower the wind velocity. Mild summers and winters. Semiarid—low relative humidity, low average precipitation: 25 inches of snow, 9 inches of rain. 227 to 274 days of sunshine a year.

Five Largest Employers: Russell Stover Candies, 650 employees; Montrose County School District, 570; Montrose Memorial Hospital, 450; federal agencies, 310; Montrose County, 300.

High School: Montrose High School enrolls 894 students in grades 10–12, graduates 82%, sends 65% to college/university. Recent composite ACT score for 65% of students taking test, 21.9.

Housing: 3BR 2BA house in good condition averages $130,000 in city, ranges from $70,000 to $170,000; county range, $110,000 to $245,000. Most people heat with natural gas. Real estate tax on a residence with market value of $150,000 is about $900.

Telecommunications: Qwest provides 56 Kbps connection speed.

Sales, Income Taxes: Retail sales tax, 6.9%. State income tax, 4.63%.

Cost of living: Movie ticket, $5.50; doctor appointment, routine, $50; plumber per hour, $68; baby-sitting, per hour, $5–10; dry cleaning, men's suit, $8.75; dinner for 4, local restaurant, $45.

Community Infrastructure & Amenities:
Community leadership training program
Main Street member
Boys Club/Girls Club
4-H
Bed-and-breakfast
Movie theater
Public library
Public parks
Public swimming pool
Airport
Golf course, 18 holes
Emergency home shelter

Religious Denominations:

Assemblies of God	Four Square
Baptist	Interdenominational
Catholic	Jehovah's Witnesses
Christian	Lutheran
Christian Science	Mennonite
Church of Christ	Pentecostal
Church of God	Presbyterian
Church of Jesus Christ	Presbyterian USA
of Latter-Day Saints	Seventh Day Adventist
Church of the Nazarene	United Church of Christ
Episcopal	United Methodist

Newspaper: *Montrose Daily Press*, 535 S. 1st St., Montrose, CO 81401. 970-249-3444. montrosepress.com. Published daily, Stephen Woody, editor. 3-month mail subscription, $24.05 in Colorado. *New York Times*, *Wall Street Journal* also sold in town.

Annual festivals and events: July 4th Weekend, Lighter than Air Balloon Affair & Great American Summer Salute; July–August, Montrose County Fair & Rodeo; September, Best of the West Food Fest.

Further information: Montrose Chamber of Commerce, 1519 E. Main St., Montrose, CO 81401. 970-249-5000 or 800-923-5515. mchamber@frontier.net

Rexburg, ID 83440

Population: 17,257 (+20%)
Banks: 11, all branches of banks headquartered elsewhere,
Hospital: Madison Memorial Hospital, 52 beds.

Location: 28 miles northeast of Idaho Falls, 70 miles southwest of Wyoming-Montana-Idaho junction, on the Snake River Plain.

Geography/Climate: High-country valley, elevation 4,850 feet, sitting atop the Upper Snake River Aquifer. Teton Mountains to the east, Targhee National Forest to the northeast and northwest. January low average temperature, 7 degrees. A week or two of 30 below not uncommon. Average annual snowfall, 54 inches. Summer daytime temperatures range 80–90. Dry heat, low humidity. Rainfall averages 11 inches.

Five Largest Employers: Brigham Young University—Idaho, 1,012 employees; Artco, wedding invitations, 700; Madison School District, 452; Basic American Foods, 264; Madison Memorial Hospital, 254.

High School: Madison High School enrolls 946 students in grades 10–12, graduates 99%, sends 85% to college/university. Composite ACT for 96% of eligible students taking test, 22.7.

Housing: 3BR 2BA house sells at median $103,840, pays $700 to $750 in real estate tax. Most people heat with natural gas.

Telecommunications: CableOne provides broadband connection to Internet.

Sales, Income Taxes: Retail sales tax, 5%, prescription drugs exempt. State income tax, scaled 2% to 8.2%.

Cost of Living: Movie ticket, $6.75; doctor appointment, routine, $58; plumber per hour, $60; baby sitting per hour, $2-$3; dry cleaning, men's suit, $6; dinner for 4, local restaurant, $40.

Community Infrastructure & Amenities:
United Way
Main Street
4-H
Bed-and-breakfast
Motion picture theater
Public library
Public parks: 7, totaling 40 acres
Public swimming slide
Airport
Golf course, 27 holes
Emergency home shelter

Religious Denominations:
Apostolic
Assemblies of God
Baptist
Catholic
Christian
Church of Jesus Christ of Latter-Day Saints
Four Square
Jehovah's Witnesses
Presbyterian

Newspaper: *Standard Journal*, 23 S. 1st East, Rexburg, ID 83440. 208-356-5441. rexburgstandardjournal.com. Published three times a week; Richard Ballou, editor. 3-month subscription, $19. *New York Times*, *Wall Street Journal*, *USA Today*, *Post Register* (Idaho Falls) also sold in town.

Annual Festivals and Events: Mid-July, Idaho International Folk Dance Festival.

Further Information: Rexburg Chamber of Commerce, 420 W. 4th South, Rexburg, ID 83440. 208-356-5700. info@rexcc.com

Salida, CO 81201

Population: 5,504 (+16%)

Banks: 5, including three locally owned.

Hospital: Heart of the Rockies Regional Medical Center, 49 beds.

Location: 130 miles southwest of Denver, in the mountains of central Colorado.

Geography/Climate: Arkansas River Valley town, with 14,000-foot peaks of the Sawatch Range to the northwest and the Sangre de Cristo Range to the south. Locals describe the area as the "Banana Belt" of the Rockies because it is not uncommon to go skiing on a January morning and golfing or biking in the afternoon. Surrounded by mountains, Salida is sunny and dry. Annual rainfall, 9–10 inches, humidity 20%–30%. January temperatures range from 19 to 49 degrees; July, 50s to upper 80s, rarely over 90.

Five Largest Employers: Monarch Ski Tow, 342 employees; Wal-Mart, 235; Regional Medical Center, 220; Salida School District R-32-J, 150; Columbine Manor, 104.

High School: Salida High School enrolls 396 students in grades 9–12, graduates 88%, sends 43% to college/university. Composite ACT, 20.7.

Housing: 3BR 2BA house sells in the range of $165,000 to $180,000, pays real estate tax of about $650 a year. Most people heat with natural gas.

Telecommunications: Qwest provides Internet connection at 56 Kbps.

Sales, Income Taxes: Retail sales tax, 6.9%. State income tax, 4.63%.

Cost of Living: Movie ticket, $5; doctor appointment, routine, $40; plumber per hour, $48; baby-sitting per hour, $3; dry cleaning, men's suit, $9; dinner for 4, local restaurant, $60.

Community Infrastructure & Amenities:
4-H
Bed-and-breakfast
Motion picture theater
Public library
Public parks
Public swimming pool
Airport
Golf course, 9 holes

Religious Denominations:
Assemblies of God
Baptist
Catholic
Christian
Church of Christ
Church of God
Church of Jesus Christ of Latter-Day Saints
Community
Episcopal
Jehovah's Witnesses
Lutheran (Missouri)
Methodist
Nondenominational
Presbyterian USA
Seventh Day Adventist
United Methodist

Newspaper: *Mountain Mail*, P.O. Box 189, Salida, CO 81201. 719-539-6691. Published 5 days a week; Lee Spaulding, editor. 3-month subscription, $16.

Annual Festivals and Events: June, Boat Races & Festival; June, Art Walk, July; Colorado Brewers Rendezvous, micro-brewers' gathering; September, Taste of Salida; September, Banana Belt Bicycle Weekend; late November, Lighting of Christmas Mountain.

Further Information: Salida-Heart of the Rockies Chamber of Commerce, 406 W. Highway 50, Salida, CO 81201. 877-772-5432. salidachamber.org.

Silver City, NM 88061

Population: 10,545 (−1.3%)
Banks: 5, including 2 branch banks.
Hospital: Gila Regional Hospital, 88 beds.

Location: 240 miles southwest of Albuquerque, 200 miles east of Tucson, in mountainous southwestern New Mexico.

Geography/Climate: Grassland valley in the Piños Altos Mountains, rimmed on three sides by low hills and mountains. Mean elevation of Grant County, 6,000 feet, creates semiarid continental climate. Topography ranges from flat semidesert to mountain peaks over 10,000 feet. January average low, 24 degrees; high, 49. July average low, 59; high, 87. Rapid cooling after sundown on summer nights. Annual rainfall, 17 inches. Snow occurs several times a year but seldom stops travel. Average relative humidity, 31%. Sun shines on 83% of days.

Five Largest Employers: Phelps Dodge, copper mining, 1,500 employees; Stream International, 724; Gila Regional Medical Center, 600; Western New Mexico University, 600; Silver City Schools, 400.

High School: Silver City High School enrolls 1,040 students in grades 9–12, graduates 90%, sends 45% to college/university. Composite ACT for 45% of eligible students taking test, 19.7.

Housing: 3BR 2BA house sells in the range of $75,000 to $110,000, pays $350 to $400 real estate tax. Most people heat with natural gas.

Telecommunications: Qwest provides Internet connection at 56 Kbps.

Sales, Income Taxes: Retail sales tax, 6.375%, prescription drugs exempt. State income tax, scaled 1.8% to 8.5%.

Cost of Living: Movie ticket, $4.50; doctor appointment, routine, $60–$70; plumber per hour, $42; baby-sitting per hour, $2.25; dry cleaning, men's suit, $5; dinner for 4, local restaurant, $40.

Community Infrastructure & Amenities:

United Way	Public library
Main Street	Public parks: 10
National Historic District	Public swimming pool
Bed-and-breakfast	Airport
Community recreational center	Country club
	Golf course, 18 holes
Motion picture theater	Emergency home shelter

Religious Denominations:
Apostolic
Assemblies of God
Baptist
Catholic
Church of Christ
Church of Jesus Christ of Latter-Day Saints
Episcopal
Friends
Jehovah's Witnesses
Jewish Congregation
Lutheran (ELCA)
Lutheran (Missouri)
Nondenominational
Presbyterian
United Methodist

Newspaper: *Silver City Daily Press*, P.O. Box 740, Silver City, NM 88062. 505-388-1576. thedailypress.com. Published daily except Sunday. Christina Ely, editor. 3-month subscription, $50. *Silver City Sun News*, 800-745-5851. Published daily; James Rosenthal, editor. 3-month subscription, $48. *New York Times, Wall Street Journal, Las Cruces Sun News* also sold in town.

Annual Festivals and Events: Memorial Day Weekend Blues Festival; May, Gila Bike Race (an international event); 4th of July, Rodeo; Lighted Christmas Parade.

Further Information: Silver City Grant County Chamber of Commerce, 201 N. Hudson, Silver City, NM 88061. 800-548-9378. scgcchamber@cybermesa.com

Steamboat Springs, CO 80477

Population: 9,815 (+47%)
Banks: 5, including one branch bank.
Hospital: Yampa Valley Medical Center, 29 beds.

Location: 157 miles northwest of Denver, 339 miles east of Salt Lake City, on the Western Slope of the Rocky Mountains in northwestern Colorado.

Geography/Climate: Broad mountain valley—the Yampa Valley—at 6,700-foot elevation, immediately west of Rocky Mountain peaks reaching 9,000 to 12,000 feet. Alpine climate, very low humidity. Average temperatures: January high, 30; low 1; July high 82, low 41. Snowfall in the mountains ranges from 170 inches to 450 inches a year. Precipitation in town averages about 24 inches. Lots of sunshine.

Five Largest Employers: Steamboat Ski & Resort Corporation, 2,000 employees in winter; Yampa Valley Medical Center, 450; TIC, construction, 180; Steamboat School District, 305; Colorado Mountain College, 163.

High School: Steamboat Springs High School enrolls 650 students in grades 9–12, graduates 92%, sends 77% to college/university. Composite SAT for 77% of eligible students taking test, 1060.

Housing: 3BR 2BA house sells for about $330,000, pays $1,800 in real estate tax. Most people heat with natural gas.

Telecommunications: AT&T provides broadband cable connection.

Sales, Income Taxes: Retail sales tax, 8.4%. State income tax, 4.63%.

Cost of Living: Movie ticket, $7; doctor appointment, routine, $40; plumber per hour, $50; baby-sitting per hour, $7; dry cleaning, men's suit, $9.50; dinner for 4, local restaurant, $120.

Community Infrastructure & Amenities:
United Way
Community foundation
Community leadership training program
Main Street
4-H
Bed-and-breakfast
Community recreational center
Motion picture theater
Public library
Public parks
Public swimming pool
Airport
Golf course
Emergency home shelter

Religious Denominations:
Baptist
Catholic
Christian
Christian Science
Church of Christ
Church of Jesus Christ of Latter-Day Saints
Episcopal
Euzoa Bible Church
Interdenominational
Jehovah's Witnesses
Jewish Congregation
Lutheran
Nondenominational
Seventh Day Adventist
United Methodist

Newspaper: *Steamboat Pilot/Steamboat Today*, 1901 Curve Plaza, Steamboat Springs, CO 80477. 970-879-1502. steamboatpilot.com. Published daily and weekly; Scott Stanford, editor. 3-month subscription, $13. *New York Times*, *Wall Street Journal*, *USA Today*, *Denver Post* also sold in town.

Annual Festivals and Events: June, Steamboat Marathon (running); July, Hot Air Balloon "Rodeo"; July 4th and all summer, Cowboy Roundup Days, Rodeo.

Further Information: Steamboat Springs Chamber Resort Association, P.O. Box 774408, Steamboat Springs, CO 80477. 970-879-0880. info@steamboatchamber.com

Telluride, CO 81435

Population: 2,220 (+70%)
Banks: 4, all branches.
Hospital: 4 ER beds at a local clinic. Nearest hospital is Montrose Memorial Hospital (67 miles), 75 beds.

Location: 341 miles southwest of Denver, 126 miles southeast of Grand Junction, tucked into the end of a canyon and surrounded by the 13,000-foot peaks of the San Juan Mountains.

Geography/Climate: At elevation 8,760 feet, Telluride is the highest town listed in this book. High alpine, semiarid conditions, and very changeable weather. Sunny summer mornings, thunderstorms in the afternoon, clear at night. Average temperatures: January low 14, high 38; July low 51, high 78. Average annual precipitation, 23.5 inches.

Five Largest Employers: Telluride Ski & Golf Company, 750 winter employees, 240 summer, plus 165 year-round; Wyndham Peaks Resort and Wyndham Peaks Lodge, 334 annual average, 47 full-time; San Miguel County, 97 full-time, 13 part-time; Telluride School District, 65; Town of Telluride, 61 full-time, 20 seasonal.

High School: Telluride High School enrolls 155 students in grades 9–12, graduates 95%, sends 85% to college/university. Composite ACT for 100% of eligible students taking test, 22.9. Composite SAT for 100% of eligible students taking test, top 25%, 1317; top 50%, 1240.

Housing: 3BR 2BA home, $700,000+. Real estate tax, $1,500. Most households heat with natural gas. Telluride is a very hot real estate market and the priciest small town listed in this book. One broker counted only five homes under $1 million on the market in early 2002. Condominiums priced under $200,000 have practically disappeared. Statistics compiled by Judi Kiernan of Telluride Consulting show $431 million in real estate transactions during 2001.

Telecommunications: Qwest provides DSL service in the area.

Sales, Income Taxes: Retail sales tax, 4.5%. State income tax, 4.63%.

Cost of Living: Movie ticket, $7; doctor appointment, routine, $40; plumber per hour, $80; baby-sitting per hour, $16; dry cleaning, ski suit, $20; dinner for 4, local restaurant, $100.

Community Infrastructure & Amenities:

Community foundation	Public swimming pool
National Historic District	Airport: Telluride
Bed-and-breakfast	Regional Airport, 9,078-
Community recreational	ft. elevation, the high-
center	est in America
Motion picture theaters, 2	Golf course, 18 holes
Public library	Emergency home shelter
Public parks: 3	

Religious Denominations

Baptist	Jewish Congregation
Catholic	Presbyterian
Christian Fellowship	

Newspapers: *Telluride Daily Planet*, P.O. Box 2315, Telluride, CO 81435. 970-728-9788. telluridegateway.com. 6-month subscription, $30. Charles Womack, publisher. *Telluride Watch*, P.O. Box 2042, Telluride, CO 81435. 970-728-4496. seth@telluride-colorado.com. 6-month subscription by mail, $25. Seth Cagin, publisher.

Annual Festivals and Events: Approximately 35 major festivals between Memorial Day and October; weekend events during the ski season, Thanksgiving through Easter. Summer highlights: June, Wine Festival; August, Jazz Celebration, Mushroom Festival, Chamber Music; Labor Day Weekend, Film Festival; September, Blues & Brews. Log on to telluride.com for current details.

Further Information: Telluride Chamber of Commerce, P.O. Box 653, Telluride, CO 81435. 970-668-0376. telluride.com

College Towns

Berea, KY 40403

Population: 10,006 (+10%)
Banks: 5, including 4 branches of out-of-town banks.
Hospital: Berea Hospital, 110 beds

Location: 114 miles southeast of Louisville, 130 miles north of Knoxville, about an hour south of Lexington, on I-75.

Geography/Climate: Gently rolling terrain, where the Blue Grass meets the foothills of the Appalachian Mountains. Elevation at airport, 900 feet; at highest point in town, 2,000 feet. Temperate, four-season climate. Average temperatures: January, high 42, low 25. July, high 86, low 66. Average 97 days below freezing, 2 days below zero, 16 days above 90. Rainfall, 46 inches; snowfall, 16 inches. The fall season can be very pleasant, with least rain, most sun, and glorious colors.

Five Largest Employers: Berea College, 600 employees; Tokico (USA), Inc., auto shock absorbers, struts, 571; NACCO Materials Handling Group, 540; Berea Hospital, 380; Dresser Industries, pressure gauges, 373.

Berea College, a nationally known liberal arts institution, ranks first among best regional schools of the South in the 2001 edition of *America's Best Colleges*, published by *U.S. News & World Report*. Founded in 1855, the college offers free tuition in a work-study program for academically able residents of Appalachia who meet a financial needs test. Current enrollment, about 1,500.

High School: Berea Community Schools enroll 320 students in grades 9–12, graduate 98%, send 80% to college/university. Composite ACT score for 87% of eligible students taking test, 21.7.

Housing: 3BR 2BA house in good condition, $102,000. Real estate taxes on such a house, $970. Most households heat with electricity.

Telecommunications: Served by Verizon and Adelphia.

Sales, Income Taxes: Retail sales tax, 6%, medicine and grocery food exempt. State income tax, scaled 2% to 6%.

Cost of Living: Doctor appointment, routine, $65; plumber per hour, $45; baby-sitting per hour, $5; dry cleaning, men's suit, $3.50; dinner for 4, local restaurant, $47.

Community Infrastructure & Amenities:

United Way	Public library
Community leadership training program	Public parks: 2
Main Street	Public swimming pool
Boys Club/Girls Club	Airport
4-H	Country club
Bed-and-breakfast	Golf course

Religious Denominations:

AME	Four Square
Apostolic	Friends
Assemblies of God	Full Gospel
Baptist	Interdenominational
Catholic	Jehovah's Witnesses
Christian	Lutheran
Church of Christ	Methodist
Church of God	Nondenominational
Church of Jesus Christ of Latter-Day Saints	Pentecostal
Church of the Nazarene	Presbyterian
Disciples of Christ	United Methodist
Episcopal	
Evangelical	

Newspaper: *Berea Citizen*, P.O. Box 207, Berea, KY 40403. 859-986-0959. Published weekly, Scott Powell, editor. 1-year subscription by mail outside of county, $26. *New York Times, Wall Street Journal,* major Kentucky dailies also sold in town.

Annual Festivals and Events: May and October, Kentucky Guild of Artists and Craftsmen; July, Berea Craft Festival; First weekend after Labor Day, Berea Spoonbread Festival. Berea is known as the folk arts and crafts capital of Kentucky.

Further Information: Berea Chamber of Commerce, P.O. Box 318, Berea, KY 40403. bereachamber@berea.com, chamber.berea.com

Bennington, VT 05201

Population: 9,168 (–4%)

Banks: 6, including 3 branch banks.

Hospital: Southwestern Vermont Health Care, 99 beds.

Location: 150 miles northwest of Boston, 127 miles south of Burlington, near the southwestern corner of Vermont.

Geography/Climate: Foothills of the Green Mountains, with peaks to the north and northeast rising to the 3,700–3,800-foot level. Harsh continental climate tempered by relative warmth of the Atlantic Ocean to the south. First frost at the end of September, very cold winters with as many as 150 days below freezing and 15 or more days below zero. Short spring. Pleasant summer days with a hot spell or two but rarely more than 8 days above 90. Cool nights. Annual rainfall, 36 inches; snowfall, 64 inches.

Five Largest Employers: Southwestern Vermont Medical Center, 1,000 employees; Southwestern Vermont Supervisory Union, 625; NASTECH, 500; Energizer-Eveready Battery, 320; Bennington College, 245.

Bennington College enrolls 450 students and is ranked in the third tier among national liberal arts colleges by *U.S. News & World Report*.

High School: Mount Anthony Union Senior High School enrolls 1,300 students in grades 9–12, graduates 86%, sends 49% to college/university. For current SAT scores, call 802-447-7511.

Housing: 3BR 2BA house in good condition sells for about $100,000, pays $2,500 in real estate tax.

Telecommunications: Verizon provides DSL service. Adelphia provides Internet access via cable.

Sales, Income Taxes: Retail sales tax, 5%. State income tax, 24% of federal tax liability.

Cost of Living: Movie ticket, $7; doctor appointment, routine, $45; plumber per hour, $45; baby-sitting per hour, $7; dry cleaning, men's suit, $9; dinner for 4, local restaurant, $80.

Community Infrastructure & Amenities:

United Way	Public swimming pool
Main Street	Airport
National Historic District	Country club
4-H	Golf course, 18 holes
Bed-and-breakfast	Emergency home shelter
Community recreational center	
Motion picture theater	
Public library	
Public parks: 2	

Religious Denominations:
Baptist
Catholic
Christian
Church of Christ
Episcopal
Jehovah's Witnesses
Jewish Congregation
Lutheran
Methodist
Pentecostal
Presbyterian
United Methodist

Newspaper: *Bennington Banner*, 425 Main Street, Bennington, VT 05201. 802-447-7567. bennington-banner.com. Published daily. Robert Larson, editor. Type "Bennington Banner" in your search engine, click on "Subscribe" for information. Online newsletter also available.

Annual Festivals and Events: Memorial Day weekend, Mayfest Craft Festival; September, Antique Car Show & Flea Market.

Further Information: Bennington Area Chamber of Commerce, 100 Veterans Memorial Drive, Bennington, VT 05201. 802-447-3311. chamber@bennington-com

Boone, NC 28607

Population: 13,472 (+4%)
Banks: 13 banks, including 5 that are branches of banks based elsewhere.
Hospital: Watauga Medical Center, 117 beds.

Location: 85 miles west of Winston-Salem, 95 miles northeast of Asheville, 15 miles from the Tennessee border, in northwestern North Carolina.

Geography/Climate: Situated in a long valley within the Appalachian Mountains at 3,333 feet elevation. Temperate, humid climate. January average temperatures range from 21 low to 42 high; July, 60 low; 81 high. Annual average snowfall, 36 inches; rainfall, 53 inches. Growing season, 158 days.

Five Largest Employers: Appalachian State University, 2,200 employees; Watauga County Board of Education, 900; Watauga Medical Center, 820; IRC, electronic components, 300; Samaritan's Purse, 251.

Appalachian State University ranks 10th among Best Regional Schools of the South in the 2001 edition of *America's Best Colleges*, published by *U.S. News & World Report*. ASU enrolls about 11,000 students.

High School: Watauga High School enrolls 1,519 students in grades 9–12, sends 85% of graduates to postsecondary study including 65% to 4-year college. Recent composite ACT score, 22.3. SAT verbal, 524; math, 530.

Housing: 3BR 2BA house in good condition sells in range of $100,000 to $200,000, pays 88.5 cents per $100 of assessed valuation in real estate tax. Most people heat with oil.

Telecommunications: BellSouth provides DSL service at 1.5 Mbps. Charter Communications provides Internet link via cable.

Sales, Income Taxes: Retail sales tax, 6.5%, grocery food exempt. State income tax, scaled 6% to 7.75%.

Cost of Living: Movie ticket, $7; doctor appointment, routine, $46; plumber per hour, $50; baby-sitting per hour, $8; dry cleaning, men's suit, $7; dinner for 4, local restaurant, $60.

Community Infrastructure & Amenities:

United Way	Motion picture theater
Community leadership training program	Public library
	Public parks: 5
Main Street	Public swimming pool
4-H	Golf course, 18 holes
Bed-and-breakfast	Emergency home shelter
Community recreational center	

Religious Denominations:

Assemblies of God	Episcopal
Baptist	Jehovah's Witnesses
Catholic	Jewish Congregation
Christian	Lutheran
Church of Christ	Mennonite
Church of God	Methodist
Church of Jesus Christ of Latter-Day Saints	Nondenominational
	Presbyterian
Church of the Nazarene	Seventh Day Adventist
Eastern Orthodox	

Newspaper: *Watauga Democrat*, 474 Industrial Park Drive, Boone, NC 28607. 828-264-3612. wataugademocrat.com. Published 3 times a week; Sandra Shook, editor. 3-month subscription by mail, $19.

Annual Festivals and Events: February, Sweetheart Ice Skating; June, Singing on the Mountain, annual gospel singing event; July, An Appalachian Summer, festival of music, theater, dance. Highland Games, on Grandfather Mountain; August, Gospel Singing Jubilee; September, Olde Boone Streetfest. The Boone area is home to some 400 artists. Fine arts and crafts are a large part of life and a commercial attraction: 14 galleries, numerous shops and showrooms.

Further Information: Boone Area Chamber of Commerce, 208 Howard Street, Boone, NC 28607. 828-262-3516. media@visitboonenc.com

Buckhannon, WV 26201

Population: 5,725 (–3%)

Banks: 5, 4 of which are branch banks.

Hospital: St. Joseph's Hospital, 95 beds.

Location: 136 miles south of Pittsburgh, 238 miles west of Washington, D.C., in north central West Virginia.

Geography/Climate: 1,400-foot elevation in the foothills of the Allegheny Mountains. Terrain varies from level to hilly to mountainous—highest point in county, 3,000 feet. Seldom extremely hot or cold, though a winter cold snap may send temperatures to zero. January average temperatures: low, 21; high, 39. July: low, 63; high, 85. Annual precipitation, 51 inches. Very pleasant fall.

Five Largest Employers: Board of education, 539 employees; Union Drilling, 475; Trus Joist, engineered wood products, 330; St. Joseph's Hospital, 325; West Virginia Wesleyan College, 301.

West Virginia Wesleyan College enrolls about 1,500 students and ranks among second-tier regional universities in the 2001 edition of *America's Best Colleges*, published by *U.S. News & World Report*.

High School: Buckhannon Upshur High School enrolls 1,170 students in grades 9–12, graduates 97%, sends 45% to college/university. Composite scores for 45% of eligible students taking tests: ACT, 20.5; SAT, 1026.

Housing: 3BR 2BA house in good condition, $65,000 to $75,000; pays $250 to $300 in real estate tax. Most people heat with natural gas.

Telecommunications: Verizon provides DSL service: 768 Kbps downstream; 128 Kbps upstream.

Sales, Income Taxes: Retail sales tax, 6%. State income tax scaled 3% to 6%.

Cost of Living: Doctor appointment, routine, $30; plumber per hour, $20–$25; baby-sitting per hour, $3; dry cleaning, men's suit, $6; dinner for 4, local restaurant, $40.

Community Infrastructure & Amenities:
United Way
Community leadership training program
4-H
Bed-and-breakfast
Community recreational center
Public library
Public parks: 2, totaling 13 acres
Public swimming pool
Airport
Country club
Golf course, 9 holes

Religious Denominations:
Assemblies of God
Baptist
Catholic
Church of Christ
Church of God
Church of Jesus Christ of Latter-Day Saints
Church of the Nazarene
Episcopal
Jehovah's Witnesses
Methodist
Nondenominational
Pentecostal
Presbyterian
Seventh Day Adventist
United Methodist

Newspaper: *Record Delta*, 213 Clarksburg Road, Buckhannon, WV 26201. 304-472-2800. www.therecorddelta.com. Published three times a week. John Scott, editor. 3-month subscription by mail, $27.77.

Annual Festivals and Events: May, West Virginia Strawberry Festival; August, Upshur County Fair; Country Roads Motorcycle Festival: call the Chamber of Commerce for dates.

Further Information: The Buckhannon Upshur Chamber of Commerce, P.O. Box 442, Buckhannon, WV 26201. 304-472-1722. cocoltchos@mountain.net

Carlinville, IL 62626

Population: 6,000 (+7%)
Banks: 5, 4 of which are branch banks.
Hospital: Carlinville Area Hospital, 30 beds.

Location: 60 miles northeast of St. Louis, 250 miles southwest of Chicago, in southwestern Illinois.

Geography/Climate: Mostly flat farmland north of town, quite hilly south, along Macoupin Creek. Tree-shaded streets in town. Continental climate. Strong seasonal swings. 119 below-freezing days, 8 below-zero days. 18 inches of snow. January averages, 39 high, 19 low. July averages, 87 high, 66 low. Summers are sunny, often hot and humid. 28 days at 90 degrees or above. Annual rainfall, 38 inches.

Five Largest Employers: Monterey Coal Company, 300 employees; Carlinville Area Hospital, 200; Carlinville Community School District, 187; corporate base of Prairie Farms Dairy, Inc., a Fortune 500 company, 150; Blackburn College, 104. Karmak, an Inc. 500 software company, also based in town.

Blackburn College enrolls about 500 students, ranks among third-tier liberal arts colleges in the 2001 edition of *America's Best Colleges*, published by *U.S. News & World Report*.

High School: Carlinville Community High School enrolls 562 students in grades 9–12, graduates 92%, sends 81% to college/university. Composite ACT for 79% of eligible students taking test, 24.8.

Housing: 3BR 2BA house sells for $125,000 to $160,000, pays upward of $4,000 a year in real estate tax.

Telecommunications: Maximum digital connection speed, 1.544 Mbps.

Sales, Income Taxes: Retail sales tax, 6.25%. State income tax, 3%.

Cost of Living: Movie ticket, $4; doctor appointment, routine, $55–$60; plumber per hour, $40; baby-sitting per hour, $3–$4; dry cleaning, men's suit, $7.25; dinner for 4, local restaurant, $25–$50.

Community Infrastructure & Amenities:
United Way
National Historic District
4-H
Bed-and-breakfast
Motion picture theater
Public library
Public parks: 4
Public swimming pool
Country club
Golf course, 18 holes

Religious Denominations:
Assemblies of God
Baptist
Catholic
Church of Christ
Church of the Nazarene
Episcopal
Lutheran (Missouri)
Pentecostal
United Methodist

Newspaper: *Macoupin County Enquirer*, 217-854-2534. Published weekly. Chris Schmidt, editor. *Carlinville Democrat*, 217-854-2561. Edward Albracht and Thomas Hatalla, editors. 6-month subscription by mail, $10. *New York Times, Wall Street Journal, St. Louis Post-Dispatch*, other regional dailies also sold in town.

Annual Festivals and Events: Christmas Market; Super Summer Weekend, sidewalk sales, band concerts, car show; Macoupin County Fair; Halloween Parade; Historical Society fall and spring festivals—crafts, agricultural re-enactments, such as blacksmithing.

Further Information: Carlinville Community Chamber of Commerce, 126 E. Main Street, Carlinville, IL 62626. 217-854-2141. www.carlinvillechamber.com

Cleveland, MS 38732

Population: 13,841 (–10%)
Banks: 6, including 2 locally owned.
Hospital: Bolivar Medical Center, 165 beds.

Location: 110 miles south of Memphis, 317 miles north of New Orleans, 19 miles east of the Mississippi River, in northwestern Mississippi.

Geography/Climate: Flat, fertile Mississippi Delta land. Short, cold winters with January lows averaging 32, highs, 55; 50 days at freezing or below; 2 to 3 inches of snow. Humid much of the year. July daily highs averaging 91, lows 70. Long, hot summers with 75 days at 90 or above. Annual rainfall, 49 inches.

Five Largest Employers: Baxter Healthcare, 1,100 employees; Delta State University, 788; Tyson Foods, 650; Cleveland School District, 540; Bolivar Medical Center, 500.

High School: Cleveland High School and East Side High School enroll a total of 1,037 students in grades 9–12 and graduate 80% of students. 91% of CHS graduates enroll in college/university. Composite ACT score for 91% of eligible students taking test, 17.7.

Housing: 3BR 2BA house in good condition sells for about $100,000, pays real estate tax of $600 to $630. Most people heat with electricity.

Telecommunications: BellSouth provides DSL service. Cable One provides Internet connection via cable.

Sales, Income Taxes: Retail sales tax, 7%. State income tax, 7%.

Cost of Living: Movie ticket, $6; doctor appointment, routine, $35–$45; plumber per hour, $50; baby-sitting per hour, $6; dry cleaning, men's suit, $5; dinner for 4, local restaurant, $60.

Community Infrastructure & Amenities:
United Way
Community leadership training program
Main Street
National Historic District
Boys Club/Girls Club
4-H
Bed-and-breakfast
Community recreational center
Motion picture theaters (4)
Public library
Public parks: 8, totaling 175 acres
Public swimming pool
Airport
Country club
Golf course

Religious Denominations:

AME	Four Square
Apostolic	Independent
Assemblies of God	Jehovah's Witnesses
Baptist	Jewish Congregation
Catholic	Lutheran
Christian	Methodist
Church of Christ	Nondenominational
Church of God	Pentecostal
Church of Jesus Christ of	Presbyterian
Latter-Day Saints	Seventh Day Adventist
Church of the Nazarene	United Methodist
Episcopal	

Newspaper: *Bolivar Commercial*, P.O. Box 1050, Cleveland, MS 38732. 662-843-4241. www.bolivar-com.com. Published daily except weekends. 3-month subscription by mail, $22.50.

Annual Festivals and Events: April, Crosstie Arts Festival, paintings, arts and crafts; September, Peavine Awards for Artistic Excellence in the Blues, Delta State University; October, Octoberfest, Memphis-in-May BBQ contest, arts and crafts, entertainment, food.

Further Information: Cleveland-Bolivar County Chamber of Commerce, 600 Third Street, Cleveland, MS 38732. 662-843-2712. www.clevelandchamberms.com

Clinton, SC 29360

Population: 8,091 (+1.3%)

Banks: 7, including 2 branch banks.

Hospital: Laurens County Health Care System, 90 beds.

Location: 60 miles northwest of Columbia, 40 miles southeast of Greenville, in western South Carolina.

Geography/Climate: Rolling terrain in a transition zone between the Piedmont and the Coastal Plain. Appalachian Mountains offer some protection from the worst wintry blasts from the north. On average, 58 days at 32 degrees or below but none below zero. An inch or two of snow perhaps. January average temperatures range from freezing to the 50s. Summers are long and hot, with an average 77 days at 90 or above, including several over 100 degrees. July average temperatures, from low 70s to upper 80s.

Five Largest Employers: Whitten Center, state institution for the mentally handicapped, 1,941; Torrington Company, ball bearings, 1,300 employees; Laurens County Health Care Systems, 480; School District 56, 450; Presbyterian College, 355.

Presbyterian College, a four-year, private institution, enrolls 1,073 students and ranks in the second tier nationally among liberal arts colleges, according to the 2001 survey by *U.S. News & World Report.*

High School: Clinton High School enrolls about 1,200 students in grades 9–12, graduates 74%, sends 46% of graduates to college/university. Composite SAT for 39% of seniors taking test, 974.

Housing: 3BR 2BA house sells in the range of $80,000 to $100,000, pays $500 to $600 in real estate tax. Most people heat with LP gas.

Telecommunications: Charter Communication provides broadband connection to the Internet.

Sales, Income Taxes: Retail sales tax, 6%. State income tax, scaled 2.5% to 7%.

Cost of Living: Doctor appointment, routine, $45; plumber per hour, $40; dry cleaning, men's suit, $8; dinner for 4, local restaurant, $50.

Community Infrastructure & Amenities:
United Way
Community leadership training program
National Historic District
YMCA/YWCA
Boys Club/Girls Club
4-H
Public library
Public parks: 4
Public swimming pool
Country club
Golf course

Religious Denominations:

AME	Interdenominational
Assemblies of God	Jehovah's Witnesses
Baptist	Lutheran
Catholic	Methodist
Church of Christ	Pentecostal
Church of God	Presbyterian
Episcopal	United Methodist
Independent	

Newspaper: *Clinton Chronicle*, P.O. Box 180, Clinton, SC 29325. 864-833-1900. Published weekly. Larry Franklin, editor. 1-year subscription, $45.

Annual Festivals and Events: Pride in Clinton Festival. Call Chamber of Commerce for dates.

Further Information: Laurens County Chamber of Commerce, P.O. Box 248, Laurens, SC 29340. 864-833-2716.

Decorah, IA 52101

Population: 8,172 (+1%)
Banks: 4, including 3 branch banks.
Hospital: Winneshiek County Memorial Hospital, 88 beds.

Location: 215 miles northeast of Des Moines, 130 miles southeast of Minneapolis, in the northeast corner of Iowa.

Geography/Climate: Scenic farm country, hilly enough to support commercial skiing operations— and snowy enough, with 42 inches of snow on average, 31 inches of rain. The continental climate means frequent changes in temperature. Cold, humid winters, with frequent snow. Warm, moderately humid summers. Seasonally, 154 days below freezing, 24 days below zero; 13 days at 90 degrees or above. January average temperatures range from upper teens to upper 20s; July, mid-60s to upper-80s.

Five Largest Employers: Textron, fastening systems, 600 employees; Luther College, 560; Heco Products, 435; Rockwell-Collins, communications equipment, 365; Fred Carlson Co., ready-mix concrete, 330.

Luther College enrolls 2,500 students and is ranked by *U.S. News & World Report* in the third tier of national liberal arts colleges.

High School: Decorah High School enrolls 942 students in grades 7–12, graduates 99.7%, sends 89% to college/university. Composite ACT, 23.7

Housing: 3BR 2BA house in good condition, $115,000. Real estate tax, $1,500. Most households heat with natural gas and LP gas.

Telecommunications: U.S. Qwest provides DSL service. Telnet provides digital connection via cable.

Sales, Income Taxes: Retail sales tax, 7%. State income tax, scaled 0.36% to 8.98%.

Cost of Living: Movie ticket, $5; doctor appointment, routine, $50; plumber per hour, $50; baby-sitting per hour, $2; dry cleaning, men's suit, $8; dinner for 4, local restaurant, $40.

Community Infrastructure & Amenities:

United Way	Public parks
Community foundation	Public swimming pool
(Assets $300,000)	Airport
Community leadership	Golf course
training program	Emergency home shelter
National Historic District	
Boys Club/Girls Club	
4-H	
Bed-and-breakfast	
Motion picture theater	
Public library	

Religious Denominations:

Assemblies of God	Methodist
Baptist	Presbyterian
Catholic	Seventh Day Adventist
Christian	United Church of Christ
Episcopal	
Friends	
Interdenominational	
Jehovah's Witnesses	
Lutheran	
Lutheran (ELCA)	
Lutheran (Missouri)	

Newspaper: *The Decorah Public Opinion*, *The Decorah Journal*, P.O. Box 350, Decorah, IA 52101. 563-382-4221. www.decorahnewspaper.com. Published twice weekly. Rick Fromm, editor. $31 a year. *New York Times, Wall Street Journal, Cedar Rapids Gazette* also sold in town.

Annual Festivals and Events: July, Nordic Fest, 3-day celebration of Norwegian ancestry; October, Northeast Iowa Artist Studio Tour; musical programs at Luther College, call 563-387-1357; Christmas Celebration at Luther College. (Call for times.)

Further Information: Decorah Area Chamber of Commerce, 300 W. Water, Decorah, IA 52101. 563-382-3990. www.decorah-iowa.com

Elkins, WV 26241

Population: 7,699 (+ 3.7%)
Banks: 5 banks, including 3 branch banks.
Hospital: Davis Memorial Hospital, 115 beds.

Location: 208 miles west of Washington, D.C.; 176 miles south of Pittsburgh; 147 miles northeast of Charleston, in the mountain region of east central West Virginia.

Geography/Climate: Situated at 1,920-feet elevation in the Tygart Valley, beside Monongahela National Forest, at the northwest corner of Randolph County, largest county east of the Mississippi River. Spruce Knob, highest point in West Virginia at 4,861 feet, is 23 miles southeast. Backbone Mountain, highest point in Maryland at 3,360 feet, is 30 miles northeast. January average temperature, 27 degrees. Storms can dump 1 to 2 feet of snow on the region. Because of its elevation, Elkins often is cited as one of the coldest spots in the East. July averages: temperature, 72 degrees; rainfall, 6.4 inches.

Davis & Elkins College, a 4-year liberal arts institution affiliated with the Presbyterian Church, enrolls 900 and ranks among the best regional institutions in a survey by *U.S. News & World Report.*

Five Largest Employers: Bruce Hardwood Flooring, 753 employees; Randolph County Board of Education, 705; Davis Memorial Hospital, 635; West Virginia Department of Highways, 302; Wal-Mart, 210.

High School: Elkins High School enrolls 950 students in grades 9–12. Graduation rate, 96%. College/university enrollment rate, 65%. Composite ACT for 85% of eligible students taking test, 20.2.

Housing: 3BR 2 BA house in good condition, $65,000. Annual real estate tax on such a house, $300.

Telecommunications: Verizon, Cablevision.

Sales, Income Taxes: Retail sales tax, 6%. State income tax, scaled 4% to 6.5%.

Cost of living: Movie ticket, $5.50; doctor appointment, routine, $35; plumber per hour, $25–35; baby-sitting, per hour, $1.75; dry cleaning, men's suit, $11; dinner for 4, local restaurant, $45.

Community Infrastructure & Amenities:
United Way
National Historic District
YMCA/YWCA
4-H
Bed-and-breakfast
Movie theater
Public library
Public parks: 3, totaling 32 acres
Airport
Country club
Golf course, 9 holes
Emergency home shelter

Religious Denominations:

Assemblies of God	Independent
Baptist	Jehovah's Witnesses
Cathedral of Deliverance	Lutheran
Catholic	Methodist
Christian	Nondenominational
Church of Brethren	Presbyterian
Church of Christ	Seventh Day Adventist
Church of God	Sound of Triumph
Church of Jesus Christ Of	United Methodist
Latter-Day Saints	
Church of the Nazarene	
Community	
Episcopal	

Newspaper: *The Inter-Mountain*, Elkins, WV 26241. 304-636-2121. intermtn@neumedia.net. Published daily. Don Smith, editor. 3-month subscription by mail, $43.50. *USA Today* also sold in town.

Annual Festivals and Events: Spring, Ramp Cook-Off & Festival, celebrating the ramp, a wild leek/onion regarded as a spring tonic; Summer, Augusta Heritage Festival of music, dance, and the arts; October, Mountain State Forest Festival.

Further information: Randolph County Convention & Visitors Bureau, 315 Railroad Ave., Suite 1, Elkins, WV 26241. pbritt@randolphcountywv.com

Ellensburg, WA 98926

Population: 15,414 (+25%)
Banks: 7, all branches of banks headquartered elsewhere.
Hospital: Kittitas Valley Community, 50 beds.

Location: 180 miles southwest of Spokane, 108 miles southeast of Seattle, smack-dab in the middle of Washington State.

Geography/Climate: Located in the Kittitas Valley between foothills rising to the west toward Mt. Rainier National Park and to the northeast toward the Wenatchee Mountains. A relatively mild climate thanks to the mountain barriers. Located in the rain shadow east of the Cascades, Ellensburg is comparatively dry: annual rainfall, 8 inches; snowfall, 24 inches. Dry, hot summers. Average humidity, 61%. January average temperatures range from upper 20s to upper 30s but with as many as four days below zero; July, from the 50s to the 80s but with 33 days at 90 degrees or above.

Five Largest Employers: Central Washington University, 1,230 employees; Ellensburg School District, 350; Kittitas County, 279; Kittitas Valley Community Hospital, 260; City of Ellensburg, 160.

Central Washington University enrolls 6,000 students and is ranked among second-tier regional universities by *U.S. News & World Report.*

High School: Ellensburg High School enrolls 950 students in grades 9–12, graduates 98%, sends 70% to colleges/university. Composite SAT scores: verbal, 531; math, 525.

Housing: 3BR 2BA house in good condition sells in the $120,000 to $150,000 range. Real estate tax on a house valued at $120,000: $1,079. Most households heat with natural gas.

Telecommunications: Ellensburg Telephone (Elltel) provides DSL service. Charter Cable provides a broadband connection to the Internet.

Sales, Income Taxes: 7% retail sales tax, grocery food exempt. No state income tax.

Cost of Living: Movie ticket, $6; doctor appointment, routine, $80; plumber per hour, $50; baby-sitting per hour, $2; dry cleaning, men's suit, $8; dinner for 4, local restaurant, $50.

Community Infrastructure & Amenities:

United Way	Motion picture theater
Community leadership	Public library
training program	Public parks
Main Street	Public swimming pool
National Historic District	Airport
4-H	Golf course, 27 holes
Bed-and-breakfast	Emergency home shelter
Community recreational	
center	

Religious Denominations:

Assemblies of God	Full Gospel
Baptist	German Baptist
Campus Ministries	Jehovah's Witnesses
Catholic	Lutheran
Christian	Lutheran (ELCA)
Church of Christ	Lutheran (Missouri)
Church of God	Methodist
Church of Jesus Christ of	Nondenominational
Latter-Day Saints	Presbyterian
Church of the Nazarene	Presbyterian USA
Community	Seventh Day Adventist
Episcopal	United Methodist
Evangelical	
Four Square	

Newspaper: *Daily Record,* 401 N. Main Street, Ellensburg, WA 98926. www.kvnews.com. Published daily except Sunday. Bill Kunerth, editor. 3-month subscription by mail, $27.

Annual Festivals and Events: third weekend in May, Western Art Festival—National Art Show & Auction; first Saturday in June, Gustfest; last weekend in July, Jazz Festival; Labor Day Weekend, Ellensburg Fair & Rodeo; second weekend in September, Threshing Bee.

Further Information: Ellensburg Chamber of Commerce, 609 N. Main Street, Ellensburg, WA 98926. www.ellensburg-chamber.com

Grinnell, IA 50112

Population: 9,105 (+2.3%)
Banks: 6 banks, including 5 branches.
Hospital: Grinnell Regional Medical Center, 83 beds.

Location: 4 miles north of I-80, 60 miles east of Des Moines, in central Iowa.

Geography/Climate: Gently rolling mid-continent farmlands. Four sharply etched seasons. A few brittle cold winter days may not rise above zero. Summer highs in the 90s. Precipitation averages 32 inches, snowfall 31 inches. Spring and fall each last about 6 weeks.

Five Largest Employers: Grinnell College, 659 employees; Grinnell Mutual Reinsurance, 631; Grinnell Regional Medical Center, 300; Donaldson Co., mufflers, 220; Iowa Telecom, 182.

Grinnell College ranks 14th on the *U.S. News & World Report* 2001 "Top 50 list of Best National Liberal Arts Colleges."

High School: Grinnell-Newburg High School enrolls 566 students in grades 9–12, graduates 98%, and sends 80% on to college or university. Recent composite ACT score for 80% of eligible students taking test, 23.1.

Housing: 3BR 2BA house in good condition sells in the $80,000 to $125,000 range. Annual real estate tax on such a house, $2,500 to $4,500. Most households heat with natural gas.

Telecommunications: Iowa Telecom provides DSL service at 1.024 Mbps.

Sales, Income Taxes: Retail sales tax, 5%, food exempt. State income tax, ranges from 0.4% to 9.98%.

Cost of Living: Movie ticket, $5; doctor appointment, routine, $40; plumber per hour, $56; baby-sitting, per week, $115–125; dry cleaning, men's suit, $8.40; dinner for 4, local restaurant, $50.

Community Infrastructure & Amenities:

United Way	Public library
Community foundation (Assets $175,755)	Public parks: 10 parks, totaling 75 acres
Community leadership training program	Public swimming pool
National Historic District	Airport
Boys Club/Girls Club	Country club
4-H	Golf courses: 9 holes in town, 18 holes nearby
Bed-and-breakfast	Emergency home shelter
Community recreational center	
Motion picture theater	

Religious Denominations:

Apostolic	Episcopal
Assemblies of God	Friends
Baptist	Lutheran
Catholic	Lutheran (ELCA)
Christian	Methodist
Christian Science	Pentecostal
Church of Christ	Presbyterian
Church of God	United Church of Christ
Church of the Nazarene	United Methodist
Community	

Newspaper: *Grinnell Herald Register*, 813 5th Ave., Grinnell, IA 50112. 641-236-3113. Published twice weekly. Al Pinder, editor and publisher. 6-month subscription by mail, $50. *New York Times*, *Wall Street Journal*, other Iowa newspaper, also sold in town.

Annual Festivals and Events: March, Home Show & Business Expo; June, Bike Rodeo; June–July, Concerts in the Park; July, Poweshiek County Fair; First Thursday September, Ag Appreciation Day; September, Shakespeare in the Park; November, Jingle Bell Holiday, Festival of Trees.

Further Information: Grinnell Area Chamber of Commerce, 833 Fourth Ave., Grinnell, IA 50112. 641-236-6555. chamberc@pcpartner.net

Lewisburg, PA 17837

Population: 5,620 (–2.9%)
Banks: 5 branch banks.
Hospital: Evangelical Community Hospital, 155 beds.

Location: 165 miles northwest of Philadelphia, 70 miles north of Harrisburg, in the Central Susquehanna Valley.

Geography/Climate: Elevation 460 feet, bordered on the east by the Susquehanna River; Appalachian Mountains to the northwest; Shamokin Mountain, Montour Range to the southeast. Prime agricultural land. Changeable weather, a mixture of drier continental and more humid eastern seaboard weather patterns. Annual rainfall, 36 inches; snowfall, 35. January daily high, 35; low, 20, with one day below zero. July highs average 86, with 20 days into the 90s. Though humid and quite cloudy, nice summers and falls.

Lewisburg is the home of **Bucknell University**, ranked among the top 50 national liberal arts colleges by U.S. News & World Report.

Five Largest Employers: American Home Foods, 1,700 employees; Evangelical Community Hospital, 1,170; Bucknell University, 1,020; Pennsylvania House Furniture, 600; Ritz Craft Modular, 375.

Public Schools: Lewisburg schools enroll 1,820 students in grades K–12. Graduation rate, 99%. 80% of graduates enroll in college/university. Composite scores for 84% of eligible students taking SAT exam: 539 verbal; 542 math.

Housing: 3BR, 2 BA house in good condition ranges from $85,000–$120,000. Taxes on such a house, $2,000. Most residents heat with natural gas.

Telecommunications: Conestoga Communications offers DSL service. Cable operator offers Internet connection.

Sales, Income Taxes: 6% retail sales tax, food exempt. 2.8% flat-rate state income tax.

Cost of living: Movie ticket, $5; doctor appointment, routine, $70; plumber per hour, $45; baby-sitting, per hour, $10; dry cleaning, men's suit, $8; dinner for 4, local restaurant, $60.

Community Infrastructure & Amenities:
United Way
Community foundation
Community leadership training program
Main Street member
National Historic District
Bed-and-breakfast
Community recreational center
Movie theater
Public library
Public parks: 5 parks total 75 acres
Public swimming pool
Emergency home shelter

Religious Denominations
Assemblies of God
Baptist
Catholic
Church of Christ
Episcopal
Evangelical
Lutheran
Lutheran (ELCA)
Methodist
Presbyterian
Presbyterian USA
United Methodist

Newspaper: *Lewisburg Daily Journal*, 21 Arch St., Milton, PA 17847. 570-742-9671. Published daily. 3-month subscription, $26.60. Michael Redding, editor. *New York Times*, *USA Today* also sold in town.

Annual festivals and events: April, Arts Festival; July 4, Hymn Sing at Soldiers Park; October, Wooly Warm, Prognostication of Warm or Cold Weather, Halloween Parade; December, Victorian Parade.

Further information: Dr. David L. Clouser, 101 S. 3rd St., Lewisburg, PA 17837. 570-524-4303.

Lexington, VA 24450

Population: 6,867 (–1%)
Banks: 7, 3 of which are branch banks.
Hospital: Stonewall Jackson Hospital, 200 beds.

Location: 69 miles southwest of Charlottesville, 54 miles northeast of Roanoke, in the Shenandoah Valley of southwestern Virginia.

Geography/Climate: Mountain valley town located between the Blue Ridge range on the southeast and Shenandoah range on the northwest. Mild continental climate. January temperatures range on average from 26 low to 47 high; July, 61 to 86. Seasonally, 92 days below freezing, 31 days above 90. Annual precipitation, 40 inches; snowfall, 25 inches.

Five Largest Employers: Burlington Industries— Lees Carpet, 1,250 employees; Virginia Military Institute, 740; Washington & Lee University, 626; Stonewall Jackson Hospital, 419; Dana Corporation, 415.

Washington & Lee University ranks 12th on the list of Best National Liberal Arts Colleges, as compiled by *U.S. News & World Report* in 2001. The private institution, founded in 1749, enrolls about 1,750 students. **Virginia Military Institute,** also located in Lexington, is ranked in the third tier of national liberal arts colleges by *USN&WR*. VMI enrolls about 1,350 students.

High School: Rockbridge County High School enrolls 1,060 students in grades 9–12, graduates 96%; sends 45% to 4-year college, 28% to 2-year, 4% to technical school. Composite SAT: verbal, 541; math, 536.

Housing: 3BR 2BA house ranges from $150,000 to $375,000 and higher depending on location. Most households heat with natural gas.

Telecommunications: Sprint provides DSL service. Adelphia provides Internet connection via cable.

Sales, Income Taxes: Retail sales tax, 4.5%. State income tax, 2% to 5.75%.

Cost of Living: Movie ticket, $6.50; doctor appointment, routine, $40; plumber per hour, $50; baby-sitting per hour, $5; dry cleaning, men's suit, $6; dinner for 4, local restaurant, $75+.

Community Infrastructure & Amenities:
United Way
Community leadership training program
Main Street
National Historic District
4-H
Bed-and-breakfast
Motion picture theater
Public library
Public parks
Public swimming pool
Country club
Golf course
Emergency home shelter

Religious Denominations:
Assemblies of God
Baptist
Catholic
Church of Christ
Church of God
Church of Jesus Christ of Latter-Day Saints
Episcopal
Jehovah's Witnesses
Lutheran
Methodist
Presbyterian
United Methodist

Newspaper: *News-Gazette,* Box 1153, Lexington, VA 24450. 540-463-3113. www.thenews-gazette.com. 6-month subscription, $19.95. *New York Times, Wall Street Journal, USA Today, Washington Post, Richmond Times Dispatch* also sold in town.

Annual Festivals and Events: February, Chocolate Lovers Weekend; March, Home & Business Expo; plus dozens of events annually at the two prestigious college campuses in town. Check the chamber Web site (below) for current details.

Further Information: *Chamber of Commerce,* 100 E. Washington Street, Lexington, VA 24450. 540-463-5375. chamber@lexrockchamber.com.

Middlebury, VT 05753

Population: 8,183 (+36%)
Banks: 5, including 4 branch banks.
Hospital: Porter Medical Center, 45 beds.

Location: 34 miles south of Burlington, 35 miles north of Rutland, 200 miles west of Boston, 265 miles north of New York City, in west central Vermont.

Geography/Climate: Scenic New England village in the Champlain Valley, backed up to the east by Green Mountain peaks rising 3,000 to 4,000 feet. Typical Northern New England weather—cold, sometimes intensely cold, winters; pleasant summers; cool, colorful falls. January temperatures average 18 degrees, with range of 8 to 26. July averages 70, with range of 60 to 80. Five or so 90-degree days during summer; average 28 days below zero through the 5-month winter season. Average rainfall 33 inches; snowfall, up to 80.

Five Largest Employers: Middlebury College, 1,095 employees; Counseling Service of Addison County, 250–500; Porter Hospital, 400; Middlebury School District, 100–250; Specialty Filaments, 138.

Middlebury College ranks 6th (along with Carleton, Haverford, and Bowdoin) among "Best National Liberal Arts Colleges" as compiled by *U.S. News & World Report* in 2001.

High School: Middlebury Union High School enrolls 730 students in grades 9–12, graduates 83%, sends 50% to 65% to college/university. Composite SAT in 2001: math 540, verbal 528.

Housing: 3BR 2 BA house in good condition sells in the range of $150,000 to $199,000. Real estate taxes on such a house, $3,000 to $4,000. Most households heat with oil.

Telecommunications: Adelphia provides Internet connection via cable.

Sales, Income Taxes: 5% retail sales tax, except for clothing and shoes up to $100. State income tax, 24% of federal tax liability.

Cost of Living: Movie ticket, $7; doctor appointment, routine, $45; plumber per hour, $48; baby-sitting per hour, $2 per child; dry cleaning, men's suit, $9.25; dinner for 4, local restaurant, $65 without drinks.

Community Infrastructure & Amenities:

United Way	Motion picture theater
Community foundation:	Public library
($60 million assets)	Public parks: 4
Main Street	Public swimming pool
National Historic District	Airport
4-H	Golf course, 18 holes
Bed-and-breakfast	
Community recreational	
center	

Religious Denominations:

Baptist	Episcopal
Buddhist	Friends
Catholic	Jehovah's Witnesses
Christian Science	Jewish Congregation
Church of Jesus Christ of	Unitarian Universalist
Latter-Day Saints	United Church of Christ
Community	United Methodist
Eastern Orthodox	

Newspaper: *Addison Independent*, P.O. Box 31, Middlebury, VT 05753. 802-388-4944. www.addisonindependent.com. Published biweekly, Angelo Lynn, editor. 3-month subscription by mail, $23. *New York Times, Wall Street Journal, Boston Globe* also sold in town.

Annual Festivals and Events: July, Festival on the Green, free entertainment for a week, with Brown Bag Specials at noon, evening performances, street dance; Lobsterfest benefit for conservation and recreation programs; After Dark Music Series during winter months, featuring blues, folk, and acoustic performers.

Further Information: Addison County Chamber of Commerce, 2 Court Street, Middlebury, VT 05753. 802-388-7951. info@midvermont.com

Oxford, MS 38655

Population: 11,756 (+15%)
Banks: 7 banks, 6 of which are branches.
Hospital: Baptist Memorial Hospital—North Mississippi, 200 beds.

Location: 165 miles north of Jackson, 75 miles south of Memphis, in the hill country of northern Mississippi.

Geography/Climate: Hilly, rolling land; average elevation 500 feet. Short winters, January daily lows averaging 32 degrees—57 days at freezing or below; highs, 50; 5 inches of snow. Long summers, with hot, humid stretches. July averages: low, 72; high, 92; 66 days into the 90s. Annual precipitation, 52 inches.

Five Largest Employers: University of Mississippi, 2,500 employees; North Mississippi Regional Center, 1,100; Baptist Memorial Hospital, North Mississippi, 950; Emerson Electric, 530; Whirlpool Corporation, 375.

University of Mississippi—Ole Miss—enrolls about 11,000 students and ranks among third tier institutions on the 2001 rankings of *U.S. News & World Report*.

High School: Oxford High School enrolls 850 students in grade 9–12, graduates 95%, and sends 84% to college/university. Recent composite ACT score for 75% of eligible students taking test, 21.1.

Housing: 3BR 2BA house in good condition sells for $100,000–$150,000. Taxes on such a house, about $1,000. Most people heat with natural gas.

Telecommunications: Bell South provides DSL service. Galaxy Cable provides Internet connection.

Sales, Income Taxes: Retail sales tax, 7%. State income tax 3%–5%. (Certified retirement income for persons age 65+ is not subject to state tax.)

Cost of Living: Movie ticket, $5; doctor appointment, routine, $54; plumber per hour, $55; babysitting, per hour, $7; dry cleaning, men's suit, $7; dinner for 4, local restaurant, $75.

Community Infrastructure & Amenities:

United Way	Motion picture theater
Community leadership training program	Public library
	Public parks: 8 parks, totaling 150 acres
National Historic District	
Boys Club/Girls Club	Public swimming pool
4-H	Airport
Bed-and-breakfast	Golf courses, two 18-hole
Community recreational center	Emergency home shelter

Religious Denominations:

Apostolic	Full Gospel
Assemblies of God	Interdenominational
Baptist	Jehovah's Witnesses
Catholic	Lutheran
Church of Christ	Methodist
Church of God	Pentecostal
Church of Jesus Christ of Latter-Day Saints	Presbyterian
	Presbyterian USA
Church of the Nazarene	Unitarian Universalist
Covenant	United Methodist
Episcopal	

Newspaper: *Oxford Eagle*, 916 Jackson Ave., Oxford, MS 38655. 662-234-4331. oxfordeagle.com. Published daily, Monday–Friday. Mrs. J. C. Goolsby, editor. *New York Times, Wall Street Journal, Memphis Commercial-Appeal*, other Mississippi newspapers sold in town.

Annual Festivals and Events: Spring, Oxford Conference for the Book; 4th weekend April, Double-Decker Arts Festival; July, Faulkner Conference; Fall, Southern Foodway Symposium, History Symposium.

Further Information: Oxford–Lafayette County Chamber of Commerce, 299 W. Jackson Ave., Oxford, MS 38655. 662-234-4651. info@oxfordms.com

Plymouth, NH 03223

Population: 5,892 (+1.3%)
Banks: 5, 4 of which are branches.
Hospital: Speare Memorial Hospital, 35 beds.

Location: 59 miles north of Manchester, 112 miles north of Boston, 200 miles south of Montreal, between the Lakes Region and the White Mountains of north central Vermont

Geography/Climate: Elevation 514 feet. Located at confluence of Baker and Pemigewasset Rivers in central New Hampshire. Scenic, heavily forested area 5 miles west of Squam Lake, where *On Golden Pond* was filmed. Long, snowy, sometimes bitterly cold winters. January average temperature 15.6 degrees, with range of 8 to 30. July temperature averages: low, 53; high, 81. Warm summer days, cool nights. Colorful, pleasant falls. Annual rainfall, 38 inches; up to 90 inches of snow.

Five Largest Employers: Plymouth State College, 487 employees; Speare Memorial Hospital, 220; New Hampshire Electric Cooperative, 208; Shop-n-Save Supermarket, 180; Plymouth Regional High School, 125.

Plymouth State College enrolls about 4,000 students and is listed among third-tier regional universities in 2001 rankings by *U.S. News & World Report*.

High School: Plymouth Regional High School enrolls 848 students in grades 9–12, graduates 97%, sends 85% to 4- or 2-year college. Recent composite scores: SAT, 989; ACT, 23.

Housing: 3BR 2BA house in good condition sells in $110,000–$115,000 range. Real estate tax on such a house, $3,800 to $4,000. Most people heat with oil.

Telecommunications: Verizon provides DSL service. Adelphia provides Internet cable connection.

Sales, Income Taxes: None.

Cost of Living: Movie ticket, $7; doctor appointment, routine, $61; plumber per hour, $60; baby-sitting, per hour, $4–$6; dry cleaning, men's suit, $26; dinner for 4, local restaurant, $60–$80.

Community Infrastructure & Amenities:
Main Street
Bed-and-breakfast
Community recreational center
Motion picture theater
Public library
Public parks: 3 parks, totaling 18 acres
Airport
Golf course, 9 holes
Emergency home shelter

Religious Denominations:
Assemblies of God
Baptist
Catholic
Church of Christ
Church of Jesus Christ of Latter-Day Saints
Congregational
Episcopal
Gateway Alliance
Seventh Day Adventist
United Methodist
Universalist Fellowship

Newspapers: *Record Enterprise*, P.O. Box 148, Plymouth, NH 03264. 603-536-1311. Published weekly. 6-month subscription by mail, $16. Brian McCarthy, editor. *Citizen*, 171 Fair Street, Laconia, NH 03246. 603-524-3800. citizen.com. Published daily. John Howe, editor. *New York Times*, *Wall Street Journal* also sold in town.

Annual Festivals and Events: March, Cardboard Box Derby at Tenney Mountain, Friends of the Arts Art Auction; Memorial Day, St. Jude's Bike-a-thon; July–August, Summer Concert on the Common, New Hampshire Music Festival; September, Townwide Yard Sale; October, Art Show on the Common, Antique Appraisal Day at Episcopal Church, Railroad Promotion Day/Campaign Train.

Further Information: Plymouth Chamber of Commerce, P.O. Box 65, Plymouth, NH 03264. 603-536-1001. info@plymouthnh.org

Ripon, WI 54971

Population: 6,828 (–6%, under appeal)
Banks: 5, of which 4 are branches of outside banks.
Hospital: Ripon Medical Center, 30 beds.

Location: 70 miles northwest of Milwaukee, in east central Wisconsin.

Geography/Climate: Picturesque farm country. Continental climate with four sharply etched seasons. Long winters: first freeze occurs in early October and the last in mid-May. Pleasant summers, with cool evenings and nights. January average temperatures range from the teens to the 20s; July, 50s to 80s. Year-round the area may experience 160 days at freezing or below and 25 days below zero; 7 days at 90 or above. 29 inches of rain, 45 inches of snow.

Five Largest Employers: Alliance Laundry Systems, 850 employees; Bremner, cookies and crackers, 630; Admanco, 500; Ripon Community Printers, 380; Smuckers Specialty Foods, 162.

Ripon College, the widely know liberal arts institution enrolling 900 students, received a "Best Value" ranking by *U.S. News & World Report* in its *America's Best Colleges* 2002 edition. The ranking considers both academic quality and cost. Ripon tied for fifth place with Claremont-McKenna College, Claremont, Calif.

High School: Ripon High School enrolls 542 students in grades 9–12, graduates 98.5%, sends 77% to college/university. Composite ACT for 66% of eligible students taking test, 22.4.

Housing: 3BR 2BA house in good condition sells in the range of $90,000 to $125,000, pays about $2,800 in real estate tax. Most people heat their homes with natural gas.

Telecommunications: Charter Communication provides a broadband Internet connection.

Sales, Income Taxes: 5% retail sales tax. State income tax scaled 4.6% to 6.75%.

Cost of Living: Movie ticket, $6.50; doctor appointment for routine physical exam, $40–$60; plumber per hour, $50; baby-sitting per hour, $2.25; dry cleaning, men's suit, $8.30; dinner for 4, local restaurant, $30 low end to $125 high end.

Community Infrastructure & Amenities:

United Way	Bed-and-breakfast
Community leadership training program	Motion picture theater
Main Street	Public library
National Historic District	Public parks
4-H	Emergency home shelter

Religious Denominations:
Assemblies of God
Baptist
Catholic
Christian
Episcopal
Evangelical
Methodist
Nondenominational
United Methodist

Newspaper: *Commonwealth Express*, P.O. Box 344, Ripon, WI 54971. 920-748-3017. Published weekly, Randy Radtke, editor. 6-month subscription by mail, $28. *New York Times* and *Wall Street Journal* also sold in town.

Annual Festivals and Events: Ripon, where the Republican Party was given its name in 1854, is a cookie-baking center and produced the World's Biggest Cookie in 1992, according to the *Guinness Book of World Records*. Annually, the town celebrates Cookie Daze, in early August. Other events: March, Farm Toy & Craft Show; May, Birth of a Clydesdale; late June, Jazz Festival; October, Pumpkin Fest; early December, Dickens of a Quilt Show.

Further Information: Ripon Area Chamber of Commerce, P.O. Box 305, Ripon, WI 54971. 920-748-6764. racc@vbe.com

Rolla, MO 65401

Population: 16,367 (+14.2%)
Banks: 6 banks, including 3 branches.
Hospital: Phelps County Regional Medical Center, 235 beds

Location: 103 miles southwest of St. Louis, 61 miles southeast of Jefferson City, on the northern edge of the Missouri Ozarks.

Geography/Climate: Rolling hills. Temperate, four-season climate with relatively mild winters, hot and humid summers. Average rainfall, 37 inches; snowfall, 12. January is driest month; May the wettest, with average 4.7 inches of rain. January temperatures range from 23 low to 40 high, with two or three days dipping below zero per season. July averages, 70 low to 86 high. Average 38 days at 90 degrees or above.

Five Largest Employers: University of Missouri-Rolla and governmental agencies, 5,113 employees; Phelps County Regional Medical Center, 1,100; Briggs & Stratton, 725; Brewer Science, chemicals, 170; Lowe's, 170.

University of Missouri-Rolla is the backbone of the economy. Known for its engineering programs, the Rolla campus is on the second-tier list of best national universities in 2001 rankings by *U.S. News & World Report*.

High School: Rolla High School enrolls 1,000 students in grades 10–12, graduates 88%, sends 43% to college/university. Recent composite score on ACT test for 72% of eligible students taking test, 23.2.

Housing: 3BR 2BA house in good condition, $85,000–$95,000. Real estate taxes, $500–$600. Most people heat with electricity.

Telecommunications: Sprint provides DSL service at 3.0 Mbps. Fidelity Cablevision offers Internet access.

Sales, Income Taxes: Retail sales tax, 7.725%, prescription drugs exempt. State income tax, 3% flat rate.

Cost of Living: Movie ticket, $6.25; doctor appointment, routine, $65; plumber per hour, $50; baby-sitting, per hour, $5; dry cleaning, men's suit, $6.25; dinner for 4, local restaurant, $60.

Community Infrastructure & Amenities:

United Way
Community leadership training program
Main Street
4-H
Bed-and-breakfast
Community recreational center
Motion picture theater
Public library
Public parks: 27 parks, totaling 490 acres
Public swimming pool
Airport
Country club
Golf courses, 9-hole and 18-hole
Emergency home shelter

Religious Denominations:

Apostolic
Assemblies of God
Assembly of Yahweh
Baha'i
Baptist
Catholic
Christian
Christian Science
Church of Christ
Church of God
Church of Jesus Christ of Latter-Day Saints
Church of the Nazarene
Disciples of Christ
Episcopal
Full Gospel
Independent
Islamic Center of Rolla
Jehovah's Witnesses
Lutheran
Lutheran (ELCA)
Lutheran (Missouri)
Methodist
Nondenominational
Pentecostal
Presbyterian
Quaker
Seventh Day Adventist
Unitarian
United Methodist

Newspaper: *Rolla Daily News*, 101 W. 7th, Rolla, MO 65401. 573-364-2468. therolladailynews.com. Published daily and Sunday. Steve Sowers, editor. 3-month subscription by mail, $25.67.

Annual Festivals and Events: St. Pat's Parade; Route 66 Summerfest; Fall Arts & Crafts Festival.

Further Information: Rolla Area Chamber of Commerce, 1301 Kingshighway, Rolla, MO 65401. 573-364-3577. rollacc@rollachamber.org

Shippensburg, PA 17257

Population: 5,586 (+5%)

Banks: 7, including 6 branch banks.

Hospital: Chambersburg Hospital (9 miles), 232 beds; Carlisle Regional Medical Center (16 miles), 200 beds.

Location: 130 miles west of Philadelphia, 180 miles southeast of Pittsburgh, in the Cumberland Valley of Pennsylvania.

Geography/Climate: Rolling terrain against a backdrop of low mountain ranges to the south and east. Four-season climate buffered by the Appalachians and coastal influence of the Atlantic Ocean. January average temperatures: low, 23; high, 41. July: low, 62; high, 87. Average annual rainfall, 40 inches; snowfall, 31 inches.

Five Largest Employers: Shippensburg University, 850 employees; Ingersoll Rand, 650; The Beistle Company, 489; Hoffman Mills, 450; Shippensburg Area School District, 390.

Shippensburg University enrolls 5,500 students, ranks fifth among "Top Regional Public Schools in the North" in 2001 rankings by *U.S. News & World Report*.

High School: Shippensburg Area Senior High enrolls 950 students in grades 9–12, sends 62% to college/university. Composite SAT: verbal, 479; math 484.

Housing: 3BR 2BA house in good condition sells for about $99,000; pays $1,000 a year in real estate tax. Most people heat with electricity.

Telecommunications: Sprint provides DSL service. Comcast offers Internet connection via cable.

Sales, Income Taxes: Retail sales tax, 6%. State income tax, 2.8% flat rate.

Cost of Living: Movie ticket, $6.50; doctor appointment, routine, $44–$57; plumber per hour, $35; baby sitting per hour, $3; dry cleaning, men's suit, $7.25; dinner for 4, local restaurant, $28.

Community Infrastructure & Amenities:

United Way	Public parks: 3, totaling
Community leadership	123 acres.
training program	Public swimming pool
Main Street	Airport
National Historic District	Country club
4-H	Golf course, 18 holes
Bed-and-breakfast	Emergency home shelter
Community recreational	
center	
Public library	

Religious Denominations:

AME	Interdenominational
Assemblies of God	Jewish Congregation
Baptist	Lutheran
Brethren	Mennonite
Catholic	Methodist
Christian	Nondenominational
Church of Christ	Pentecostal
Church of God	Presbyterian
Church of the Nazarene	Presbyterian, Reformed
Community	United Brethren
Eastern Orthodox	United Church of Christ
Episcopal	United Methodist
Evangelical	Wesleyan
Full Gospel	

Newspaper: *Pubic Opinion*, 77 N. Third Street, Chambersburg, PA 17201. 717-264-6161. pubop@epix.net. Published daily except Sunday. John Mason, publisher. 3-month subscription by mail, $35.75.

Annual Festivals and Events: Last Saturday in August, Corn Festival, crafts, vendors, food; first Saturday in December, Dickens Day: Dickens carolers, Christmas parade.

Further Information: Shippensburg Area Chamber of Commerce, 75 W. King Street, Shippensburg, PA 17257. 717-532-5509. chamber@shippensburg.org

Williamstown, MA 01267

Population: 8,424 (+3%)

Banks: 4, all branches of larger banks.

Hospital: North Adams Regional Hospital, 10 miles.

Location: 140 miles west-northwest of Boston, 155 miles north-northwest of New York City, 15 miles south of Bennington, Vermont, in the northwest corner of Massachusetts.

Geography/Climate: Elevation in town at Field Park, 725 feet; near peak of Mount Greylock, 5 miles southeast, 3,317 feet, the highest point in Massachusetts. Berkshire Hills setting. A half dozen brooks and streams flow through community. Cold, snowy winters produce great skiing. Very pleasant summers. Temperature averages: January, high 31; low 11. July, high 82; low 56. Annual rainfall, 43 inches; snowfall 56 inches.

Five Largest Employers: Steinerfilm, 200 employees; Town of Williamstown; Williams College; Williamstown Medical Associates; Northern Berkshire Health Systems.

Williams College, enrolling 2,000 students, ranks number 3 on the list of liberal arts colleges serving a national clientele, according to *U.S. News & World Report.*

High School: Mount Greylock Regional High School enrolls 800 students in grades 7–12, sends 59% of graduates to 4-year college and 22% to 2-year college. Mean SAT scores: verbal, 541; math, 537. Total, 1078.

Housing: 3BR 2BA house in good condition, $215,000. Real estate tax rate, $13.95 per $1,000 of assessed valuation.

Telecommunications: Verizon provides DSL service.

Sales, Income Taxes: Retail sales tax, 5%. State income tax, 5.6% flat rate.

Cost of Living: Movie ticket, $8; doctor appointment, routine, $65; plumber per hour, $30; baby sitting per hour, $5; dry cleaning, men's suit, $10; dinner for 4, local restaurant, $100.

Community Infrastructure & Amenities:
Main Street
National Historic District
Bed-and-breakfast
Community recreational center
Motion picture theater
Public library
Public parks
Country club
Golf courses (2), 18 holes each

Religious Denominations:
Baptist
Catholic (2)
Community Bible
Congregational (3)
Episcopal
Methodist
United Methodist

Newspaper: *The Advocate*, 38 Spring Street, Williamstown, MA 01267. 413-458-5713. Published weekly. news@advocateweekly.com

Annual Festivals and Events: 2nd weekend December, Holiday Walk Weekend; April, Williamstown Jazz Festival; August, A Taste of Williamstown.

Further Information: Williamstown Chamber of Commerce, P.O. Box 357, Williamstown, MA 01267. 413-458-9077. commerce@williamstown.net

Big City/Small Town Pairs

Baraboo, WI 53913

Population: 10,537 (+14%)
Banks: 3, including 1 branch.
Hospital: St. Clare Hospital and Health Services, 70 beds.

Location: 100 miles west of Milwaukee, 41 miles northwest of Madison, 200 miles southeast of Minneapolis-St. Paul, in south central Wisconsin.

Geography/Climate: To the west, gently rolling plain, deeply cut by streams and broken by occasional hills or ridges. To the east, glacial landscape of moraines, bogs, marshes, and fens. Pleasant summers; long, severe winters. January daily highs average 25; lows, 8. Average 164 days below freezing, 25 days below zero. July daily highs, 81; lows, 59. Twelve days into the 90s. Annual rainfall, 32 inches; snowfall, 39 inches.

Five Largest Employers: Ho-Chunk Casino, 1,975 employees; Baraboo Sysco Food Service, 675; Perry Judd's, printer, 620; Flambeau Corp., plastics, 600; Baraboo School System, 500.

High School: Baraboo High School enrolls 1,025 students in grades 9–12, graduates over 100% including GED and other nontraditional students, sends 55% to college/university. Recent composite ACT for college-bound, 23.1.

Housing: 3BR 2BA house in good condition sells for about $120,000 and pays about $2,800 in real estate tax. Most people heat with natural gas.

Telecommunications: Charter Communications provides Internet connection via cable.

Sales, Income Taxes: Retail sales tax, 5.5%, most food items exempt. State income tax, 5%.

Cost of Living: Movie ticket, $6.50; doctor appointment, routine, $75; plumber per hour, $60; baby-sitting, per hour, $3; dry cleaning, men's suit, $8.45; dinner for 4, local restaurant, $40.

Community Infrastructure & Amenities:

United Way
Community leadership training program
Boys Club/Girls Club
4-H
Bed-and-breakfast
Motion picture theater
Public library
Public parks: 12 parks, totaling 123 acres
Public swimming pool
Airport
Country club
Golf course, 18 holes
Salvation Army

Religious Denominations:
Advent Christian
Apostolic
Assemblies of God
Baptist
Catholic
Christian Science
Church of Christ
Church of God
Church of Jesus Christ of Latter-Day Saints
Church of the Nazarene
Episcopal
Independent
Jehovah's Witnesses
Lutheran (WELS)
Lutheran (ELCA)
Lutheran (Missouri)
Nondenominational
Presbyterian USA
Seventh Day Adventist
United Church of Christ
United Methodist
Wesleyan

Newspaper: *Baraboo News Republic*, 219 First Street, Baraboo, WI 53913. 608-356-4808. Baraboo.scwn.com. Published daily. Judy Juenger, editor. *New York Times*, *Wall Street Journal*, and Madison, Milwaukee, and Chicago dailies also sold in town.

Annual Festivals and Events: 3rd Saturday in May, Spring Arts & Crafts Fair; 4th Saturday in July, Old Fashioned Day; 2nd Saturday in August, Summer Classic Art Festival; 2nd Saturday in October, Fall Arts & Crafts Fair.

Further Information: Baraboo Area Chamber of Commerce, P.O. Box 442, Baraboo, WI 53913. 608-356-8333. 1-800-BARABOO. chamber@baraboo.com

Bardstown, KY 40004

Population: 7,594 (+12%)
Banks: 6, including 2 branch banks.
Hospital: Flaget Memorial Hospital, 52 beds.

Location: 34 miles south of Louisville, 58 miles west of Lexington.

Geography/Climate: Hilly Kentucky country called The Knobs. Continental climate with four distinct seasons. Moderately cold winters with average 15 inches of snow. Warm, humid summers with average 26 days at 90 degrees or higher. 44 inches of rain a year. Intense rainstorms common in spring and summer. Colorful falls.

Five Largest Employers: American Greetings, 750 employees; Jideco of Bardstown, 530; Tower Automotive, 380; Heaven Hill Distilleries, bourbon, 375; American Fuji Seal, 350.

High School: Bardstown High School enrolls about 450 students in grades 10–12.

Housing: 3BR 2BA house in good condition sells in $100,000 range. Households use both natural gas and electricity for heating.

Telecommunications: Bell South provides DSL service. City of Bardstown cable system (municipally owned) provides Internet connection by cable. (128K, $24.95 a month; 512K, $40 a month.)

Sales, Income Taxes: Retail sales tax, 6%. State income tax, scaled 2% to 6%.

Cost of Living: Movie ticket, $7; doctor appointment, routine, $40; baby-sitting, per hour, $3; dinner for 4, local restaurant, $25.

Community Infrastructure & Amenities

United Way	Public library
Community leadership training program	Public parks: 7
Main Street	Public swimming pool
National Historic District	Airport
4-H	Country club
Bed-and-breakfast	Golf courses (4), 18-hole; (1) 9-hole
Community recreational center	Emergency home shelter
Motion picture theater	

Religious Denominations:

AME
Assemblies of God
Baptist
Catholic
Charismatic
Christian
Church of Christ
Church of God
Disciples of Christ
Episcopal
Independent
Interdenominational
Jehovah's Witnesses
Lutheran
Methodist
Nondenominational
Presbyterian
United Methodist

Newspaper: *Kentucky Standard*, 110 W. Stephen Foster Avenue, Bardstown, KY 40004. 502-348-9003. www.kystandard.com. Published 3 times a week. 3-month subscription by mail, $15.37. Melissa Newman, editor. *Wall Street Journal* also sold in town.

Annual Festivals and Events: Spring, Kentucky Quilt Festival; fall, Bourbon Festival, Regional Arts & Crafts Festival.

Further Information: City of Bardstown, 220 N. 5th Street, Bardstown, KY 40004. emeece@bardstowncable.net

Brewton, AL 36426

Population: 5,498 (–6.6%)
Banks: 5.
Hospital: D.W. McMillan Memorial Hospital, 85 beds.

Location: 60 miles north of Pensacola, Florida; 98 miles southwest of Montgomery, in extreme southern Alabama.

Geography/Climate: Pine forest flatlands. Proximity to the Gulf of Mexico moderates the weather, tempering the cold northern blasts of winter. But summers are long, hot, and humid. Growing season of 220-240 days. Average annual rainfall, 70 inches. Best season is spring, when dogwoods and azaleas are in bloom.

Five Largest Employers: Smurfit-Stone Container Corp., 580 employees; T.R. Miller Mill Co., wood products, 455; Citation Alabama Ductile, iron pipe, 350; NewSouth Apparel, 235; Natural Decorations, Inc., 85. Oil and gas production in Escambia County. Brewton is the county seat.

High School: T.R. Miller High Schools enrolls 395 students in grades 9–12, graduates 96%, sends 87% to college/university. Composite score on ACT for 100% of 11th and 12th graders taking test, 22.1.

Housing: 3BR 2BA house in good condition sells for $75,000 to $85,000, pays $200 in real estate tax with homestead exemption. Most people heat with electricity.

Telecommunications: BellSouth offers DSL at 1 Mbps maximum; Mediacom offers Internet connection via cable.

Sales, Income Taxes: Retail sales tax, 8%. State income tax, scaled 2% to 5%.

Cost of Living: Doctor appointment, routine, $54; plumber per hour, $58; baby-sitting, per hour, $6; dry cleaning, men's suit, $6.50; dinner for 4, local restaurant, $70.

Community Infrastructure & Amenities:
United Way
YMCA/YWCA
4-H
Public library
Public parks: 4, totaling 8 acres
Public swimming pool
Airport
Country club
Golf course, 9 holes

Religious Denominations:
AME
Assemblies of God
Baptist
Catholic
Church of Christ
Church of God
Church of Jesus Christ of Latter-Day Saints
Church of the Nazarene
Episcopal
Interdenominational
Jehovah's Witnesses
Mennonite
Methodist
Nondenominational
Pentecostal
Presbyterian
United Methodist

Newspaper: *Brewton Standard*, P.O. Box 887, Brewton, AL 36427. 251-867-4876. Published twice weekly. 3-month subscription by mail, $18. Bill Crist, editor. *USA Today* also sold in town.

Annual Festivals and Events: 3rd Saturday in June, Alabama Blueberry Festival.

Further Information: Greater Brewton Area Chamber of Commerce, 1010-B Douglas Avenue, Brewton, AL 36426. 251-867-3224. jcrane@cetl.acet.net.

Bryan, OH 43506

Population: 8,333 (–0.01%)

Banks: 4.

Hospital: Community Hospitals of Williams County, 88 beds.

Location: 60 miles southwest of Toledo, 56 miles northeast of Fort Wayne, Indiana, in northwestern Ohio.

Geography/Climate: Flat farmlands. Cold winters, hot and humid summers. Averages: January, high 33 degrees, low 18; July, high 84, low 62. 140 days at freezing or below, 14 at 90 degrees or above. Ground usually snow-covered 30 days through winter. Annual rainfall, 34 inches; snowfall, 34 inches.

Five Largest Employers: Ingersoll-Rand/ARO, 750 employees; Community Hospitals of Williams County, 544; Plastech, plastics, 500; Spangler Candy Co. (Dum-Dums and other popular candies), 450; ITW-Illinois Tool Works (Tomco), 400.

High School: Bryan High School enrolls 760 students in grades 9–12, graduates 94%, sends 77% to college/university. Recent composite ACT for 70% of eligible students taking test, 21.5.

Housing: 3BR 2BA house in good condition, $100,000 to $110,000. Real estate taxes on such a house, $940 to $1,000. Most people heat their homes with natural gas.

Telecommunications: Verizon provides DSL service. Bryan Utilities offer Internet connection via cable on the community-owned fiber optic transmission system

Sales, Income Taxes: Retail sales tax, 6%. State income tax scaled from 0.743% to 7.5%.

Cost of Living: Movie ticket, $5.50; doctor appointment, routine, $42; plumber per hour, $50; baby-sitting, per hour, $2 to $3; dry cleaning, men's suit, $7.95; dinner for 4, local restaurant, $50 to $60.

Community Infrastructure & Amenities:
United Way
Community foundation (assets total $9.2 million)
Community leadership training program
National Historic District
YMCA/YWCA
4-H
Bed-and-breakfast
Community recreational center
Motion picture theater
Public library
Public parks
Public swimming pools: 2
Airport
Country club
Golf courses: (2) 18-hole
Emergency home shelter

Religious Denominations:

Assemblies of God	Methodist
Baptist	Nondenominational
Catholic	Pentecostal
Christian	Presbyterian
Church of Christ	Seventh Day Adventist
Church of God	United Methodist
Church of Jesus Christ of	
Latter-Day Saints	
Church of the Nazarene	
Community	
Episcopal	
Evangelical	
Full Gospel	
Lutheran	

Newspaper: *Bryan Times*, 121-127 S. Walnut, Bryan, OH 43506. 419-636-1111. www.bryantimes.com. Published daily except Sunday. Don Allison, editor. 3-month subscription by mail, $23.25. *New York Times*, *Wall Street Journal*, *USA Today*, and regional city dailies also sold in town.

Annual Festivals and Events: June, Bryan Jubilee, a week-long celebration around the town square; Fountain City Festival, yearly musical production.

Further Information: Bryan Area Chamber of Commerce, 138 S. Lynn Street, Bryan, OH 43506. 419-636-2247. bryancc@locl.net

Clarksdale, MS 38614

Population: 20,645 (–2%)
Banks: 5, including 3 branch banks.
Hospital: Northwest Mississippi Regional Medical Center, 194 beds.

Location: 65 miles southwest of Memphis, 60 miles west of Oxford, in the Delta country of northwestern Mississippi.

Geography/Climate: Flat, fertile Delta land, a dozen or so miles east of the Mississippi River. Short, cold winters, with January lows at about freezing, midday highs around 55. Seasonally, 50 or so days at 32 or below, a few inches of snow. Humid much of the year. July daily highs average 90; lows, 70. Long, hot summers with 86 days at 90 or above. Annual rainfall, 52 inches.

Five Largest Employers: Northwest Mississippi Regional Medical Center, 600 employees; Clarksdale Public Schools, 535; Cooper Tire & Rubber Co., 250; Coahoma Community College, 230; Wal-Mart, 175.

High School: Clarksdale High School enrolls 523 students in grades 10–12, graduates 75%, sends about 85% to college/university. Recent composite ACT score for 80% of eligible students taking test, 18.

Housing: 3BR 2 BA house in good condition sells for $65,000 to $80,000. A house valued at $75,000 pays $1,074 in real estate tax. Most people heat with natural gas.

Telecommunications: South Central Bell offers DSL service. Cable One offers Internet connection.

Sales, Income Taxes: Retail sales tax, 7%. State income tax, scaled from 3% to 5%.

Cost of Living: Movie ticket, $6; doctor appointment, routine, $35; plumber per hour, $50; baby-sitting, per hour, $5; dry cleaning, men's suit, $6; dinner for 4, local restaurant, $45.

Community Infrastructure & Amenities:
Community leadership training program
National Historic District
4-H
Motion picture theater
Public library
Public parks
Public swimming pool
Airport
Country club
Golf course, 18-hole private, 9-hole public
Emergency home shelter

Religious Denominations

AME	Mennonite
Apostolic	Methodist
Assemblies of God	Nondenominational
Baptist	Pentecostal
Catholic	Presbyterian
Christian	Seventh Day Adventist
Church of Christ	United Methodist
Church of God	
Church of the Nazarene	
Episcopal	
Jehovah's Witnesses	
Jewish Congregation	

Newspaper: *Clarksdale Press Register*, P.O. Box 1119, Clarksdale, MS 38614. 662-627-2201. www.pressregister.com. Published daily except Sunday. 3-month subscription by mail, $30. Steve Stewart, editor. *Memphis Commercial Appeal, New York Times, Wall Street Journal* also sold in town.

Annual Festivals and Events: Clarksdale is a mecca for blues enthusiasts from throughout the world. Home to many blues greats including Muddy Waters, John Lee Hooker, Ike Turner. First weekend June: Delta Jubilee, a 2-day event with live music, BBQ cooking contest, hot air balloons, fishing rodeo for children. August: Sunflower River Blues and Gospel Festival, 2-day event. October: Tennessee Williams Festival, 2-day event including plays, student drama competition, ethnic dinner.

Further Information: Clarksdale-Coahoma County Chamber of Commerce, P.O. Box 160, Clarksdale, MS 38614. 662-627-7337. ccoc@clarksdale.com

Columbus, IN 47201

Population: 38,059 (+19%)

Banks: 6, including 2 branch banks.

Hospital: Columbus Regional Hospital, 225 beds.

Location: 45 miles south of Indianapolis, 67 miles north of Louisville, in south central Indiana.

Geography/Climate: Mostly level or slightly rolling terrain. Continental climate with warm, often humid summers influenced by air masses from the Gulf of Mexico but relieved by cooler air from the northern Plains and Great Lakes. Average humidity, 73%. Moderately cold winters. Annual snowfall average, 20 inches; rainfall 40 inches. January average temperatures ranging from low-20s to low-30s; July, mid-60s to upper-80s. 115 days at 32 degrees or lower; 22 days at 90 or above.

Five Largest Employers: Cummins, diesel engines, 5,048 employees; ArvinMeritor, automobile exhaust systems, 2,715; Dorel Juvenile Group, 1,064; NTN Driveshaft, 725; Enkei America, 627.

High School: Columbus East High School enrolls 1,329 students in grades 9–12, graduates 93.3%, sends 70% of graduates to college. Composite SAT for 61% of eligible students taking test: math, 517; verbal, 509. Columbus North High School enrolls 1,698 students in grades 9–12, graduates 94%, sends 81% of graduates to college. Composite SAT for 81% of eligible students taking test: math, 539; verbal, 527.

Housing: 3BR 2BA house in good condition sells for $125,000 to $132,000, pays about $1,300 a year in real estate tax. Most households heat with natural gas or electricity.

Telecommunications: Ameritech provides DSL service. Insight Communications offers Internet connection via cable.

Sales, Income Taxes: Retail sales tax, 5%. State income tax, 3.4%.

Cost of Living: Movie ticket, $6.50; doctor appointment, routine, $45; plumber per hour, $40; baby-sitting per hour, $6; dry cleaning, men's suit, $6; dinner for 4, local restaurant, $35–$40.

Community Infrastructure & Amenities:

United Way	Boys Club/Girls	Public library
Community	Club	Public parks: 18
foundation	4-H	parks, totaling
(Assets $2.12	Bed-and-break-	537 acres
million)	fast	Public swim-
Community	Community	ming pool
leadership	recreational	Airport
training pro-	center	Country club
gram	Motion picture	Golf courses, 9,
Main Street	theater	18, 27 holes
		Emergency
		home shelter

Religious Denominations:

Apostolic	Episcopal	Missionary
Assemblies of	Evangelical	Alliance
God	Friends	Moravian
Baptist	Full Gospel	Nondenomina-
Catholic	Independent	tional
Christian	Interdenomina-	Pentecostal
Church of Christ	tional	Presbyterian
Church of God	Jehovah's	Presbyterian
Church of Jesus	Witnesses	USA
Christ of Latter-	Jewish	Seventh Day
Day Saints	Congregation	Adventist
Church of the	Lutheran	United Church
Nazarene	Lutheran (ELCA)	of Christ
Community	Lutheran	United
Disciples of	(Missouri)	Methodist
Christ	Methodist	Wesleyan

Newspaper: *The Republic*, 500 Franklin Street, Columbus, IN 47201. 812-372-7811. therepublic.com. Published daily, John Harmon, editor. 2-month subscription by mail, $26. *New York Times, Wall Street Journal, Indianapolis Star, Louisville Courier-Journal* also sold in town.

Annual Festivals and Events: March, Bluegrass Festival; May, Jazz Festival; July, Scottish Festival; August, Gospel Music Festival; September, Chautauqua of the Arts; October, Ethnic Expo, County Music Festival; December, Boar's Head and Yule Log Festival.

Further Information: Columbus Area Visitors Center, P.O. Box 1589, Columbus, IN 47202. 812-378-2622. www.columbus.in.us

Crawfordsville, IN 47933

Population: 15,243 (+11%)
Banks: 8, including 4 branches.
Hospital: St. Clare Medical Center, 120 beds.

Location: 49 miles northwest of Indianapolis, 132 miles south-southeast of Chicago, in west central Indiana.

Geography/Climate: Basically flat, farmland. Continental climate: moderately cold winters; nice spring, warm to hot, often humid summers; pleasant, dry fall. Average temperatures: January, low, 19; high, 36. July, low, 65; high, 86. Average rainfall, 39 inches; snowfall, 17 inches.

Five Largest Employers: R.R. Donnelley & Sons, printers, 1,800 employees; Raybestos, automotive aftermarket products, 750; Lithonia Lighting, 500; Nucor Steel, 480; Alcoa CSI, closures, 426. Crawfordsville is home of Wabash College, ranked in the second tier among national liberal arts colleges by *U.S. News & World Report*.

High School: Crawfordsville High School enrolls 680 students in grades 9–12, graduates 95%, sends 63% to college/university. Composite SAT for 72% of eligible students taking test, 1020.

Housing: 3BR 2BA house in good condition sells for about $95,000. Real estate taxes on such a house, $1,200. Most people heat with natural gas.

Telecommunications: Ameritech provides Internet connection at maximum 56 Kbps.

Sales, Income Taxes: Retail sales tax, 5%, excluding grocery foodstuffs. State income tax, 3.4%.

Cost of Living: Movie ticket, $6.50; doctor appointment, routine, $55; plumber per hour, $40; baby-sitting, per hour, $3; dry cleaning, men's suit, $7; dinner for 4, local restaurant, $30.

Community Infrastructure & Amenities:
United Way
Community Foundation ($22 million in assets)
Community leadership training program
Boys Club/Girls Club
4-H
Bed-and-breakfast
Community recreational center
Motion picture theater
Public library
Public parks: 7, totaling 104 acres
Public swimming pool
Airport
Country club
Golf course, 18 holes
Emergency home shelter

Religious Denominations:

AME	Episcopal
Apostolic	Four Square
Assemblies of God	Full Gospel
Baptist	Lutheran (ELCA)
Catholic	Lutheran (Missouri)
Christian	Methodist
Church of Christ	Nondenominational
Church of Jesus Christ of	Pentecostal
Latter-Day Saints	Presbyterian
Church of the Nazarene	United Methodist
Community	Wesleyan
Eastern Orthodox	

Newspaper: *Crawfordsville Journal Review*, 119 N. Green Street, Crawfordsville, IN 47933. 765-362-1200. www.journalreview.com. Published daily. 3-month subscription by mail, $29. *Wall Street Journal, USA Today*, and state metro dailies also sold in town.

Annual Festivals and Events: Second weekend of June, The Strawberry Festival, featuring strawberries, other foods; arts, crafts, and entertainment. Attracts upward of 100,000 visitors. At a 4th of July celebration in 1836, one of the speakers proposed a toast to Crawfordsville as "The Athens of Indiana," and by the end of the century, the town had become known widely for its authors, including Lew Wallace, author of *Ben Hur*.

Further Information: Crawfordsville/Montgomery County Chamber of Commerce, 200 S. Washington Street, 3rd Floor, Crawfordsville, IN 47933. 765-362-6800.

Danville, KY 40422

Population: 15,477 (+7%)

Banks: 13, including 5 branches.

Hospital: Ephraim McDowell Regional Medical Center, 177 beds.

Location: 35 miles southwest of Lexington, 85 miles southeast of Louisville, in the Bluegrass Region of central Kentucky.

Geography/Climate: Gently rolling hills, elevations varying from 900 to 1,000 feet. Temperate, four-season continental climate. Average snowfall, 16 inches; rainfall, 45 inches. January lows average 25, highs 42, with two winter days below zero and 97 at freezing or below freezing. July average temperatures, 59 low, 81 high, with 16 days reaching into the 90s. 46 thunderstorm days annually. Fall weather typically clear and dry.

Five Largest Employers: Ephraim McDowell Health, medical center, 1,300 employees; R.R. Donnelley & Sons, printer, 1,100; Matsushita, floor sweepers, 967; American Greetings, 800; ATR Wire & Cable, 600. Danville is the home of Centre College, ranked no. 42 on the *U.S. News & World Report* list of best national liberal arts colleges.

High School: Danville High School enrolls 490 students in grades 9–12, graduates 98%, sends 85% to college/university. Recent composite scores: SAT, 1125, for 20% of eligible students taking test; ACT, 20.5, for 83% of eligible students taking test. Kentucky School for the Deaf also located in town, enrolls 151 students.

Housing: 3BR 2BA house in good condition sells in range of $85,000 to $95,000, pays $10 per assessed $1,000 in real estate tax.

Telecommunications: BellSouth provides DSL service.

Sales, Income Taxes: 6% retail sales tax. 6% state income tax.

Cost of Living: Movie ticket, $3; doctor appointment, routine, $45; plumber per hour, $50; baby sitting, per hour, $3; dry cleaning, men's suit, $8.15; dinner for 4, local restaurant, $32.

Community Infrastructure & Amenities:

United Way	Public parks: 3, totaling
Community leadership	179 acres
training program	Public swimming pool
Main Street	Airport
National Historic District	Country club
YMCA/YWCA	Golf course, 18 holes
4-H	
Bed-and-breakfast	
Community recreational	
center	
Motion picture theater	
Public library	

Religious Denominations:

AME	Church of the Nazarene
Assemblies of God	Episcopal
Baptist	Interdenominational
Catholic	Islamic
Christian	Jehovah's Witnesses
Christ the Head	Lutheran
Missionary	Pentecostal
Church of Christ	Presbyterian
Church of God	Presbyterian PCA
Church of Jesus Christ of	Salvation Army
Latter-Day Saints	United Methodist

Newspaper: *Advocate Messenger*, 330 S. 4th Street, Danville, KY 40422. 859-236-2551. www.amnews.com. Published daily. 3-month subscription by mail, $35.25. *New York Times, Wall Street Journal*, Kentucky metro dailies also sold in town.

Annual Festivals and Events: Mid-June, Great American Brass Band Festival; mid-August, participant in 450-mile-long outdoor sale along U.S. Hwy. 127, the "127 Corridor" sale. Danville was site of the vice-presidential debate in October 2000.

Further Information: Danville-Boyle County Chamber of Commerce, 304 S. 4th Street, Danville, KY 40422. 859-236-2361. www.dcc@searnet.com

Easton, MD 21601

Population: 11,708 (+25%)
Banks: 8 banks, including 6 branch banks.
Hospital: The Memorial Hospital at Easton, 159 beds.

Location: 59 miles southeast of Baltimore, 69 miles east of Washington, D.C., 117 miles south of Philadelphia, on the Eastern Shore of Maryland.

Geography/Climate: Flat, tidewater country. Continental climate moderated by Chesapeake Bay, Atlantic Ocean. High humidity. Average 100 winter days at freezing or below, 15 inches of snow. July daily highs average 87; lows, 67. 31 days into the 90s. Annual rainfall 42 inches, concentrated in late summer and early fall.

Largest Employers: Black & Decker, 1,700; Easton Memorial Hospital, 1,000; Cadmus Journal Services, 340; Chesapeake Publishing, 165.

High School: Easton High School enrolls 1,138 students in grades 9–12. Graduation rate, 98%. College entrance rate, 85%. Composite SAT score for 80% of eligible students taking test, 1034.

Housing: 3BR, 2BA house in good condition sells in range of $125,000 to $225,000. Real estate taxes on such a house, $1,600+. Households use natural gas for heat. Deep wells supply town drinking water.

Telecommunications: Easton Utilities offers Internet connection via cable.

Sales, Income Taxes: 5% retail sales tax; does not apply to medicines, professional services. State income tax ranges from 2% to 4.85%.

Cost of living: Movie ticket, $6; doctor appointment, routine, $85; plumber per hour, $48; baby-sitting, per hour, $5; dry cleaning, men's suit, $8.25; dinner for 4, local restaurant, $100.

Community Infrastructure & Amenities:
United Way
Community foundation ($13 million assets)
Main Street member
National Historic District
YMCA/YWCA
4-H
Bed-and-breakfast
Movie theater
Public library
Public parks: 11, totaling 104 acres
Airport
Golf course, 18 holes
Emergency home shelter

Religious Denominations:

AME	Lutheran
Anglican	Lutheran (ELCA)
Apostolic	Lutheran (Missouri)
Baptist	Methodist
Catholic	Nondenominational
Christian Science	Presbyterian
Church of Christ	Unitarian Universalist
Church of God	United Methodist
Church of the Nazarene	Wesleyan
Episcopal	
Friends	
Holiness	
Independent	
Jewish Congregation	

Newspaper: *Star Democrat* & *Sunday Star*, P.O. Box 600, Easton, MD 21601 www.stardem.com (410) 770-4034. Larry Effingham, editor. 3-month subscription by mail, $27.43.

Annual Festivals and Events: May, Memorial Hospital Classic; June, Eastern Shore Chamber Music Festival; July, Old Tyme July 4th Celebration; November, Waterfowl Festival, Festival of Trees; New Year's Eve, First Night Talbot.

Further Information: Talbot County Chamber of Commerce, 101 Marlboro Ave., Suite 53, Easton, MD. 21601-1366. asilver@talbotchamber.org

Elkhorn, WI 53121

Population: 7,305 (+37%)
Banks: 6, including 5 branch banks.
Hospital: Lakeland Medical Center, 99 beds.

Location: 45 miles southwest of Milwaukee, 75 miles northwest of Chicago, in southeastern Wisconsin.

Geography/Climate: Rolling terrain of the southern kettle moraine country. Continental climate, influenced by storms that move in from the west, across upper Ohio Valley and Great Lakes, as well as high pressure systems rolling down from Canada. Winters can be severe and long. January temperature averages: low, 8; high, 24. Twenty days at zero or below, average through winter. Sunny summers. July averages: low, 60..

Five Largest Employers: Mann Brothers, Inc., sand and gravel, 300 employees; Coleman Group, 139; Snap-On Diagnostics, 130; Frank Holton & Co., band instruments, 120; Getzen Co., band instruments, 120; Intertractor America Corp., Grouser shoes, 100.

High School: Elkhorn Area High School enrolls 826 students in grades 9–12, graduates 96%, sends 82% to college/university. Recent composite ACT for 60% of eligible students taking test, 22.2.

Housing: 3BR 2BA house in good condition, $140,000. Annual taxes on that house, $3,000. Most households heat with natural gas.

Telecommunications: DSL service available from telephone company at 768 Kbps. Cable operator also offers Internet connection.

Sales, Income Taxes: 5.5% retail sales tax. State income tax, scaled 4.85% to 6.87%.

Cost of Living: Doctor appointment, routine, $48; plumber per hour, $65; baby-sitting, per hour, $3; dry cleaning, men's suit, $8.65; dinner for 4, local restaurant, $50.

Community Infrastructure & Amenities:
4-H
Public library
Public parks: 7, totaling 97 acres
Public swimming pool
Golf course, 27 holes

Religious Denominations:
Assemblies of God
Baptist
Catholic
Christian
Church of Christ
Church of Jesus Christ of Latter-Day Saints
Community
Episcopal
Evangelical
Jehovah's Witnesses
Lutheran
Lutheran (ELCA)
Nondenominational
United Church of Christ
United Methodist

Newspaper: *Elkhorn Independent*, 11 W. Walworth Street, Elkhorn, WI 53121. 262-723-2250. www.elkhornindependent.com. Published weekly. 6-month subscription by mail, $15. Judy Franklin Knudsen, editor.

Annual Festivals and Events: First weekend of June, Harley Fest; mid-June through July, Holton/Elkhorn Community Band concerts on Friday evenings; Walworth County Fair, the largest in the Midwest, begins 6 days before Labor Day; December, Elkhorn Christmas Parade. Elkhorn is known as "The Christmas Card Town," stemming from a *March of Time* TV show in the 1950s featuring Elkhorn and Elkhorn scenes on Christmas cards for many years thereafter.

Further Information: Elkhorn Chamber of Commerce, 9 S. Broad Street, Elkhorn, WI 53121. 262-723-5788. www.elkchamber@elkhorn-wi.org

Essex, CT 06426

Population: 6,370 (+8%)
Banks: 5, 4 of which are branch banks.
Hospital: Middlesex Hospital and Medical Center in Middletown, 20 miles upriver.

Location: 35 miles east of New Haven, 20 miles west of New London, 5 miles upriver from Long Island Sound, on the west bank of the Connecticut River.

Geography/Climate: Lower river valley approaching the Atlantic Ocean. Old town center is on a narrow peninsula jutting into the Connecticut River. Three villages composing the town—Ivoryton, Centerbrook, and Essex—cover about 10 square miles, with hills in the western section and flat marshlands near the river. Proximity to Long Island Sound brings cooling southerly breezes in summer and moderates the winter lows. Averages: snowfall, 30 inches; rainfall, 44 inches; days below freezing, 80; days above 90, 15. Generally mild summer and fall.

Five Largest Employers: Domcasters; Essex Meadows, nursing home, 167 employees; Incarnation Center; Griswold Inn, 104 employees; Middlesex Medical Center Shoreline.

High School: Valley Regional High School enrolls 199 students in grades 9–12, graduates 98%, sends 93% to college/university. Composite SAT score for 93% of eligible students taking test, 1094.

Housing: 3BR 2BA house sells for $350,000 or more. Most people heat with oil.

Telecommunications: Southern New England Telephone provides DSL service. Comcast Cable provides Internet connection.

Sales, Income Taxes: Retail sales tax, 6%, shoes and clothing exempt up to $75 per item. State income tax, scaled 3% to 4.5%.

Cost of Living: Doctor appointment, routine, $75; plumber per hour, $65; baby-sitting per hour, $5; dry cleaning, men's suit, $10.65; dinner for 4, local restaurant, $80.

Community Infrastructure & Amenities:
Public library
Public parks: 5

Religious Denominations:
Baptist
Catholic
Congregational (3)
Episcopal
Lutheran

Newspaper: *Main Street News*, 242 Essex Plaza, Essex, CT 06426. 860-767-3434. mainstnews.com. Published weekly, Cary Hull, editor. 3-month subscription by mail, $21. *New York Times*, *Wall Street Journal*, numerous other East Coast dailies sold in town.

Annual Festivals and Events: February, Essex Ground Hog Parade, Eagle Festival; June, Shad Bake; August, Lobster Bake; September, Blue Fish Bake, Family Day; October, Pumpkin Festival Parade, Halloween Parade; December, Christmas Tree Lighting.

Further Information: Town of Essex, P.O. Box 98, Essex, CT 06426. selectman@essexct.net

Fredericksburg, TX 78624

Population: 8,911 (+28%)
Banks: 8, including 3 locally owned banks.
Hospital: Hill Country Memorial Hospital, 77 beds.

Location: 70 miles west of Austin, 65 miles northwest of San Antonio, in the Texas Hill Country.

Geography/Climate: Rolling, grassy hill country dotted with mesquite, live oak, and cacti. Humid subtropical climate with two seasons: mild winters and long, hot summers. Average 23 days below 32 degrees, 101 days at 90 or above. Close enough to the Gulf of Mexico to feel the influence of hot, moist air. Thunderstorms can occur any month but are most likely in May–June and September–November. 32 inches of precipitation on average; an inch of snow or less. Best weather for a visit: February–May and October–November.

Five Largest Employers: Hill Country Memorial Hospital System, 475 employees; Fredericksburg Independent School District, 397; Knopp Nursing and Retirement Homes, 230; HEB Food Store, 158; Central Texas Electric Cooperative, 127.

High School: Fredericksburg High School enrolls 987 students in grades 9–12, graduates 99%, and sends 84% to college/university. Recent composite SAT score for 100% of eligible students taking test, 1026.

Housing: 3BR 2BA house in good condition, $140,000. Taxes on such a house, about $3,000. Wells supply the municipal water system. Voluntary conservation during summertime.

Telecommunications: Verizon provides digital connection speeds at up to 5.1 Mbps. Time Warner offers Internet connection through the cable system.

Sales, Income Taxes: Retail sales tax 8.25%, grocery food exempt. No state income tax.

Cost of Living: Doctor appointment, routine, $58; plumber per hour, $35; baby-sitting per hour, $5; dry cleaning, men's suit, $8; dinner for 4, local restaurant, $40–$100.

Community Infrastructure & Amenities:

United Way	Community recreational
Community foundation	center
Community leadership	Public library
training program	Public parks: 6, totaling
Main Street	334 acres
National Historic District	Public swimming pool
YMCA/YWCA	Airport
Boys Club/Girls Club	Country club
4-H	Golf course, 18 holes
Bed-and-breakfast: 328	Emergency home shelter
establishments in county	

Religious Denominations:

Assemblies of God	Disciples of Christ	Methodist
Baptist	Episcopal	Nondenomina-
Bible	Evangelical	tional
Catholic	Independent	Pentecostal
Church of Christ	Jehovah's	Presbyterian
Church of Jesus	Witnesses	Seventh Day
Christ of Latter-	Lutheran	Adventist
Day Saints	Lutheran (ELCA)	Spanish
Community	Lutheran (Missouri)	United Methodist

Newspaper: *Fredericksburg Standard*, 108 E. Main Street, Fredericksburg, TX 78624. 830-997-2155. fredericksburgstandard.com. Published weekly; 3-month subscription, $6. Terry Collier, editor. *New York Times*, *Wall Street Journal*, major Texas dailies also sold in town.

Annual Festivals and Events: February, Wine Lovers Trail; March, Country Peddlers Show; April, Pedernales Valley Wildflower Celebration, Herb Fest, Stonewall Peach JAMboree and Rodeo; August, Gillespie County Fair, the oldest in Texas; September, Texas Renewable Energy Roundup, Texas Woodcarvers' Guild; October, Oktoberfest, Mesquite Art Festival; November, Die Künstler Fine Art Exhibit; December, Weinachten in Fredericksburg, traditional German Christmas market.

Further Information: Fredericksburg Chamber of Commerce/Convention & Visitor Bureau, 106 N. Adams, Fredericksburg, TX 78624. 830-997-6523. visitorinfo@fbg.net

Greencastle, IN 46135

Population: 9,880 (+11%)

Banks: 4, all branches of banks headquartered elsewhere.

Hospital: Putnam County Hospital, 50 beds.

Location: 40 miles southwest of Indianapolis, 160 miles south-southeast of Chicago, in west central Indiana.

Geography/Climate: Rolling terrain in town, quite hilly toward the south and west. Continental climate: moderately cold winters; pleasant spring commencing March; warm to hot, often humid summers; pleasant, dry fall. Average temperatures: January, low 19, high 36. July, low 65, high 86. Average rainfall, 39 inches; snowfall, 17.

Five Largest Employers: Lear Corp., pickup truck interiors, 1,000 employees; Wal-Mart Distribution, 816; DePauw University, 650; HAPPICO, automobile trim, 460; Heartland Automotive, auto industry supplier, 366.

DePaw University enrolls 2,200 students and is ranked number 40 among the top 50 liberal arts colleges serving a national clientele, according to *U.S. News & World Report.*

High School: Greencastle High School enrolls 600 students in grades 9–12, graduates 99%, sends 47% to college/university. Composite SAT score for 62% of students taking test, 1001.

Housing: 3BR 2BA house in good condition sells in the $100,000 to $150,000 range, pays $800 to $1,200 a year in real estate tax. Most people heat with natural gas.

Telecommunications: Verizon provides Internet connection at 56 Kbps.

Sales, Income Taxes: 5% retail sales tax. 3.4% state income tax.

Cost of Living: Movie ticket, $5; doctor appointment, routine, $45; plumber per hour, $65; baby-sitting per hour, $5; dry cleaning, men's suit, $9; dinner for 4, local restaurant, $40.

Community Infrastructure & Amenities

United Way
Community foundation (Assets $10 million. In 2001, the foundation awarded $340,000 in grants to nonprofit organizations in the area.)
Community leadership training program
Main Street
National Historic District
4-H
Bed-and-breakfast
Motion picture theater
Public library
Public parks: 2, totaling 47 acres
Public swimming pool
Airport
Country club
Golf course, 18 holes
Emergency home shelter

Religious Denominations:

Apostolic	Evangelical
Assemblies of God	Four Square
Baptist	Full Gospel
Catholic	Interdenominational
Christian	Jehovah's Witnesses
Church of Christ	Lutheran
Church of God	Methodist
Church of Jesus Christ of	Nondenominational
Latter-Day Saints	Presbyterian
Church of the Nazarene	Seventh Day Adventist
Disciples of Christ	United Methodist
Episcopal	

Newspaper: *Banner-Graphic*, 100 N. Jackson St., Greencastle, IN 46135. 765-653-5151. bannergraphic.com. Published daily, Eric Bernsee, editor. 3-month subscription by mail, $24.75. *New York Times, Wall Street Journal, Indianapolis Star* also sold in town.

Annual Festivals and Events: May, Heritage Fair, a celebration of county history. Late July, Putnam County Fair.

Further Information: Greater Greencastle Chamber of Commerce, 2 S. Jackson St., Greencastle, IN 46135. 765-653-4517. gogreencastle.com

Hastings, MI 49058

Population: 7,095 (+8%)
Banks: 3, including two that are locally owned.
Hospital: Pennock Health Services, 88 beds.

Location: 35 miles southeast of Grand Rapids, 30 miles northeast of Kalamazoo, in southwestern Lower Michigan.

Geography/Climate: Hilly, wooded countryside dotted with spring-fed lakes. Elevation 790 feet. Westerly winds pick up moisture from Lake Michigan, 75 miles west, boosting the number of cloudy, wet days. But the large lake also moderates winter lows and summer highs. Average snowfall, 49 inches. 149 days below freezing, 8 days below zero. January temperature averages, low 16, high 30. Average date of last frost, May 16. July averages, 60 low, 84 high. Moderate humidity. Annual rainfall, 46 inches, heaviest in May.

Five Largest Employers: Flexfab, flexible tubing, 500 employees; Hastings Manufacturing Company, auto filters and piston rings, 465; Viking Corporation/Tyden Seal, railway car seals, sprinkler systems, 400; Hastings Mutual Insurance Company, 350; Hastings Area Schools, 250.

High School: Hastings High School enrolls 999 students in grades 9–12, graduates 96.5%, sends 50% to college/university. Composite ACT for 50% of eligible students taking test, 21.7.

Housing: 3BR 2BA house in good condition sells for $80,000 to $90,000 and pays real estate taxes of about $1,700. Most residents heat with natural gas.

Telecommunications: Ameritech provides DSL service. Millenium, the cable provider, provides Internet connection.

Sales, Income Taxes: Retail sales tax, 6%. State income tax, 4.2%.

Cost of Living: Movie ticket, $6.50; doctor appointment, routine, $50; plumber per hour, $60; baby-sitting, per hour, $2–$4; dry cleaning, men's suit, $10; dinner for 4, local restaurant, $40–$50.

Community Infrastructure & Amenities:
United Way
Community foundation ($4.9 million in assets)
Community leadership training program
Main Street
National Historic District
YMCA/YWCA
4-H
Bed-and-breakfast
Motion picture theater
Public library
Public parks: 5
Airport
Country club
Golf course, 27 holes

Religious Denominations:

Apostolic	Lutheran
Assemblies of God	Methodist
Baptist	Nondenominational
Catholic	Pentecostal
Christian	Presbyterian
Church of Christ	Seventh Day Adventist
Church of God	United Methodist
Church of Jesus Christ of	Wesleyan
Latter-Day Saints	
Church of the Nazarene	
Episcopal	
Jehovah's Witnesses	

Newspaper: *The Reminder*, 1952 N. Broadway, Hastings, MI 49058. 616-945-9554. www.localcounties.com. Published weekly. 3-month subscription by mail, $7.50. David Young, editor. *New York Times*, *Wall Street Journal*, *Detroit Free Press*, and other state dailies also sold in town.

Annual Festivals and Events: Springfest & Chamber Show; Summerfest & Craft Show; Christmas Festival.

Further Information: Barry County Area Chamber of Commerce, 221 W. State Street, Hastings, MI 49058. bcacc@voyager.net

Hermann, MO 65041

Population: 2,674 (–2.9%)
Banks: 3, including 1 branch bank.
Hospital: Hermann Area District Hospital, 44 beds.

Location: 70 miles west of St. Louis, 45 miles northeast of Jefferson City, 55 miles southeast of Columbia, on the banks of the Missouri River, in east central Missouri.

Geography/Climate: Four-season climate but generally avoiding extremes because of mid-continental location. Intersection of warm, moist air from the Gulf of Mexico and cold, dry air from the north produces a variety of weather conditions. Winter months can register 100+ days below freezing and a few below zero; summers average 38 days at 90 degrees or above. 38 inches of rain, 20 inches of snow, on average. Humid: average humidity 71%.

Five Largest Employers: Stone Hill Winery, 150 employees; Pretium Packaging, 134; Hermann Hospital, 120; Lennertson, Inc., 70; Moore Gear, 35.

High School: Hermann High School enrolls 429 students in grades 7–12, graduates 83%, sends 60% to college/university. Composite ACT for 60% of eligible students taking test, 22.7.

Housing: 3BR 2BA house in good condition sells for between $85,000 and $100,000, pays about $750 in real estate tax. Most people heat with natural gas.

Telecommunications: Kingdom Telephone provides digital connection at 56 Kbps.

Sales, Income Taxes: Retail sales tax, 6.7%. State income tax, scaled 1.5% to 6%.

Cost of Living: Doctor appointment, routine, $45; plumber per hour, $35; baby-sitting per hour, $6; dry cleaning, men's suit, $7.50; dinner for 4, local restaurant, $50.

Community Infrastructure & Amenities:
National Historic District
State historic site
4-H
Bed-and-breakfast (about 50 establishments in the area)
Public library
Public parks: 6 parks, totaling 10 acres
Public swimming pool
Airport
Country club
Golf course, 9 holes
Emergency home shelter

Religious Denominations:
Baptist
Catholic
Christian
Independent
Lutheran (Missouri)
Methodist
Pentecostal
United Church of Christ

Newspaper: *Hermann Advertiser-Courier*, 136 E. 4th Street, Hermann, MO 65041. 573-486-5418. Published weekly, Don Kruse, editor. 6-month subscription by mail, $14.

Annual Festivals and Events: Fourth weekend March, Wurstfest, a gathering of sausage makers from around the state; third weekend May, Maifest; Octoberfest, all month; first weekend in December, Kristkindl Markt. Settled in the 1830s by Germans from Philadelphia, Hermann is known as "Missouri's Rhine Village."

Further Information: Hermann Area Chamber of Commerce, 207 Schiller Street, Hermann, MO 65041. 573-486-2313. chamber@ktis.net

Kosciusko, MS 39090

Population: 7,372 (+5%)

Banks: 4, including one locally owned and 3 branch banks.

Hospital: Monfort Jones Hospital, 72 beds.

Location: 71 miles northeast of Jackson, 155 miles south of Memphis, in north central Mississippi.

Geography/Climate: Gently rolling terrain. One short cold season, with 48 days below freezing and sometimes a trace of snow; followed by long and pleasant spring rolling into long warm season. Southerly winds transport Gulf air, producing hot, humid summer days—and often humid summer nights, as well. Average rainfall, 57 inches; 76 days at 90 degrees or above.

Five Largest Employers: M&F Bank, with 450 employees systemwide and 150 locally; LuVel Dairy Products, 300; Kosciusko School District, 265; Attala County School District, 235; Milwaukee Electric Tool Corporation, 230. Also, Interstate Industries of Mississippi, wiring harnesses, 190; MS Sportswear, 155.

High School: Kosciusko High School enrolls 597 students in grades 9–12, graduates 84%, sends 70% to college/university. Composite ACT for 70% of eligible students taking test, 19.4.

Housing: 3BR 2BA house in good condition sells in range of $85,000 to $125,000, pays $400 to $800 in real estate tax. Most people heat with natural gas.

Telecommunications: Bell South provides digital connection at maximum 56 Kbps.

Sales, Income Taxes: 7% retail sales tax. State income tax scaled 3% to 5%.

Cost of Living: Movie ticket, $5; doctor appointment, routine, $38–$52; plumber per hour, $35; baby-sitting, per hour, $4; dry cleaning, men's suit, $6.50; dinner for 4, local restaurant, $40.

Community Infrastructure & Amenities:
Community foundation
Community leadership training program
Main Street
Boys Club/Girls Club
4-H
Bed-and-breakfast
Motion picture theater
Public library
Public parks: 4, totaling 70 acres
Public swimming pool
Airport
Country club
Golf course, 9 holes

Religious Denominations:
AME
Apostolic
Assemblies of God
Baptist
Catholic
Church of Christ
Church of God
Church of Jesus Christ of Latter-Day Saints
Church of the Nazarene
Episcopal
Interdenominational
Jehovah's Witnesses
Methodist
Missionary Baptist
Nondenominational
Pentecostal
Presbyterian
United Methodist

Newspaper: *Star Herald*, 207 N. Madison, Kosciusko, MS 39090. 662-289-2251. thestarherald.net. Published weekly. Layne Bruce, editor. 6-month subscription by mail, $16. *New York Times*, *Wall Street Journal*, Jackson and Memphis dailies also sold in town.

Annual Festivals and Events: Last Saturday in April, Natchez Trace Festival, a 3-day celebration that draws about 12,000 people. Early August, Central Mississippi Fair, a 75-year tradition. Kosciusko is the hometown of Oprah Winfrey.

Further Information: Kosciusko-Attala Chamber of Commerce, 124 N. Jackson Street, Kosciusko, MS 39090. 662-289-2981. chamber@kopower.com

Litchfield, CT 06759

Population: 1,328 (–6%)
Banks: 3 banks, including 1 branch bank.
Hospital: Charlotte Hungerford Hospital in Torrington, 8 miles distant, 109 beds.

Location: 85 miles northeast of New York City, 34 miles west of Hartford, in the foothills of northwestern Connecticut.

Geography/Climate: Westerly winds bring most of the weather systems, but proximity to the Atlantic Ocean, 40 miles southeast, delivers storms moving up the coast. Average January temperature, 25 degrees; July, 78. Annually, average 20 days at 90 degrees or above; 130 days at 32 degrees or below, including 6 days below zero. Annual rainfall and snowfall both measure about 45 inches.

Five Largest Employers: GE Aerospace, Connecticut Power & Light, Bridgeport Hydraulic, Dowling Toyota, Litchfield Ford.

High School: Litchfield High School enrolls 410 students in grades 7–12, graduates 97%, sends 85% to college/university. Composite SAT for 85% of eligible students taking test, 540 math, 530 verbal.

Housing: 3BR 2BA house sells for about $325,000, pays $5,000 a year in real estate tax. Most households heat with oil.

Telecommunications: Southern New England Telephone provides DSL service.

Sales, Income Taxes: Retail sales tax, 6%, food and clothing under $50 exempt. State income tax, 4%.

Cost of Living: Movie ticket, $8; doctor appointment, routine, $75; plumber per hour, $50; baby-sitting per hour, $7; dry cleaning, men's suit, $10.30; dinner for 4, local restaurant, $150.

Community Infrastructure & Amenities:
Community foundation
National Historic District
4-H
Bed-and-breakfast
Community recreational center
Motion picture theater
Public library
Public parks: several very large parks in immediate area
Country club
Golf course, 9 holes

Religious Denominations:
Baptist
Catholic
Congregational
Episcopal
Methodist

Newspaper: *Litchfield Enquirer*, P.O. Box 547, Litchfield, CT 06759. 860-567-8766. Published weekly, Ken Paul, editor. 3-month subscription, $15.

Annual Festivals and Events: Third Sunday in May, Blessing of the Motorcycles, Lourdes Shrine; second Saturday June, Gallery on the Green Craft Show, Litchfield Hills Road Race; fourth Saturday–Sunday June, A Taste of Litchfield; second Saturday July, Litchfield Open House Tour; fourth Saturday September, Nature Day, White Memorial Conservation Center.

Further Information: Litchfield Hills Visitors Bureau, 499 Bantam Road, Litchfield, CT 06759. 860-567-4506. lhcvbnwct@aol.com

Madison, GA 30650

Population: 3,636 (+4%)

Banks: 4, including 2 branch banks.

Hospital: Morgan Memorial Hospital, 41 beds.

Location: 60 miles east of Atlanta, 85 miles west of Augusta, in north central Georgia.

Geography/Climate: Generally flat terrain, with trees a mixture of southern yellow pine, oak, hickory. A warm and mild climate with hot spells. Long growing season—241 days. January temperatures range from 30s to 60s; 55 days at 32 degrees or below during the winter months. Measurable snow is rare. July temperatures range from upper 60s to mid-90s. Through summer months, 76 days at 90 degrees or above. Precipitation, 45 inches. Thunderstorms on 56 days, typically.

Five Largest Employers: Wellington Leisure Products, 450 employees; Georgia Pacific, 415; Denon Digital, 215; Pennington Seed, 200; Bard Manufacturing, 150.

High School: Morgan County High School enrolls 850 students in grades 9–12, graduates 93%, sends 84% to college/university. Composite SAT for 65% of eligible students taking test, 995; ACT for 30% of eligible students, 19.26.

Housing: 3BR 2BA house in good condition, $150,000. Taxes on such a house, about $1,200. Households heat with natural gas and electricity.

Telecommunications: BellSouth provides DSL service. Communicomm provides Internet connection via cable.

Sales, Income Taxes: Retail sales tax, 7%. State income tax, 2%.

Cost of Living: Doctor appointment, routine, $30; plumber per hour, $45; baby-sitting per hour, $5–$6; dry cleaning, men's suit, $7; dinner for 4, local restaurant, $30–$100.

Community Infrastructure & Amenities:

Community leadership training program	Public library
Main Street	Public parks: 6, totaling 30 acres
National Historic District	Public swimming pool
4-H	Airport
Bed-and-breakfast	Golf course
Community recreational center	

Religious Denominations:

AME	Independent
Apostolic	Interdenominational
Assemblies of God	Jehovah's Witnesses
Baptist	Lutheran
Catholic	Methodist
Christian	Nondenominational
Church of Christ	Pentecostal
Church of God	Presbyterian
Community	Presbyterian USA
Episcopal	Seventh Day Adventist
Four Square	United Methodist
Full Gospel	

Newspaper: *Morgan County Citizen*, 235 S. Main Street, Madison, GA 30650. 706-342-7440. www.morgancountycitizen.com. Published weekly. 6-month subscription by mail, $11. Patrick Yost, editor. *New York Times*, *Wall Street Journal*, *Atlanta Journal-Constitution* also sold in town.

Annual Festivals and Events: March, Taste of Madison; May, Spring Tour of Homes; June, Madison Fest; July, Theater Festival. Madison is known as "the town that Sherman refused to burn" in the Civil War, and is described in a state guide from the nineteenth century as "the most cultured and aristocratic town on the stagecoach route from Charleston to New Orleans." Streets lined with enormous live oaks dripping Spanish moss. Plantation-era mansions. Madison was declared "The No. 1 Small Town in America" in 2001 *Travel Holiday* magazine.

Further Information: Madison Welcome Center, P.O. Box 826, Madison, GA 30650. 800-709-7406. marguerite@madisonga.org

Madison, IN 47250

Population: 12,004 (–3%)
Banks: 6, including 2 branch banks.
Hospital: King's Daughters Hospital, 142 beds.

Location: 55 miles northeast of Louisville, 65 miles southwest of Cincinnati, on the banks of the Ohio River in southeastern Indiana.

Geography/Climate: Continental, four-season climate, but variable because of the influence of westerly winds at mid-latitudes and the upper reach of Gulf weather. Moderately cold winters, with 16 inches of snow; 90 days at 32 degrees or below, 2 days below zero. Spring arrives in early April. Warm, humid summers with rainstorms common. 44 inches of precipitation on average; 35 days at 90 degrees or above.

Five Largest Employers: King's Daughters Hospital, 952 employees; Grote Manufacturing Co., automobile parts, 840; Madison Consolidated Schools, 611; Arvin Sango, automotive supplier, 581; Madison State Hospital, 515.

High School: Madison Consolidated High School enrolls 1,000 students in grades 9–12, graduates 97%, sends 85% to college/university. Composite SAT score for 60% of eligible students taking test, 1013.

Housing: 3BR 2BA house in good condition sells for $115,000 to $140,000, pays real estate taxes of $1,500 to $2,000. Most people heat with electricity.

Telecommunications: Verizon provides DSL service at 768 Kbps.

Sales, Income Taxes: Retail sales tax, 5%, grocery food exempt. State income tax, 3.4%.

Cost of Living: Movie ticket, $5.50; doctor appointment, routine, $40; plumber per hour, $50; baby-sitting per hour, $6; dry cleaning, men's suit, $7.45; dinner for 4, local restaurant, $60.

Community Infrastructure & Amenities:

United Way	Motion picture theater
Community foundation	Public library
(Assets $8 million)	Public parks
Main Street	Public swimming pool
National Historic District	Airport
Boys Club/Girls Club	Country club
4-H	Golf courses (4) 18-hole
Bed-and-breakfasts (10)	Emergency home shelter

Religious Denominations:

AME	Lutheran
Apostolic	Mennonite
Assemblies of God	Methodist
Baptist	Nondenominational
Catholic	Pentecostal
Christian	Presbyterian
Church of Christ	Seventh Day Adventist
Church of God	United Church of Christ
Church of Jesus Christ of	United Methodist
Latter-Day Saints	Wesleyan
Church of the Nazarene	
Community	
Episcopal	
Evangelical	
Jehovah's Witnesses	

Newspaper: *Madison Courier*, One Courier Drive, Madison, IN 47250. 812-265-3641. www.madison-courier.com. Published daily. 3-month subscription by mail, $26. Elliott Tompkin, editor.

Annual Festivals and Events: Last weekend April, first weekend May; Madison InBloom garden tour; 4th of July, Madison Regatta, hydroplane races, attracts 60,000; third weekend August; Madison Ribberfest, barbeque, blues, balloons; last weekend September, Madison Chatauqua, juried fine arts and crafts show, attracts 80,000 people.

Further Information: Madison Area Convention & Visitors Bureau, 301 E. Main, Madison, IN 47250. 812-265-2956. info@visitmadison,org

McPherson, KS 67460

Population: 13,770 (+10.85%)
Banks: 6 banks, including 4 branch banks.
Hospital: Memorial Hospital, 70 beds.

Location: 55 miles northwest of Wichita at inter-section of I-135 and U.S. 56. 230 miles southwest of Kansas City; 450 miles east of Denver.

Geography/Climate: Flatlands of the Great Plains, relieved by a few gentle slopes. Four seasons, with summer the most intense. Typically more than 60 days over 90 degrees. Annual rainfall, 31 inches. Annual snowfall, 16 inches. Temperatures will dip below freezing 114 days, below zero 2 days, on average.

Five Largest Employers: Abbott Laboratories, 700 employees; National Cooperative Refinery Association (oil and gas), 525; CertainTeed Corp., plastic pipe, windows, siding, 457; Farmers Alliance Mutual Insurance, 375; JohnsManville, 349. McPherson is the county seat.

High School: McPherson High School enrolls 951 students in grades 9–12, graduates 92%, sends 85% to college/university. Composite score on recent ACT exam for 68% of eligible students taking test, 22.2.

Housing: 3BR 2BA in good condition sells for $120,000–$150,000. Taxes on such a house, $2,100. Natural gas and electricity used for heating. (Electricity rates are the lowest in Kansas and among lowest in nation: 4.4 cents per kWh for resi-dential, 3.1 cents for industrial.)

Telecommunications: Southwestern Bell (SBC) provides DSL service at 380 Kbps to 1.5 megabits. Cox Communications provides Internet connection via cable.

Sales, Income Taxes: Retail sales tax, 5.9%. State income tax, 3.5%–6.45%.

Community Infrastructure & Amenities:

United Way	Motion picture theater
Community foundation	Public library
Community leadership training program	Public parks: 13, totaling about 300 acres
Main Street	Public swimming pool
National Historic District	Airport
YMCA/YWCA	Country club
4-H	Golf course, 18 holes
Community recreational center	Emergency home shelter

Religious Denominations:

Assemblies of God	Evangelical
Baptist	Four Square
Bible	Free Methodist
Calvary Baptist	Friends
Catholic	Jehovah's Witnesses
Christian	Lutheran
Christian Science	Mennonite
Church of Christ	Methodist
Church of God	Pentecostal
Church of the Brethren	Presbyterian
Church of the Nazarene	Seventh Day Adventist
Congregational	United Methodist
Covenant	Word of Faith
Episcopal	

Newspaper: *The McPherson Sentinel*, P.O. Box 926 (301 S. Main Street), McPherson, KS 67460. 620-241-2422. mcphersonsentinel.com. Published daily. Kathy Hackleman, editor. 3-month subscription by mail, $29. Other state dailies and *Wall Street Journal* also sold in town.

Cost of Living: Movie ticket, $6.25; doctor appointment, routine, $62; plumber per hour, $45; baby-sitting, per hour, $2.50; dry cleaning, men's suit, $8.90; dinner for 4, local restaurant, $40.

Annual Festivals and Events: All Schools Day, a countywide celebration held each May since 1914 honoring students; September, Scottish Festival, annual salute to McPherson, the Scot for whom the town is named.

Further Information: McPherson Chamber of Commerce, P.O. Box 616 (306 N. Main St.), McPherson, KS 67460. chamber@mcphersonks.org

Monroe, WI 53566

Population: 14,420 (+5%)
Banks: 7, including 3 locally owned.
Hospital: Monroe Clinic-Hospital, 100 beds.

Location: 35 miles south of Madison, 108 miles southwest of Milwaukee, 139 miles northwest of Chicago, in south central Wisconsin.

Geography/Climate: Dairy-farm country with a gentle contour, punctuated by some hilly, rugged landscape. Continental climate, four distinct seasons. Typically long, hard winters with January average lows of 8 degrees. Annual snowfall, 39 inches; rainfall, 34 inches, mostly between May and September. Thunderstorms on 45 days average. Pleasant spring and summer leading to a colorful fall. Average 12 days at 90-plus.

Five Largest Employers: Swiss Colony, mail order foods, 990 employees full-time, 2,285 during the busy season; Monroe Clinic, 1,024; Monroe Truck Equipment, 650; Philips Advance Transformer, 415; Charlton Group, 250.

High School: Monroe High School enrolls 865 students in grades 9–12, graduates 97%, sends 77% to college/university. Composite ACT for 50% of eligible students taking test, 21.6.

Housing: 3BR 2BA house, about $125,000. Real estate tax on such a house, about $3,300. Most people heat with natural gas and LP gas.

Telecommunications: TDS Telecom provides DSL service. Charter Communications provides broadband Internet connection via cable.

Sales, Income Taxes: Retail sales tax, 5%, grocery food exempt. State income tax, scaled 4.6% to 6.75%.

Cost of Living: Movie ticket, $6.50; doctor appointment, routine, $55-$80; plumber per hour, $45; baby sitting per hour, $3; dry cleaning, men's suit, $8.45; dinner for 4, local restaurant, $28.

Community Infrastructure & Amenities:
United Way
Community foundation (Assets $3 million+)
Community leadership training program
National Historic District
YMCA/YWCA
4-H
Bed-and-breakfast
Community recreational center
Motion picture theater
Public library
Public parks: 6 parks, totaling 173 acres
Public swimming pool
Airport
Country club
Golf course, 18 holes
Emergency home shelter

Religious Denominations:

Apostolic	Episcopal
Assemblies of God	Evangelical Free
Baptist	Jehovah's Witnesses
Bible	Lutheran
Catholic	Lutheran (ELCA)
Christian Science	Lutheran (Missouri)
Church of Christ	Pentecostal
Church of Jesus Christ of	Presbyterian USA
Latter-Day Saints	United Church of Christ
Church of the Nazarene	United Methodist
Community	

Newspaper: *The Monroe Times*, 1065 4th Avenue West, Monroe, WI 53566. 608-328-4202. themonroetimes.com. Published daily. Judie Heintzman, editor. 3-month subscription by mail, $39. *Wall Street Journal*, *Wisconsin State Journal* also sold in town.

Annual Festivals and Events: June, World Honda Grand Prix Balloon Competition, Monroe Balloon Rally; September, Cheese Days, Berghoff & Blues Jazz Festival.

Further Information: Monroe Chamber of Commerce & Industry, 1505 9th Street, Monroe, WI 53566. 608-325-7648. monroechamber.org

Mount Airy, NC 27030

Population: 8,484 (+18.6%)
Banks: 11, including 2 locally owned.
Hospital: Northern Surry Hospital, 137 beds.

Location: 35 miles northwest of Winston-Salem, 10 miles south of the Virginia state line, in northwestern North Carolina.

Geography/Climate: Elevation 1,100 feet in the foothills of the Blue Ridge Mountains, with 2,400-foot Pilot Mountain to the southeast. Appalachian Mountains offer a bit of a barrier to cold wintry blasts from the north. January average temperature, 40. Up to 90 days at freezing or below. None below zero. July daily highs average 87; lows, 65. 25 days into the 90s. Annual snowfall, 11 inches; rainfall, 41 inches.

Five Largest Employers: Renfro Hosiery, 1,500 employees; Kentucky Derby Hosiery, 1,500; Cross Creek Apparel, 1,000; Sara Lee Socks, 900; Northern Hospital of Surry County, 600.

High School: Mount Airy High School enrolls 535 students in grades 9–12, graduates 99%, sends 80% to college/university. Composite SAT for 50% of eligible students taking test, 970.

Housing: 3BR 2BA house in good condition sells in the range of $100,000 to $200,000. Real estate taxes for property in that price range, $1,170 to $2,340. Most people heat with oil and electricity.

Telecommunications: Sprint provides digital connection at 56 Kbps.

Sales, Income Taxes: Retail sales tax, 6.5%. State income tax, 6% to 7.75%.

Cost of Living: Movie ticket, $6.50; doctor appointment, routine, $60; plumber per hour, $40; baby sitting per hour, $4; dry cleaning, men's suit, $8.90; dinner for 4, local restaurant, $50.

Community Infrastructure & Amenities:
United Way
Community foundation
Community leadership training program
Main Street
National Historic District
Community recreational center
Motion picture theater
Public library
Airport
Country club
Golf course

Religious Denominations:
Baptist
Catholic
Christian
Church of God
Church of Jesus Christ of Latter-Day Saints
Evangelical
Friends
Jehovah's Witnesses
Jewish Congregation
Lutheran
Methodist
Presbyterian USA
Seventh Day Adventist
United Methodist

Newspaper: *Mount Airy News*, P.O. Box 808, Mount Airy, NC 27030. 336-786-4141. mtairynews.com. Published daily. Angela Leonard, editor. 3-month subscription, $27. *New York Times*, *Wall Street Journal*, other state dailies also sold in town.

Annual Festivals and Events: Last weekend September, Mayberry Days, celebration of Andy Griffith's hit TV series modeled on life in Mount Airy. Autumn Leaves Festival, crafts, foods, music. Call for dates.

Further Information: Greater Mount Airy Chamber of Commerce, P.O. Box 913, Mount Airy, NC 27030. 336-786-6116. visitmayberry.com

Nevada, IA 50201

Population: 6,758 (+12.2%)
Banks: 4, including 2 locally owned.
Hospital: Story County Medical Center, 122 beds.

Location: 40 miles north of Des Moines, 9 miles east of Ames, in central Iowa.

Geography/Climate: Flat to gently rolling prairie. Continental climate. Long, cold winters averaging 23 degrees but with 16 days at zero or below, 31 inches of snow. Hot, frequently humid summers with average 20 days into the 90s, 32 inches of rain.

Five Largest Employers: Story County Courthouse, 325 employees; Burke Corporation, pizza toppings, 275; Nevada Community Schools, 230; Story County Medical Center, 200; General Financial Supply, 125.

High School: Nevada Senior High School enrolls about 550 students in grades 9–12, graduates 89%, sends 81% of graduates to college/university. Composite ACT for 63% of eligible students taking test, 22.3.

Housing: 3BR 2BA house priced at a mid-range of $95,000 to $105,000, pays about $1,750 in real estate tax.

Telecommunications: Iowa Telecom offers DSL service. Mediacom offers Internet connection via the cable system.

Sales, Income Taxes: Retail sales tax, 6%. State income tax scaled 5% to 9%.

Cost of Living: Doctor appointment, routine, $57; plumber per hour, $45; baby-sitting per hour, $2–$3; dry cleaning, men's suit, $8.20; dinner for 4, local restaurant, $32.

Community Infrastructure & Amenities:
United Way
Community foundation
Community leadership training program
National Historic District
Boys Club/Girls Club
4-H
Community recreational center (The foundation for a community sports complex has received 58 acres of donated land and raised more than $6 million.)
Public library
Public parks: 9 parks, totaling 193 acres
Public swimming pool
Country club
Golf course, 9 holes

Religious Denominations:
Assemblies of God
Baptist
Catholic
Christian
Disciples of Christ
Evangelical
Lutheran (ELCA)
Lutheran (Missouri)
Methodist
Presbyterian
Seventh Day Adventist
United Methodist

Newspaper: *Nevada Journal*, 1210 6th Street, Nevada, IA 50201. 515-382-2161. nevadaiowajournal.com. Published weekly. Marlys Barker, editor. 3-month subscription by mail, $12.75.

Annual Festivals and Events: Annual craft fair in the fall attracts visitors from throughout the state. Lincoln Highway Days commemorates the original Lincoln Highway, the first transcontinental highway. Call for dates.

Further Information: Nevada Chamber of Commerce and Economic Development Council, 1015 6th Street, Nevada, IA 50201. 515-382-6538. nevadaiowa.org

Northfield, MN 55057

Population: 17,147 (+14%)

Banks: 4, including 2 branches of banks headquartered elsewhere.

Hospital: Northfield Hospital, 39 beds.

Location: 37 miles south of Minneapolis/St. Paul.

Geography/Climate: Rolling farmland, continental climate, with a long winter season. January average temperatures range from single digits to upper 20s; July averages range from lower 60s to middle 80s. Year-round, average 150 or so days below freezing, 15 days above 90, 28 inches of rain, 48 inches of snow. Minnesota gets all kinds of weather, from blizzards to tornadoes, with hail and fog for variety. This part of the state also experiences about 100 sunny days a year.

Five Largest Employers: St. Olaf College, 825 employees; Malt-O-Meal, cereal manufacturer, 740; Sheldahl, flexible circuits, 700; Carleton College, 640; Northfield Public Schools, 500.

Carleton College ranks sixth on the 2001 list of "Best National Liberal Arts Colleges," and **St. Olaf College** ranks on the "Second Tier," according to *U.S. News & World Report*.

High School: Northfield High School enrolls 1,200 students in grades 9–12, sends 73% to college/university. Composite ACT, 22.7. Composite SAT, 625 verbal, 612 math.

Housing: 3BR 2BA house in good condition, $179,000. Real estate taxes on such a house, $2,100.

Telecommunications: Qwest provides DSL service. Charter Communications provides Internet connection via cable.

Sales, Income Taxes: Retail sales tax, 6.5%; food, prescription drugs, clothing exempt. State income tax, scaled 5.35% to 7.85%.

Cost of Living: Movie ticket, $5; doctor appointment, routine, $35; plumber per hour, $60; baby-sitting per hour, $1.50; dry cleaning, men's suit, $4; dinner for 4, local restaurant, $44.

Community Infrastructure & Amenities

United Way
Community foundation
National Historic District
4-H
Bed-and-breakfast
Motion picture theater
Public library
Public parks: 25 parks, totaling 425 acres
Public swimming pool
Country club
Golf course, 18 holes
Emergency home shelter

Religious Denominations:

Assemblies of God	Lutheran (Missouri)
Baptist	Methodist
Catholic	Presbyterian
Episcopal	Presbyterian USA
Friends	Unitarian-Universalist
Jehovah's Witnesses	United Church of Christ
Lutheran	United Methodist
Lutheran (ELCA)	

Newspaper: *Northfield News*, 115 5th Street West, Northfield, MN 55057. 507-645-5615. Published twice weekly. Renee Pranger, editor. 6-month subscription, $30. *New York Times, Wall Street Journal, Minneapolis Star-Tribune, St. Paul Pioneer-Press* also sold in town.

Annual Festivals and Events: "Defeat of Jesse James Days," held each year the week after Labor Day to celebrate Northfield citizens' victory over Jesse James and his gang during an attempted bank robbery on September 7, 1876.

Further Information: Economic Development Manager, 801 Washington Street, Northfield, MN 55057.

Penn Yan, NY 14527

Population: 5,219 (−0.5%)
Banks: 3, all branches of out-of-town banks.
Hospital: Soldiers & Sailors Memorial Hospital has 54 acute beds, 5 ICU, 152 long-term, 12 psychiatric.

Location: 56 miles southeast of Rochester, at the top of Keuka Lake, in the Finger Lakes region of western New York.

Geography/Climate: Located on the shores of Keuka Lake, surrounded by rolling hills dotted with farms and vineyards. Rigorous continental climate. Cloudy, cold winters with 135 freezing days, 10 below-zero days. January daily high averages 31; low, 16. Typical July range of 61 to 82, with six days at 90 or above. Annual rainfall, 36 inches; snowfall can total into the 90-inch range.

Five Largest Employers: Soldiers & Sailors Memorial Hospital, 500 employees; Keuka College, 300; Penn Yan Central Schools, 300; Yates County Government, 275; Yates County ARC, 175.

High School: Penn Yan Academy enrolls about 800 students in grades 9–12, graduates 98%, sends 80% to college/university. Composite SAT for 70% of eligible students taking test, 1076.

Housing: 3BR 2BA house sells between $60,000 and $85,000, pays real estate tax of $1,900 to $3,000. Most households heat with natural gas.

Telecommunications: Adelphia provides broadband connection via the cable system.

Sales, Income Taxes: Retail sales tax, 7%. State income tax, 4% to 6.85%.

Cost of Living: Movie ticket, $5.50; doctor appointment, routine, $35; plumber per hour, $40; baby-sitting per hour, $3; dry cleaning, men's suit, $8.70; dinner for 4, local restaurant, $40–$50.

Community Infrastructure & Amenities:
United Way
Main Street
National Historic District
4-H
Bed-and-breakfast
Motion picture theater
Public library
Airport
Country club
Golf course
Emergency home shelter

Religious Denominations:
Assemblies of God
Baptist
Catholic
Christian
Church of Jesus Christ of Latter-Day Saints
Church of the Nazarene
Episcopal
Evangelical
Jehovah's Witnesses
Lutheran
Mennonite
Methodist
Presbyterian
United Methodist

Newspaper: *Chronicle Express*, 138 Main Street, Penn Yan, NY 14527. 315-536-4422. Published weekly, Eric Reuscher, editor. 6-month subscription by mail, $26. *New York Times*, *Wall Street Journal*, *Finger Lakes Times* also sold locally.

Annual Festivals and Events: June, Cruisin' Night, Classic Car Show; July, Yates County Fair; December, StarShine, Christmas Celebration.

Further Information: Yates County Chamber of Commerce, 2375 Route 14A, Penn Yan, NY 14527. 315-536-3111. yatesny.com

Red Wing, MN 55066

Population: 15,792 (+4%)
Banks: 5, including 2 branch banks.
Hospital: Fairview Red Wing Medical Center, 50 beds.

Location: On the Mississippi River, 50 miles southeast of Minneapolis-St. Paul.

Geography/Climate: Bluffy contour along the Mississippi River gives way to bottomlands and prairie. Rigorous climate—long and often severely cold winters with average 16 days below zero and 39 inches of snow; short spring and fall; warm summers with average 14 days into the 90s. Average annual precipitation, 27 inches.

Five Largest Employers: Treasure Island Resort & Casino, 1,355 employees; Red Wing Shoe Company, 1,100; Northern States Power, 435; Fairview Red Wing Hospital, 373; Jostens, Diploma Division, 300.

High School: Red Wing High School enrolls 1,105 students in grades 9–12, graduates 95%, sends 70% to college/university. Composite ACT for 95% of eligible students taking test, 23.

Housing: 3BR 2BA house in good condition sells in the range of $130,000 to $140,000. Most households heat with natural gas.

Telecommunications: Qwest Communication provides DSL service. Charter Communications provides Internet connection via cable.

Sales, Income Taxes: 6.5% retail sales tax, clothing and grocery food exempt. State income tax, scaled 5.35% to 7.85%.

Cost of Living: Movie ticket, $7; doctor appointment, routine, $65; plumber per hour, $40; baby-sitting per hour, $4; dry cleaning, men's suit, $9; dinner for 4, local restaurant, $40.

Community Infrastructure & Amenities:
United Way
Community foundation
Community leadership training program
Main Street
National Historic District
YMCA/YWCA
4-H
Bed-and-breakfast
Motion picture theater
Public library
Public parks
Public swimming pool
Airport
Country club
Golf course, 36 holes

Religious Denominations

Assemblies of God	Lutheran
Baptist	Lutheran (ELCA)
Catholic	Lutheran (Missouri)
Christian	Lutheran (Wisconsin
Church of Christ	Synod)
Church of Jesus Christ of	Methodist
Latter-Day Saints	Nondenominational
Covenant	Pentecostal
Episcopal	Presbyterian
Evangelical	Seventh Day Adventist
Four Square	United Methodist
Jehovah's Witnesses	

Newspaper: *Red Wing Republican Eagle*, 2760 N. Service Drive, Red Wing, MN 55066. 651-388-8235. www.republican-eagle.com. Published daily except Sunday. Jim Pumarlo, editor. 3-month subscription by mail, $30.50. *New York Times*, *Wall Street Journal*, Twin Cities dailies, *USA Today* also sold in town.

Annual Festivals and Events: For a detailed monthly calendar, go to www.redwing.org.

Further Information: Red Wing Area Chamber of Commerce, 420 Levee Street, Red Wing, MN 55066. 651-388-4719. chamber@redwingchamber.com

Ste. Genevieve, MO 63670

Population: 4,478 (+1%)
Banks: 4, including 1 branch bank.
Hospital: Ste. Genevieve County Memorial Hospital, 53 beds.

Location: 50 miles southeast of St. Louis, 70 miles northwest of Cape Girardeau, by the Mississippi River.

Geography/Climate: Location at mid-continent gives Ste. Genevieve (Missouri's oldest community, founded in about 1750) four seasons but none severe, without prolonged periods of heat or cold. Warm, moist air from the Gulf of Mexico competes for attention with cold polar air masses and produces a variety of weather conditions. Snowfall averages less than 20 inches per season. Summers can be very warm and humid—average humidity, 71%. Seasonally, 105 days at 32 degrees or below; 39 days at 90 degrees or above. Annual rainfall, 36 inches.

Five Largest Employers: Mississippi Lime, 800+ employees; Ste. Genevieve County Memorial Hospital, 320; Ste. Genevieve School District, 312; Silvanus, 183; BiltBest Windows, 220.

High School: Ste. Genevieve High School enrolls 728 students in grades 9–12, graduates 97%, sends 40% of graduates to college. Composite ACT score for 70% of eligible students taking test, 21.

Housing: 3BR 2BA house in good condition sells in range of $90,000 to $150,000, pays $5.78 per $1,000 of assessed valuation. Most people heat with natural gas.

Telecommunications: Southwestern Bell provides digital connections at 28 Kbps.

Sales, Income Taxes: Retail sales tax, 7.25%; food taxed at 4.22%. State income tax, 6%.

Cost of Living: Doctor appointment, routine, $54; plumber per hour, $35; baby-sitting per hour, $2.50; dry cleaning, men's suit, $8.50; dinner for 4, local restaurant, $50.

Community Infrastructure & Amenities:
Community leadership training program
Main Street
National Historic District
4-H
Bed-and-breakfast
Community recreational center
Public library
Public parks: 2
Public swimming pool
Golf course, 18 holes

Religious Denominations:
Assemblies of God
Baptist
Catholic
Church of God
Jehovah's Witnesses
Lutheran (Missouri)
Presbyterian USA

Newspaper: *Ste. Genevieve Herald*, Ste. Genevieve, MO 63670. 573-883-2222. stegenevieveherald.com. Published weekly, Jean Feld Rissover, editor. 6-month subscription by mail, $11.

Annual Festivals and Events: Memorial Day Weekend, French Festival; second Weekend August, Jour de Fete; September, Promenade des Arts; first Weekend December, Christmas Walk.

Further Information: Great River Road Interpretive Center, 66 S. Main, Ste. Genevieve, MO 63670. 573-373-7097.

Thomaston, GA 30286

Population: 9,411 (+3%)
Banks: 4, including 3 that are locally owned.
Hospital: Upson Regional Medical Center, 119 beds.

Location: 61 miles south of Atlanta, 39 miles west of Macon, in west central Georgia.

Geography/Climate: Rolling terrain at about 900 feet elevation in the southern reaches of the Piedmont Plateau, forested in white oak and southern pine. Mild winters; hot, humid summers. Average 50 inches of rain, rare snowfall. Winter temperatures seldom drop below 20. January averages: low, 35; high, 57. Relative humidity, 72%. July averages: low, 71; high, 91. Relative humidity, 74%. Average number of 90+ degree days, 74.

Five Largest Employers: Quad Graphics, printers, 700 employees; Thomaston-Upson County Schools, 687; Upson Regional Medical Center, 464; Yamaha Music Manufacturing, 300; Westek, tire cord, industrial fabric, 277.

High School: Upson-Lee High School enrolls 1,356 students in grades 9–12, graduates about 60%, sends about 46% of graduates to college/university. Composite SAT for 100% of eligible students taking test, 970.

Housing: 3BR 2BA house costs about $125,000 and pays about $1,445 a year in real estate tax. People heat their dwellings with natural gas and electricity.

Telecommunications: Alltel offers DSL service. Charter Communications offers broadband connection via cable.

Sales, Income Taxes: Retail sales tax, 6%; some food items exempt. State income tax, scaled 1% to 6%.

Cost of Living: Movie ticket, $5; doctor appointment, routine, $40; baby-sitting per hour, $4; dry cleaning, men's suit, $5.25; dinner for 4, local restaurant, $32.

Community Infrastructure & Amenities:
United Way
Community leadership training program
Main Street
National Historic District
4-H
Bed-and-breakfast
Community recreational center
Motion picture theater
Public library
Public park: 1,372 acres
Public swimming pool
Airport
Country club
Golf course, 36 holes

Religious Denominations:
AME
Assemblies of God
Baptist
Catholic
Church of Christ
Church of God
Church of Jesus Christ of Latter-Day Saints
Episcopal
Full Gospel
Independent
Jehovah's Witnesses
Methodist
Pentecostal
Presbyterian USA
Seventh Day Adventist
United Methodist

Newspaper: *Thomaston Times*, 621 E. Main Street, Thomaston, GA 30286. 706-647-5414. Published Monday, Wednesday, Friday. Ruth Bryant, editor. 3-month subscription, $24. *Upson Citizen*, Thomaston, GA 30286. 706-647-4444. Published weekly. Cindy Anderson, editor.

Annual Festivals and Events: Fourth Saturday in May, Emancipation Proclamation Celebration; first Saturday in June, Summer Solstice Auction; Saturday before July 4, Star Spangled Celebration at The Rock Ranch; first Saturday in December, Red Cross Christmas Tour of Homes.

Further Information: Thomaston-Upson Chamber of Commerce, 213 E. Gordon Street, Thomaston, GA 30286. 706-647-9686. thomaston@alltel.net

Warsaw, IN 46580

Population: 12,415 (+13%)
Banks: 14, of which 6 are branches of banks headquartered elsewhere.
Hospital: Kosciusko Community Hospital, 72 beds.

Location: 40 miles northwest of Fort Wayne, 47 miles southeast of South Bend, in north central Indiana.

Geography/Climate: Generally flat terrain, 825 feet elevation. Continental climate—cold winters, hot, often humid summers. January average low temperature, 18; high, 33. 140 days at or below freezing. July average low, 62; high, 84. 14 days into the 90s across summer. Annual rainfall, 36 inches; snowfall, 31 inches.

Five Largest Employers: R. R. Donnelley & Sons, printers, 1,800 employees; three companies that manufacture orthopedic implants—Zimmer, Inc., 1,500 employees; DePuy, Inc., 1,100; Biomet, Inc., 1,060; and Dalton Corporation, gray iron castings, 800. Warsaw is generally regarded as the world manufacturing center of prosthetics, such as hip and knee replacements.

High School: Warsaw Community High School enrolls 1,837 students in grades 9–12, graduates 89%, sends 67% of graduates to college/university. Composite SAT for 63% of eligible students taking test: 506 verbal, 494 math. Composite ACT, 23.3.

Housing: 3BR 2BA house sells in range of $85,000 to $200,000, pays real estate tax in range of $700 to $3,000. Most households heat with natural gas.

Telecommunications: Sprint provides DSL service in a limited area.

Sales, Income Taxes: Retail sales tax, 5%. State income tax, 3.4%.

Cost of Living: Movie ticket, $7; doctor appointment, routine, $55; plumber per hour, $45; baby-sitting per hour, $3; dry cleaning, men's suit, $7; dinner for 4, local restaurant, $85.

Community Infrastructure & Amenities:

United Way	Public library
Community foundation	Public parks: 17 parks,
Community leadership	totaling 36 acres
training program	Public swimming pool
Main Street	Airport
YMCA/YWCA	Country club
Boys Club/Girls Club	Golf course, 36 holes
4-H	Emergency home shelter
Bed-and-breakfast	
Motion picture theater	

Religious Denominations:

Assemblies of God	Interdenominational
Baptist	Jehovah's Witnesses
Brethren	Lutheran
Catholic	Lutheran (ELCA)
Christian	Lutheran (Missouri)
Christian Science	Mennonite
Church of Christ	Methodist
Church of God	Missionary
Church of Jesus Christ of	Nondenominational
Latter-Day Saints	Pentecostal
Church of the Nazarene	Presbyterian
Community	Salvation Army
Episcopal	Seventh Day Adventist
Four Square	United Church of Christ
Friends	United Methodist
Independent	

Newspaper: *Times-Union*, P.O. Box 1448, Warsaw, IN 46581-1448. 574-267-3111. timeswrsw.com. Published daily. Norm Hagg, editor in chief. 3-month subscription by mail, $33. *New York Times*, *Wall Street Journal* also sold in town.

Annual Festivals and Events: Cinco de Mayo, a celebration of the Hispanic culture; June through August, Friday Evening Performing Arts Series at Central Park: bands, blues, classic rock, folk, Dixieland; Back to the Days of Kosciuszko, September weekend celebration honoring the memory of Gen. Thaddeus Kosciuszko, a hero of the Revolutionary War: battle demonstrations, parades, encampment.

Further Information: Kosciusko County Convention & Visitors Bureau, 111 Capital Drive, Warsaw, IN 46582. 800-800-6090. koscvb.org

Washington, CT 06794

Population: 4,045 (+4%)

Banks: 4, all branches of out-of-town banks.

Hospital: New Milford Hospital, 10 miles.

Location: 45 miles southwest of Hartford, 80 miles northeast of New York City, in western Connecticut.

Geography/Climate: Situated on a plateau above the Shepaug River, in a region of deep valleys and lush forests. Robust Continental climate tempered by the Atlantic Ocean. Average January temperature, 25 degrees; July, 78. Annually, average 21 days at 90 degrees or above; 130 days at 32 degrees or below, including several below zero. Annual snowfall and rainfall both about 45 inches.

Five Largest Employers: Shepaug Valley Regional School District, 225 employees; Devereux-Glenholme School, 150; The Mayflower Inn, 100; The Gunnery School, 95; Rumsey Hall School, 72.

High School: Shepaug Valley High School enrolls 354 students in grades 9–12, graduates 99%, sends 81% to college/university. Composite SAT for 97% of eligible students taking test, 1054.

Housing: 3BR 2BA house sells in the range of $250,000 to $375,000, pays upward of $3,500 in real estate tax. Most people heat with oil.

Telecommunications: Southern New England Telephone (SNET) provides DSL service.

Sales, Income Taxes: Retail sales tax, 6%; clothing under $100 and grocery food exempt. State income tax, 3% to 4.5%.

Cost of Living: Doctor appointment, routine, $75; plumber per hour, $55; baby-sitting per hour, $7.50 to $10 (plus snacks!); dry cleaning, men's suit, $10.50; dinner for 4, local restaurant, $120.

Community Infrastructure & Amenities:
United Way
Community foundation
Historic District
Boys Club/Girls Club
4-H
Bed-and-breakfast
Community recreational center
Public library
Public swimming pool
Country club
Golf course, 9 holes

Religious Denominations:
Baha'i
Catholic
Congregational
Episcopal
Evangelical
Independent
Jewish Congregation
United Church of Christ

Newspaper: No local newspaper. Dailies covering the area include *Waterbury Republican-American*, *Danbury News Times*, *New Milford Spectrum*. *New York Times*, *New York Post*, *New York Daily News*, *New Haven Register*, *Wall Street Journal* also sold in town.

Annual Festivals and Events: Holiday in the Depot, 4th of July Fireworks Display, Sidewalk Sale, Antique Show at Gunn Library, Clothesline Sale of the Washington Art Association. Details and dates available from gunnlib@biblio.org

Further Information: Washington Town Clerk, P.O. Box 383, Washington, CT 06794. twn.of.wshngtn@snet.net

Winfield, KS 67156

Population: 12,206 (+3%)

Banks: 6, 2 of which are locally owned.

Hospital: William Newton Memorial Hospital, 100 beds.

Location: At crossroads of U.S. 77 and U.S. 160, 50 miles southeast of Wichita, 120 miles northwest of Tulsa.

Geography/Climate: Gently rolling Kansas farmlands subject to abrupt weather changes as warm Gulf air collides with polar cold on the Great Plains. Thunderstorms on average 55 days. Tornado country. Four seasons with some torrid midsummer days, mild winters. Average 37 inches rain, 12 inches snow.

Five Largest Employers: General Electric, jet engine overhaul, 1,002 employees; USD 465, school district, 680; Newell Rubbermaid, plastic products, 525; Winfield Correctional Facility, minimum security, 300; William Newton Memorial Hospital, 233.

High School: Winfield High School enrolls 900 students in grades 9–12, graduates 94%, sends 80% of graduates to college/university. Composite ACT for 100% of eligible students taking test, 22.

Housing: 3BR 2BA house sells for $94,400 at midmarket, pays $1,300 in real estate tax. Most people use natural gas for heat.

Telecommunications: Southwestern Bell provides DSL service. Cox Communications provides broadband connection through the cable system.

Sales, Income Taxes: Retail sales tax, 5.9%. State income tax, 3.5% to 6.45%.

Cost of Living: Movie ticket, $6.25; doctor appointment, routine, $55; plumber per hour, $49; baby-sitting per hour, $2; dry cleaning, men's suit, $7.50; dinner for 4, local restaurant, $60.

Community Infrastructure & Amenities:

United Way	Community recreational
Community foundation	center
(Assets $350,000)	Motion picture theater
Community leadership	Public library
training program	Public swimming pool
Main Street	Country club
4-H	Golf course, 18 holes

Religious Denominations:

AME	Episcopal
Assemblies of God	Evangelical
Baha'i	Full Gospel
Baptist	Jehovah's Witnesses
Catholic	Lutheran
Christian	Methodist
Church of Christ	Nondenominational
Church of God	Presbyterian
Church of Jesus Christ of	United Methodist
Latter-Day Saints	
Church of the Nazarene	

Newspaper: *Winfield Daily Courier*, 201 E. 9th Street, Winfield, KS 67156. 620-221-1050. www.winfieldcourier.com. Published daily, Dave Seaton, editor. 3-month subscription by mail, $21.69. *New York Times*, *Wall Street Journal*, *USA Today*, *Wichita Eagle* also sold in town.

Annual Festivals and Events: First weekend in May, KANZA Days, celebrating the history of Winfield; June–July, Horsefeathers & Applesauce Dinner Theater; third weekend in June, Wheatland Jam Music Fest, classic rock; third weekend September, Walnut Valley Festival & National Flatpicking Contest, bluegrass and acoustical music; November–December, Winfield Isle of Lights.

Further Information: Winfield Area Chamber of Commerce, P.O. Box 640, Winfield, KS 67156. 620-221-2420. win@winfieldchamber.org, winfieldks.gov

Far-Out Towns

Alliance, NE 69301

Population: 8,959 (–9%)
Banks: 7, including 4 branch banks.
Hospital: Box Butte General Hospital, 44 beds.

Location: 452 miles west of Omaha, 250 miles northeast of Denver, in the Nebraska Panhandle.

Geography/Climate: High Plains country at 4,000-foot elevation, with the Nebraska Sand Hills to the east. Dry and sunny much of the time, thanks to the elevation and dehydrating effect of the Rocky Mountains to the west. January average temperatures: low, 12 degrees; high, 38. July: low, 59; high, 90. Seasonally, average 25 days below zero, 32 days above 90. Average annual precipitation, 15 inches; snowfall, 43 inches.

Five Largest Employers: Burlington Northern Santa Fe Railroad, 1,500 employees; Parker-Dayco, hose manufacturer, 390; Alliance Public Schools, 315; AEP Pro Serv, 25; Perrin Manufacturing, 18.

High School: Alliance High School enrolls 680 students in grades 9–12, graduates 96%, sends 72% to college/university. Composite ACT for 86% of students taking test, 21.

Housing: 3BR 2BA house in good condition sells for about $65,000, pays $1,200 to $1,400 in real estate tax. Most households heat with natural gas.

Telecommunications: Qwest provides residential Internet connection at 56 Kbps.

Sales, Income Taxes: 6.5% retail sales tax, grocery food and prescription drugs exempt. State income tax, scaled 2.51% to 6.68%.

Cost of Living: Movie ticket, $6; local restaurant, $50.

Community Infrastructure & Amenities:
United Way
Community leadership training program
Main Street
YMCA/YWCA
4-H
Bed-and-breakfast
Motion picture theater
Public library
Public parks
Public swimming pool
Airport
Country club
Golf course, 18 holes

Religious Denominations:
Assemblies of God
Baptist
Catholic
Christian
Church of Christ
Church of God
Church of Jesus Christ of Latter-Day Saints
Church of the Nazarene
Community
Episcopal
Evangelical
Jehovah's Witnesses
Lutheran
Methodist
Pentecostal
Presbyterian
Seventh Day Adventist
United Church of Christ
United Methodist
Wesleyan

Newspaper: *Alliance Times Herald*, 114 E. 4th Street, Alliance, NE 69301. 308-762-3060. www.alliancetimes.com. Published daily except Sunday. 3-month subscription, $20.

Annual Festivals and Events: Third Thursday–Sunday July, Heritage Days; first Thursday of December, Parade of Lights; Saturday before Easter, Easter Egg Hunt.

Further Information: Alliance Chamber of Commerce, 111 W. 3rd Street, Alliance, NE 69301. 308-762-1520. commerce@premaonline.com

Alpine, TX 79830

Population: 6,750 (+13%)
Banks: 2 branch banks.
Hospital: Big Bend Regional Medical Center, 40 beds.

Location: 223 miles southeast of El Paso, 57 miles south of I-10, on the Texas Mountain Trail in Big Bend country.

Geography/Climate: Elevation 4,481 feet, located near the center of the grassy highlands and mountains of far West Texas. David Mountains, about 30 miles northwest, reach 6,000 to 8,000 feet. Del Norte Mountains in the south, 6,800 feet. Alpine's elevation and distance from moisture sources in the Pacific Ocean and Gulf of Mexico yield a dry, sunny climate. Average humidity in summer months, 25% to 30%. Air conditioning seldom needed at night. Sunny, averaging 78% of possible sunshine annually. Rainfall averages 15–16 inches, mostly in midsummer to early fall. Daytime temperatures reach 90 or higher on about half of summer days. Winter generally dry with mild days and brisk nights, seldom below freezing for more than a day.

Five Largest Employers: Sul Ross State University, 400 employees; Alpine Independent School District, 173; Big Bend Regional Medical Center, 140; Brewster County offices, 76; City of Alpine, 60.

Public Schools: District enrolls 1,100 students in K–12. 99% graduate, 70% enroll in college.

Housing: 3BR 2BA house in good condition, $100,000–$200,000. Taxes, $1,100–$2,200. Most people heat with natural gas or electricity.

Telecommunications: Southwestern Bell; no DSL.

Sales, Income Taxes: 7.25% retail sales tax, food and drugs exempt; no state income tax.

Cost of Living: Movie ticket, $6; doctor appointment, routine, $60; plumber per hour, $40; baby-sitting, per hour, $5; dry cleaning, men's suit, $6; dinner for 4, local restaurant, $30.

Community Infrastructure & Amenities:
Community leadership training program
Main Street member
Boys Club/Girls Club
4-H
Bed-and-breakfast
Community recreational center
Movie theater
Public library
Public parks: 1 park, 20 acres.
Public swimming pool
Airport
Country club
Golf course: 9 holes
Emergency home shelter

Religious Denominations:

Apostolic	Episcopal
Assemblies of God	Jehovah's Witnesses
Baptist	Lutheran
Catholic	Methodist
Christian	Presbyterian USA
Church of Christ	Seventh Day Adventist
Church of God	United Methodist
Church of Jesus Christ of Latter-Day Saints	

Newspaper: *The Alpine Avalanche*, 112 N. 5th St., Alpine, TX 79830. www.alpineavalanche.com 915-837-3334. Published weekly. 3 months, $5.50. Ed Sterling, editor. *San Angelo Standard Times*, *Odessa American* also sold in town.

Annual Festivals and Events: February, Taste of Texas Big Bend Style; March, Cowboy Poetry Gathering and Trappings of Texas; April, Big Bend Gem and Mineral Show; May, Cinco de Mayo; July, Goat Field Day; August, Big Bend Ranch Rodeo; September, Big Bend Balloon Bash; November, Gallery Night.

Further Information: Alpine Chamber of Commerce, 106 N. 3rd St., Alpine, TX 79830. chamber@alpinetexas.com

Batesville, AR 72501

Population: 9,445 (+3%)
Banks: 5, including 2 that are branches of larger banks based elsewhere.
Hospital: White River Medical Center, 180 beds.

Location: 90 miles northeast of Little Rock, 120 miles northwest of Memphis, on U.S. Hwy. 167 in north central Arkansas.

Geography/Climate: Rolling hill country approaching the Arkansas Ozarks. Elevation 365 feet. Long, warm summers including some high humidity and heat waves. Short, mild winters but with occasional ice and sleet. Annual average rainfall, 49 inches. Snowfall, 4 inches.

Five Largest Employers: Townsends of Arkansas, poultry, 1,150 employees; ConAgra, frozen foods, poultry, feed, 1,137; White River Medical Center, 902; White Rodgers, thermostats, gas burners, 743; Arkansas Operations, Eastman Chemical, 562.

High School: Batesville High School enrolls 441 students in grades 10–12, graduates 87%, sends 80% of graduates to college/university. Composite ACT for 77% of eligible students taking test, 22.2.

Housing: 3BR 2BA house in good condition sells in range of $65,000 to $85,000. A home with market value of $75,000 pays about $420 a year in real-estate tax. Most people heat with natural gas and electricity.

Telecommunications: Southwestern Bell Telephone provides DSL service. Cox Communications provides cable connection to Internet.

Sales, Income Taxes: Retail sales tax, 1.25%. State income tax, scaled 1% to 7%.

Cost of Living: Movie ticket, $6.25; doctor appointment, routine, $45; plumber per hour, $45; baby-sitting per hour, $3; dry cleaning, men's suit, $6.50; dinner for 4, local restaurant, $40.

Community Infrastructure & Amenities
United Way
Main Street
National Historic District
4-H
Bed-and-breakfast
Motion picture theater
Public library
Public parks: 5 parks, totaling 130 acres
Public swimming pool
Airport
Country club
Golf course, 9 holes
Emergency home shelter

Religious Denominations
AME
Assemblies of God
Baptist
Catholic
Charismatic
Christian
Christian Science
Church of God
Church of Jesus Christ of Latter-Day Saints
Episcopal
Full Gospel
Jehovah's Witnesses
Lutheran
Methodist
Nazarene
Pentecostal
Presbyterian
Seventh Day Adventist

Newspaper: *Batesville Daily Guard*, 258 W. Main Street, Batesville, AR 72501. 870-793-2383. Published Monday through Friday. Stacey Roberts, editor. 6-month subscription, $26.

Annual Festivals and Events: March, Ozark Hawg Barbecue; April, Ozark Foothills Film Fest; August, White River Water Carnival; October, Bean Fest & Championship Outhouse Race; December, Christmas Parade.

Further Information: Batesville Area Chamber of Commerce, 409 Vine Street, Batesville, AR 72501. 870-793-2378. batesville.dina.org

Bemidji, MN 56601

Population: 11,917 (+6%)

Banks: 6, including one bank owned out of town.

Hospital: North Country Regional Hospital, 99 beds.

Location: 229 miles northwest of Minneapolis, 110 miles east-southeast of Grand Forks, North Dakota, in north central Minnesota.

Geography/Climate: Elevation 1,356 feet. Generally flat, wooded terrain, with many lakes. January average temperatures: high, 12 degrees; low, 11 below zero. July: high, 78; low, 55. Average number of days over 90 degrees, 3. Average rainfall, 41 inches; snowfall, 41 inches. A Continental Divide marker 12 miles north of Bemidji, at elevation 1,397 feet, indicates the point separating north-flowing lakes and streams bound for Hudson Bay and south-flowing lakes and streams headed for the Gulf of Mexico. One of the south-bound streams becomes the Mississippi River.

Five Largest Employers: Bemidji Public Schools, 810 employees; North Country Health Services, 800; Bemidji State University, 550; Anderson Fabrics, 385; Beltrami County, 360.

High School: Bemidji High School enrolls 1,750 students in grades 9–12, graduates 92%, sends 71% of graduates to college/university. Composite ACT for 67% of eligible students taking test, 23.3.

Housing: 3BR 2BA house in good condition sells for about $73,000; pays $1,200 a year in real estate tax. Most people heat with natural gas.

Telecommunications: Paul Bunyan Telephone provides DSL service. Charter and PBTV provide Internet connection via cable.

Sales, Income Taxes: Retail sales tax, 6.5%. State income tax, scaled 5.35% to 7.85%.

Cost of Living: Movie ticket, $6; doctor appointment, routine, $48–$97; plumber per hour, $48; baby-sitting per hour, $2.25; dry cleaning, men's suit, $9.50; dinner for 4, local restaurant, $50.

Community Infrastructure & Amenities:
United Way
Community foundation (Assets $20 million)
Community leadership training program
Main Street
4-H
Community recreational center
Motion picture theater
Public library
Public parks: 19 parks, totaling 19.5 acres
Airport
Country club
Golf courses: (4) totaling 54 holes

Religious Denominations:

Apostolic	Lutheran (ELCA)
Assemblies of God	Lutheran (Missouri)
Baptist	Methodist
Catholic	Presbyterian
Church of Jesus Christ of	Seventh Day Adventist
Latter-Day Saints	Unitarian
Episcopal	United Methodist
Evangelical	
Independent	
Lutheran	

Newspaper: *Bemidji Pioneer*, P.O. Box 455, Bemidji, MN 56619-0455. 218-751-3740. www.bemidjipioneer.com. Published daily; 3-month subscription, $27.50. Dennis Doeden, editor. *New York Times, Wall Street Journal, Minneapolis Star-Tribune, St. Paul Pioneer Press* also sold in town.

Annual Festivals and Events: Minnesota Finlandia Ski Marathon, Paul Bunyan Sled Dog Races, Art in the Park, Peoples Art Festival, Logging Daze, Polar Daze. Inquire about times of the year.

Further Information: Bemidji Area Chamber of Commerce, P.O. Box 850, Bemidji, MN 56619-0850. chamber@paulbunyan.net

Bolivar, MO 65613

Population: 9,142 (+34%)
Banks: 6, including 3 branch banks.
Hospital: Citizens Memorial Hospital, 74 beds.

Location: 150 miles southeast of Kansas City, 210 miles southwest of St. Louis, 30 miles north of Springfield, in the Osage Lakes region of southwestern Missouri.

Geography/Climate: Gently rolling terrain, elevation about 1,000 feet. Modified continental climate generally without summer-winter extremes. January averages range from 22 low to 44 high; July, 66 low, 92 high. Average annual rainfall, 42 inches, with June the wettest month. Snowfall average, 16 inches. January is the driest month.

Five Largest Employers: Citizens Memorial Healthcare, 1,300 employees; Wal-Mart Super Center, 380; Bolivar Rural Independent Schools, 340; Southwest Baptist University, 285; Tracker Marine, boats, 225.

High School: Bolivar High School enrolls 640 students in grades 9–12, graduates 84.4%, sends 63% to college/university. Composite ACT for 57% of eligible students taking test, 21.7.

Housing: 3BR 2BA house in good condition sells on average for $95,000, pays about $450 real estate tax. Most people heat with electricity.

Telecommunications: Alltel provides DSL service and broadband connection through the cable system.

Sales, Income Taxes: Retail sales tax, 7.225%. State income tax, 6%.

Cost of Living: Movie ticket, $6.25; doctor appointment, routine, $30; plumber per hour, $40; baby sitting per hour, $3 plus $1 each additional child; dry cleaning, men's suit, $7.25; dinner for 4, local restaurant, $30–$50.

Community Infrastructure & Amenities:
United Way
YMCA/YWCA
Bed-and-breakfast
Community recreational center
Motion picture theater
Public library
Public parks: 6, totaling 130 acres
Public swimming pool
Airport
Country club
Golf courses (2), 9, 18 holes

Religious Denominations:
Assemblies of God
Baptist
Catholic
Christian
Church of Christ
Church of Jesus Christ of Latter-Day Saints
Church of the Nazarene
Episcopal
Four Square
Jehovah's Witnesses
Lutheran (Missouri)
Presbyterian
Seventh Day Adventist
United Methodist

Newspaper: *Bolivar Herald-Free Press*, P.O. Box 330, Bolivar, MO 65613. 417-326-7636. bolivarmo.com. Published twice weekly. Dave Berry, publisher; Judy Kallenbach, editor. 3-month subscription, $17. *New York Times, Wall Street Journal, USA Today, Springfield News-Leader* also sold in town.

Annual Festivals and Events: Second weekend July, Country Days & Rodeo; second weekend August, Bull Blast, bull riding, crafts; first Sunday December, Festival of Christmas.

Further Information: Bolivar Area Chamber of Commerce, 454 S. Springfield Avenue, Bolivar, MO 65613. 417-326-4118. bolivarchamber.com

Brattleboro, VT 05301

Population: 12,005 (–3%)
Banks: 8, all locally owned.
Hospital: Brattleboro Memorial Hospital, 61 beds.

Location: 120 miles northwest of Boston, 15 miles southwest of Keene, New Hampshire, in southeastern Vermont.

Geography/Climate: Valley town of the Connecticut River, elevation 310 feet, bounded by 1,351-foot Mt. Wantastiquet on the east and 1,500-foot hills approaching the Green Mountains on the west. Average January high, 29; low, 6, but with 16 days subzero. Annual snowfall, 68 inches. July average low, 56; high, 81, but with 11 days at 90 or above. Annual rainfall, 42 inches.

Five Largest Employers: C&S Wholesale Grocers, 1,046 employees; Retreat Healthcare, 615; Windham Southeast Supervisory Union, 525; Vermont Yankee Nuclear Power, 326; School for International Training, 300.

High School: Brattleboro Union High School enrolls 1,057 students in grades 9–12, graduates 85%, sends 63% to college/university. Composite SAT, 517 verbal; 505 math.

Housing: 3BR 2BA house in good condition sells for $117,000 to $190,000, pays $3,400 to $5,500 in real estate tax. Most people heat with oil.

Telecommunications: Adelphia provides broadband connection to the Internet.

Sales, Income Taxes: Retail sales tax, 5%, clothing and footwear exempt up to $100. State income tax, 24% of federal tax liability.

Cost of Living: Movie ticket, $6.75; doctor appointment, routine, $45; dry cleaning, men's suit, $9.10; dinner for 4, local restaurant, $40–$50.

Community Infrastructure & Amenities:
United Way
Community leadership training program
Main Street
Boys Club/Girls Club
4-H
Bed-and-breakfast
Community recreational center
Motion picture theater
Public library
Public park
Public swimming pool
Country club
Golf course, 18 holes
Emergency home shelter

Religious Denominations:
Assemblies of God
Baha'i
Baptist
Catholic
Christian
Church of Christ
Community
Congregational
Episcopal
Friends
Jehovah's Witnesses
Jewish Congregation
Lutheran
Presbyterian
Seventh Day Adventist
Unitarian-Universalist
United Church of Christ
United Methodist

Newspaper: *Brattleboro Reformer*, P.O. Box 802, Brattleboro, VT 05301. 802-254-2311. reformer.com. Published daily. David Emmons, editor. 3-month subscription, $46.75. *New York Times, Wall Street Journal, Rutland Herald* also sold in town.

Annual Festivals and Events: Harris Hill Ski Jump; Brattleboro Winter Carnival; May Magic Food Fest; Village Days. Call or e-mail for dates.

Further Information: Brattleboro Area Chamber of Commerce, 180 Main Street, Brattleboro, VT 05301. 802-254-4565. bratchmb@sover.net

Chelan, WA 98816

Population: 3,522 (+19%)
Banks: 4, including 3 branches of out-of-town banks.
Hospital: Lake Chelan Community Hospital, 32 beds.

Location: 170 miles west of Spokane, 185 miles east of Seattle, at the southeast end of 50-mile-long Lake Chelan, in north central Washington.

Geography/Climate: Elevation 1,200 feet. Semi-arid rolling hills in the immediate area of town morph into glacier-clad peaks of the North Cascades at the northern end of 55-mile-long Lake Chelan, the largest lake in Washington and one of the world's deepest at 1,500 feet. January average temperatures range from 19 to 32; July, 62 to 91. Mountain range to the west preserves a generally dry climate: average 12 inches of rain, 42 inches of snow.

Five Largest Employers: Trout/Blue Chelan, 350 employees; Mill Bay Casino, 205; Lake Chelan Community Hospital, 175; Lake Chelan School District, 150; Wapato Point Resort, 85.

High School: Chelan High School enrolls 407 students in grades 9–12. For SAT scores, call 509-682-4061.

Housing: Median price of a 3BR 2BA house, $127,400. Real estate tax on such a house, $576.

Telecommunications: Verizon NW provides DSL service. Millennium Digital Media provides broadband connection.

Sales, Income Taxes: Retail sales tax, 8%, grocery food exempt. No state income tax.

Cost of Living: Movie ticket, $7; doctor appointment, routine, $30–$50; plumber per hour, $60; baby-sitting per hour, $3; dinner for 4, local restaurant, $60.

Community Infrastructure & Amenities:
Bed-and-breakfast
Teen center
Motion picture theater
Public library
Public parks
Airport
Golf courses, 9, 18 holes

Religious Denominations:
Baptist
Catholic
Church of the Nazarene
Lutheran
Pentecostal
Seventh Day Adventist
United Methodist

Newspaper: *Lake Chelan Mirror*, 315 E. Woodin Avenue, Chelan, WA 98816. 509-682-2213. lakechelanmirror.com. Published weekly. Jeff Walter, editor. 6-month subscription, $15. *Wall Street Journal, Wenatchee World, Seattle Times/Post-Intelligencer* also sold in town.

Annual Festivals and Events: January, Fire & Ice Winterfest; February, Snowmobile Drag Racing; May, Cinco de Mayo Celebration; June, Habitat for Humanity Spring Fling Dance, Taste of Chelan; July, Paragliding Championships, Lake Chelan Bach Fest; August, River Walk Fine Arts; November, Community Thanksgiving Dinner; December, Christmas Caroling Cruise.

Further Information: Lake Chelan Chamber of Commerce, 102 E. Johnson, Chelan, WA 98816. 509-682-3503. lakechelan.com

Crossville, TN 38555

Population: 8,981 (+30%)

Banks: 6, including 4 banks owned out of town.

Hospital: Cumberland Medical Center, 202 beds.

Location: 110 miles east of Nashville, 74 miles north of Chattanooga, 72 miles west of Knoxville, in east central Tennessee.

Geography/Climate: Located on the Cumberland Plateau, elevation 1,980 feet. Rocky soil, not especially good for farming, but very pretty—surrounded by mountains. January average temperatures range from 21 low to 39 high; July, 64 low to 82 high. Average snowfall, 12 inches; rainfall, 52 inches. Prevailing winds from southwest. Growing season, 180 days.

Five Largest Employers: Cumberland County School System, 1,200 employees; Cumberland Medical Center, 835; Fairfield Glade, retirement community, 475; Flowers Snack of Tennessee, 400; Delbar Products, bus and truck mirrors, 300.

High School: Cumberland County High School enrolls 1,825 students in grades 9–12, graduates 95%, sends 40% to college/university. Composite ACT for 85% of eligible students taking test, 21.

Housing: 3BR 2BA house sells for about $100,000, pays $700 in real-estate taxes. Most people heat with electricity.

Telecommunications: Citizens Communications provides DSL service.

Sales, Income Taxes: Retail sales tax, 8.75%. State income tax limited to dividend and interest income.

Community Infrastructure & Amenities:

United Fund	Public parks: 4, totaling
Main Street	500 acres
Boys Club/Girls Club	Public swimming pool
4-H	Airport
Bed-and-Breakfast	Country club
Community recreational	Golf courses, 7 in imme-
center	diate area
Motion picture theater	Emergency home shelter
Public library	

Religious Denominations:

Apostolic	Independent
Assemblies of God	Jehovah's Witnesses
Baptist	Lutheran
Catholic	Lutheran (ELCA)
Christian	Lutheran (Missouri)
Church of Christ	Mennonite
Church of God	Methodist
Church of Jesus Christ of	Nondenominational
Latter-Day Saints	Pentecostal
Church of the Nazarene	Presbyterian
Episcopal	Seventh Day Adventist
Friends	United Methodist
Full Gospel	

Newspaper: *Crossville Chronicle*, 125 West Avenue, Crossville, TN 38555. 931-484-5145. crossville-chronicle.com. Published three times a week. Mike Moser, editor. 3-month subscription, $14. *New York Times, Wall Street Journal, Knoxville News-Sentinel* also sold in town.

Cost of Living: Movie ticket, $4; doctor appointment, routine, $35; plumber per hour, $30; baby-sitting per hour, $5; dry cleaning, men's suit, $5; dinner for 4, local restaurant, $60.

Annual Festivals and Events: Crossville is known as the retirement and golf capital of Tennessee. Spring and Fall, Depot Days; Pioneer Day on the Mountain; Cumberland County Fair; Christmas Parade. Call for dates.

Further Information: Greater Cumberland County Chamber of Commerce, 34 S. Main Street, Crossville, TN 38555. 931-484-8444. crossville-chamber.com

Devils Lake, ND 58301

Population: 7,222 (–7%)
Banks: 8 banks, including 3 branch banks.
Hospital: Mercy Hospital, 50 beds.

Location: 400 miles northwest of Minneapolis, 181 miles northeast of Bismarck, in northeastern North Dakota.

Geography/Climate: Flat, high plains, elevation 1,475 feet, largely treeless except some woodsy areas around the lake. Rugged climate. Average 55 days below zero, with stretches of 30 below; 35 inches of snow average. January daily temperatures: high, 14 above zero; low, 4 below. July: high, 83; low, 59. 15 or more 90-plus days through summer. Annual rainfall, 15 inches.

Five Largest Employers: Devils Lake Public Schools, The Connection, Lake Region Lutheran Home, Mercy Hospital, Camp Grafton National Guard.

High School: Devils Lake High School enrolls 710 students in grades 9–12, graduates 96%. Enrolling in college/university, 84%. Composite ACT of 22.5 for 75% of eligible students taking test.

Housing: 3BA 2BR house in good condition, $75,000–$90,000. Real-estate taxes on such a house, about $1,400. Most households heat with natural gas. Town water source, Spiritwood Aquifer.

Telecommunications: North Dakota Telephone Co. offers DSL service to residences, 768 Kbps. Midcontinent Communication is cable provider.

Sales, Income Taxes: 1.5% retail sales tax, except on natural gas, groceries, and coin-operated amusement devices. State income tax, ranges from 2.1% to 5.54%.

Cost of Living: Movie ticket, $5.50; doctor appointment, routine, $45; plumber per hour, $40; baby-sitting, per hour, $2.50; dry cleaning, men's suit, $8; dinner for 4, local restaurant, $60.

Community Infrastructure & Amenities:
United Way
Community foundation ($3 million assets)
Main Street member
National Historic District
4-H
Bed-and-breakfast
Community recreational center
Movie theater
Public library
Public parks: 4, totaling 1,257 acres
Public swimming pool
Airport
Country club
Golf course, 18 holes

Religious Denominations:
Assemblies of God
Baptist
Catholic
Church of Jesus Christ of Latter-Day Saints
Jehovah's Witnesses
Lutheran
Lutheran (ELCA)
Lutheran (Missouri)
Presbyterian
Seventh Day Adventist
United Methodist

Newspaper: *Devils Lake Daily Journal*, P.O. Box 1200, Devils Lake, ND 58301. 701-662-2127. devilslakejournal.com. Gordon Weixel, editor. 3-month subscription by mail $27. *Wall Street Journal* also sold in town.

Annual Festivals and Events: Fourth weekend January, Volunteer Fire Department Ice Fishing Tournament; second weekend February, ShiverFest (dogsled races, golfing on ice, pig roast and bonfire, etc.); first weekend June, Devils Run specialty car, truck, motorcycle show; fourth weekend June, Walleye Tournament; July, Fort Totten Little Theater; third weekend September, Rough Rider Rodeo finals.

Further Information: Devils Lake Area Chamber of Commerce, P.O. Box 879, Devils Lake, ND 58301. 701-662-4903. devilslakend.com

Douglas, WY 82633

Population: 5,288 (+8.3%)

Banks: 3, including one locally owned bank.

Hospital: Memorial Hospital of Converse County, 44 beds.

Location: 227 miles north of Denver, 447 miles northeast of Salt Lake City, on Interstate 25 in east central Wyoming.

Geography/Climate: Elevation 4,815 feet, on the Platte River, in a setting of rolling hills, with 10,200-foot Laramie Peak dominating the southern horizon. Average temperature in January, 23 degrees; July, 75. Chinooks temper the winter bite, which can include 15 days below zero. Elevation moderates summer highs—average 17 days above 90. Average annual rainfall, 6 inches; snowfall, 40 inches. Prevailing winds 11 mph from the northwest.

Five Largest Employers: School District No. 1, 283 employees; Powder River Coal Company, 206; Kennecott Antelope Coal Company, 94; City of Douglas, 65; Power Resources, uranium mining, 60.

High School: Douglas High School enrolls 549 students in grades 9–12, graduates 90%, sends 34% of graduates to college/university. Composite ACT for approximately 50% of eligible students taking test, 21.5

Housing: 3BR 2BA house sells for about $95,000. Most people heat with natural gas.

Telecommunications: Communicomm Services provides broadband Internet connection.

Sales, Income Taxes: Retail sales tax, 5%. No state income tax.

Cost of Living: Movie ticket, $4; doctor appointment, routine, $50; plumber per hour, $28; baby-sitting per hour, $1.75; dry cleaning, men's suit, $7.50; dinner for 4, local restaurant, $30.

Community Infrastructure & Amenities

United Way
Community leadership training program
Main Street
Boys Club/Girls Club
4-H
Bed-and-breakfast
Community recreational center
Motion picture theater
Public library
Public parks: 3
Public swimming pool
Airport
Country club
Golf course, 18 holes

Religious Denominations

Assemblies of God
Baptist
Catholic
Christian
Church of Christ
Church of Jesus Christ of Latter-Day Saints
Episcopal
Jehovah's Witnesses
Lutheran
Methodist
Pentecostal
Seventh Day Adventist
United Methodist

Newspaper: *Douglas Budget*, 310 Center Street, Douglas, WY 82633. 307-358-2965. douglas-budget.com. Published weekly, Matt Adelman, editor. 3-month subscription, $6.50. *Wall Street Journal*, *Casper Star-Tribune* also sold in town.

Annual Festivals and Events: January, Chariot Races; April, High Plains Country Music Festival & Craft Show; June, Fort Fetterman Pow Wow Days, Jackalope Days, Wyoming High School Rodeo Finals; July, Cowboy Shootout; August, Wyoming State Fair; August, Laramie Peak Bluegrass Festival; October, Hunters BBQ.

Further Information: Douglas Area Chamber of Commerce, 121 Brownfield Road, Douglas, WY 82633. 307-358-2950. jackalope@netcommander.com

Eureka Springs, AR 72632

Population: 2,361 (+24%)
Banks: 4, including 2 branches.
Hospital: Eureka Springs Hospital, 22 beds.

Location: 52 miles northeast of Fayetteville; 45 miles southwest of Branson, Missouri; in the Ozarks of northwestern Arkansas.

Geography/Climate: Set in a steep, narrow valley amid forested hills of Ozark country. Modified continental climate with hot, humid summers and cold but tolerable winters. Winter temperatures range from mid-20s to mid-40s, with average 1 day below zero, 105 days below 32 degrees, and 11 inches of snow. Summers range from 65 to 95 degrees, averaging 56 days at 90 or above. Annual precipitation 44 inches, with thunderstorms on 50 days in a typical year. Clear days average 123 in number; partly cloudy; 96; cloudy, 146.

Five Largest Employers: The Great Passion Play, Crescent Hotel, Inn of the Ozarks, Basin Park Hotel, Bank of Eureka.

High School: Eureka Springs High School enrolls 272 students in grades 9–12, graduates 99%, sends 55%–60% to college/university. Recent composite ACT score for 50% of eligible students taking test, 23.

Housing: 3BR 2BA house in good condition sells for about $120,000 and pays $600 to $800 annually in real-estate tax. Most people heat with natural gas.

Telecommunications: Cox Communications was preparing in early 2002 to introduce Internet connection via cable.

Sales, Income Taxes: 8.875% retail sales tax, furniture exempt. State income tax, scaled 1% to 7%.

Cost of Living: Doctor appointment, routine, $45; plumber per hour, $75; baby-sitting, per hour, $4; dry cleaning, men's suit, $6.90; dinner for 4, local restaurant, $60–$80.

Community Infrastructure & Amenities:
Main Street
National Historic District (encompasses much of the town)
Boys Club/Girls Club
Bed-and-breakfast (More than 100 in area)
Public library
Public park: 1,600 acres
Public swimming area
Country club
Golf courses, 9 and 18 holes

Religious Denominations:
Assemblies of God
Baptist
Catholic
Christian
Church of Christ
Community
Episcopal
Full Gospel
Interdenominational
Lutheran
Methodist
Nondenominational
Presbyterian
Unitarian Universalist

Newspaper: *Eureka Springs Times-Echo*, 501-253-9719. www.eurekaspringstimesecho.com. 3-month subscription by mail to an out-of-state address, $17.25. *New York Times, Wall Street Journal*, and regional metropolitan dailies also sold in town.

Annual Festivals and Events: Founded as a health resort in the mid-1800s, the town remains a picturesque village of Victorian houses and a popular tourist destination much of the year. Downtown streets lined with art galleries, shops, and restaurants. Blues Festival first weekend after Memorial Day attracts nationally known performers. Ozark Folk Festival in the fall has been staged annually since 1947.

Further Information: Greater Eureka Springs Chamber of Commerce, 1376 W. Van Buren, Eureka Springs, AR 72632. 501-253-8737. anne@eurekaspringschamber.com

Grand Marais, MN 55604

Population: 1,353 (+7%)

Banks: 3, including branches of 2 out-of-town banks.

Hospital: Cook County North Shore Hospital, 16 beds.

Location: 94 miles northeast of Duluth, 41 miles southwest of the Canadian border, on Lake Superior.

Geography/Climate: Rugged continental climate, with early snow and long and brutally cold winters. Last freeze toward the end of May. About 30 inches of rain and 55 inches of snow a year. January average temperatures range from zero to upper teens; July, mid-50s to mid-70s. The 40-degree average temperature of Lake Superior moderates summer heat and humidity.

Five Largest Employers: Cook County government, 113 employees; Cook County School District, 100; U.S. Forest Service, 97; Cook County Hospital, 86; Hedstrom Lumber Company, 48.

High School: Cook County High Schools enrolls about 250 students in grades 9–12, sends 60% of graduates to 4-year college, 20% to 2-year. Composite ACT for 75% of seniors taking test, 23.6.

Housing: 3BR 2BA house sells for $130,000 to $150,000, pays about $800 in real-estate tax.

Telecommunications: Qwest offers DSL service.

Sales, Income Taxes: Retail sales tax, 7.5%. State income tax, scaled 5.35% to 7.85%.

Cost of Living: Doctor appointment, routine, $49; plumber per hour, $60; baby-sitting per hour, $3–$5; dinner for 4, local restaurant, $75.

Community Infrastructure & Amenities:
United Way
4-H
Bed-and-breakfast
Community recreational center
Public library
Public swimming pool
Airport
Golf course, 9 holes

Religious Denominations
Baptist
Catholic
Evangelical
Jehovah's Witnesses
Jewish Congregation
Lutheran (ELCA)
Seventh Day Adventist
United Church of Christ

Newspaper: *Cook County News Herald*, P.O. Box 757, Grand Marais, MN 55604. 218-387-1025. grand-marais-mn.com. Published weekly; Brian Larsen, editor. 3-month subscription, $18. *New York Times*, *Wall Street Journal* also sold in town.

Annual Festivals and Events: February, Winter Trail Days; March, John Beargrease Sleddog Race; May, Car Show; last week June through first week July, Shakespeare Festival; end October, Moose Madness Weekend, Birding Festival.

Further Information: Grand Marais Area Tourism Association, 13 N. Broadway, Grand Marais, MN 55604. 218-387-2524. grandmarais.com

Greeneville, TN 37743

Population: 15,198 (+4%)

Banks: 9, of which 3 are branches of out-of-town banks.

Hospital: Takoma Adventist Hospital, Laughlin Memorial Hospital, 227 beds.

Location: 68 miles northeast of Knoxville, 60 miles northwest of Asheville, North Carolina, in extreme northeastern Tennessee.

Geography/Climate: Elevation 1,557 feet, in the Great Valley of East Tennessee. Sheltered by thickly forested mountains and ridges, reaching to 4,400 feet in the southwest. Moderately cold winters, warm to hot summers. January average low, 27; high 46. July: low, 65; high 86. Average 13 days into the 90s. Annual rainfall, 42 inches; snowfall, 11 inches. 45% sunshine in January; 75% in October.

Five Largest Employers: Unaka MECO, barbeque grills, folding furniture, 1,400 employees; Wal-Mart Distribution Center, 1,333; Five Rivers Manufacturing, 1,120; Plus Mark, greeting cards, giftwrap; Huf-Tennessee, 650.

High School: Greeneville High School enrolls 813 students in grades 9–12, graduates 95%, sends 74% to college/university. Composite ACT for 82% of eligible students taking test, 20.

Housing: 3BR 2BA house sells in the range of $90,000 to $100,000, pays about $1,000 in real estate tax. Most people heat with oil and electricity.

Telecommunications: Sprint provides DSL service. Adelphia Cable provides broadband connection to Internet.

Sales, Income Taxes: Retail sales tax, 8.75%. State income tax limited to dividends and interest income.

Cost of Living: Movie ticket, $6.25; doctor appointment, routine, $60; plumber per hour, $20; baby-sitting per hour, $2; dry cleaning, men's suit, $8.15; dinner for 4, local restaurant, $60.

Community Infrastructure & Amenities:

United Way	Motion picture theater
Community leadership training program	Public library
	Public parks: 4
Main Street	Public swimming pool
National Historic District	Airport
YMCA/YWCA	Country club
Boys Club/Girls Club	Golf courses, 8 in area.
4-H	Emergency home shelter
Bed-and-breakfast	
Community recreational center	

Religious Denominations:

Apostolic	Full Gospel
Assemblies of God	Jehovah's Witnesses
Baptist	Lutheran
Catholic	Lutheran (ELCA)
Christian	Mennonite
Church of Christ	Pentecostal
Church of God	Presbyterian
Church of Jesus Christ of Latter-Day Saints	Seventh Day Adventist
	United Church of Christ
Episcopal	United Methodist
Evangelical	
Friends	

Newspaper: *Greeneville Sun*, 121 W. Summer Street, Greeneville, TN 37743. 423-638-4181. greene.xtn.net. Published daily. John M. Jones, Jr., editor. 3-month subscription, $27.90. *New York Times, Wall Street Journal* also sold in town.

Annual Festivals and Events: third weekend in May, Iris Festival: juried art show, crafts, dance, stage entertainment, food.

Further Information: Greene County Partnership, 115 Academy Street, Greenville, TN 37743. 423-636-8385. greenecountypartnership.com

Harrison, AR 72602

Population: 12,152 (+22%)
Banks: 7 banks, including 5 branches.
Hospital: North Arkansas Regional Medical Center, 174 beds.

Location: 139 miles northwest of Little Rock, 235 miles southeast of Kansas City, in northwestern Arkansas.

Geography/Climate: Ozark mountain town, elevation 1,250 feet. Four seasons but generally free of extremes. One or two light snows, 45 to 60 days below freezing, generally in the 20s. Spring blooms in March. Summers warm and long, highs averaging 93 in July. 42 inches of rain. Fall colors peak in mid-October and attract throngs of sightseers.

Five Largest Employers: American Freightways, 1,000 employees; North Arkansas Regional Medical Center, 700; Millbrook Distribution Services, 700; Pace Industries, 700; North Arkansas College, 300.

High School: Harrison High School enrolls 648 students in grades 10–12, graduates 95%, sends 65% to college/university. Recent composite ACT score for 75% of eligible students taking test, 22.6

Housing: 3BR 2BA house in good condition, $55,000–$95,000. Taxes on such a house, $300–$400. Most people heat with natural gas.

Telecommunications: Alltel provides DSL service at 1,536 Kbps. Cox Communications provides Internet connection via cable.

Sales, Income Taxes: Retail sales tax, 6.625%. State income tax, 4.625%.

Cost of Living: Movie ticket, $7; doctor appointment, routine, $50; plumber per hour, $18; baby-sitting, per hour, $4; dry cleaning, men's suit, $5; dinner for 4, local restaurant, $55.

Community Infrastructure & Amenities:

United Way	Motion picture theater
Community foundations	Public library
Community leadership training program	Public parks: 10, totaling 27 acres
Main Street	Public swimming pool
National Historic District	Airport
4-H	Country club
Bed-and-breakfast	Golf course, 27 holes
Community recreational center	Emergency home shelter

Religious Denominations:

Apostolic	Full Gospel
Assemblies of God	Independent
Baptist	Interdenominational
Catholic	Jehovah's Witnesses
Christian	Lutheran (Missouri)
Church of Christ	Mennonite
Church of God	Methodist
Church of Jesus Christ of Latter-Day Saints	Nondenominational
Church of the Nazarene	Pentecostal
Community	Presbyterian
Disciples of Christ	Presbyterian USA
Episcopal	Seventh Day Adventist
Evangelical	United Methodist
	Wesleyan

Newspaper: *Harrison Daily Times*, P.O. Box 40, Harrison, AR 72601. 870-741-2325. harrisondailytimes.com. Published daily. Dwain Lair, editor. 6-month subscription by mail, $23. *New York Times, Wall Street Journal*, other Arkansas dailies sold in town.

Annual Festivals and Events: Arkansas State Hot Air Balloon Championship, Northwest Arkansas Bluegrass Festival, Crawdad Days Music Festival, Harvest Homecoming. Call for dates.

Further Information: Harrison Chamber of Commerce, 621 E. Rush St., Harrison, AR 72601. cocinfo@harrison-chamber.com

Holdrege, NE 68949

Population: 5,636 (–0.6 %)
Banks: 4, including 3 branch banks.
Hospital: Phelps Memorial Health Center, 55 beds.

Location: 206 miles southwest of Omaha, 332 miles northeast of Denver, in the fertile plains of south central Nebraska.

Geography/Climate: Flat to gently rolling high plains at 2,335 feet elevation. High-quality soil, known as Holdrege silt loam, irrigated by a large power-water project dating to the 1930s. Varied, midcontinental climate. Sunshine ranges from 55% in December to 80% in July. Worst of winter cold blasts from Canada often pass to the east. January temperatures average lows of 13 degrees, highs of 35. Snowfall October through April, 30 inches. July average temperatures: low, 64; high, 90. Elevation keeps summer humidity tolerable: 6 A.M., 82% average; 6 P.M., 49%. Average date of first frost, October 14; last frost, April 29.

Five Largest Employers: Becton Dickinson Co., medical supplies, 650 employees; Phelps Memorial Health Center, 164; Christian Homes/Holdrege Memorial Homes (nursing homes), 137 and 148 respectively; Allmand Brothers, floodlights, traffic control devices, 135; Paxar Corp., 100.

High School: Holdrege High School enrolls 431 students in grades 9–12, graduates 99%, sends 67% to 2- or 4-year college. Composite ACT for 79% of eligible students taking test, 22.1.

Housing: 3BR 2BA house in good condition, $71,000. Real estate taxes, $1,900. People heat with natural gas and electricity.

Telecommunications: Qwest provides DSL service; Charter Communications provides an Internet connection through the cable system.

Sales, Income Taxes: Retail sales tax, 6%, grocery store food items and most services exempt. State income tax, ranges from 3.49% to 5.01%.

Cost of Living: Movie ticket, $6; doctor appointment, routine, $42; plumber per hour, $38; baby-sitting, per hour, $1.50; dry cleaning, men's suit, $15; dinner for 4, local restaurant, $40.

Community Infrastructure & Amenities:
Community foundation
Community leadership training program
4-H
Bed-and-breakfast
Community recreational center
Motion picture theater
Public library
Public swimming pool
Airport
Country club
Golf course, 18 holes

Religious Denominations:
Assemblies of God
Baptist
Catholic
Church of Jesus Christ of Latter-Day Saints
Church of the Nazarene
Episcopal
Evangelical
Lutheran (ELCA)
Lutheran (Missouri)
Methodist
Presbyterian
Seventh Day Adventist
United Methodist

Newspaper: *Holdrege Daily Citizen*, 308-995-4441. Published 5 days a week. Tunney Price, editor. 6-month mail subscription, $28.

Annual Festivals and Events: June, Midsommarfest, celebration of Swedish heritage; Phelps County Fair, including Gospel Night, Outdoor Concert, Demolition Derby; Heartland Cruisers Car Show; June–September, Farmer's Market and Entertainment, Thursday nights. Call for dates: 308-995-4444.

Further Information: Holdrege Chamber of Commerce, Attn: Sheryl Vollertsen, P.O. Box 200, Holdrege, NE 68949. jared@alltel.net

Houghton, MI 49931

Population: 7,010 (–6.5%)

Banks: 5, including two locally owned.

Hospital: Portage Health System, 30 staffed beds and 30 long-term beds.

Location: On the "thumb" of the Michigan Upper Peninsula, jutting into Lake Superior. 340 miles north of Milwaukee, 340 miles northeast of Minneapolis-St. Paul.

Geography/Climate: Geologists say rugged, rocky Keweenaw Peninsula is Precambrian, the oldest land on Planet Earth. Houghton is located on the banks of the Keweenaw Waterway, surrounded by trees and water. Lake Superior is the weather controller, moderating winter lows to only 20 or so days below zero but dumping an average 210 inches of snow. Typically only two summer days above 90. 124-day growing season. Houghton is so far north that summer daylight lasts past 10 P.M.

Five Largest Employers: Michigan Technological University, 1,451 employees; Copper Country Mental Health, 255; Baraga-Houghton-Keweenaw Child Development, 237; Houghton-Portage Township Schools, 178; Wal-Mart, 176.

Michigan Tech enrolls about 5,000 students and ranks among institutions offering the best undergraduate engineering programs, according to *U.S. News & World Report* in 2001.

High School: Houghton High School enrolls 472 students in grades 9-12, graduates 100%, sends 70% to college/university. Composite ACT for 80% of eligible students taking test, 23.

Housing: 3BR 2BA house sells in the range of $130,000 to $170,000, pays about $3,300 in real-estate tax. Most people heat with natural gas.

Telecommunications: Ameritech offers digital connection at 768 Kbps. Charter Communication offers broadband connection to the Internet via cable.

Sales, Income Taxes: Retail sales tax, 6%, grocery food exempt. State income tax, 4.2% flat rate.

Cost of Living: Movie ticket, $5; doctor appointment, routine, $65; plumber per hour, $30–$50; baby-sitting per hour, $3; dry cleaning, men's suit, $8.50; dinner for 4, local restaurant, $37.

Community Infrastructure & Amenities:
United Way
Community foundation
Main Street
Bed-and-breakfast
Motion picture theater
Public library
Public parks: Beachfront plus several small parks
Public swimming pool
Golf course, 18 holes

Religious Denominations:

Apostolic	Episcopal
Baptist	Lutheran
Catholic	Lutheran (ELCA)
Christian	Nondenominational
Church of Christ	Presbyterian USA
Church of Jesus Christ of	Seventh Day Adventist
Latter-Day Saints	United Methodist
Church of the Nazarene	

Newspaper: *Daily Mining Gazette*, 206 Shelden Avenue, Houghton, MI 49931. 906-482-1500. mininggazette.com. Published daily except Sunday; Bruce Heisel, editor. 3-month subscription, $42. *Wall Street Journal, USA Today, Detroit News, Detroit Free-Press* also sold in town.

Annual Festivals and Events: February, Michigan Tech Winter Carnival; June, Bridgefest; June–July, Pine Mountain Music Festival; July–August, Waterfront Concert Series; August, Rockhound Week; September, Multicultural Festival; October, Lake Superior PPO Rally (automobile race).

Further Information: City Manager, 616 Shelden Avenue, Houghton, MI 49931. houghton@portup.com

Lander, WY 82520

Population: 6,867 (−2%)
Banks: 5, none locally owned.
Hospital: Lander Valley Medical Center, 102 beds.

Location: 369 miles northwest of Denver, 181 miles southeast of Yellowstone National Park, in west central Wyoming.

Geography/Climate: Elevation 5,357 feet, in a valley on the eastern slopes of the Wind River Range of the Rocky Mountains. Sunny most of the time. Mountains act as a wind buffer. Cool summers; snowy, cold winters. Average January temperature, 17 degrees; July, 70. Average annual rainfall, 15 inches; snowfall, 105 inches.

Five Largest Employers: National Outdoor Leadership School, 650 employees; Wyoming State Training School, 475; Fremont County School District, 396; Lander Valley Medical Center, 260; Fremont County Courthouse, 217.

High School: Lander Valley High School enrolls 707 students in grades 9–12, graduates 78%, sends 48% to 4-year college, 22% to 2-year. Composite ACT for 40% of eligible students taking test, 23–24.

Housing: 3BR 2BA house costs between $85,000 and $295,000. Real estate is assessed at 9.5% of market value. Most people heat with natural gas and electricity.

Telecommunications: DSL not available.

Sales, Income Taxes: Retail sales tax, 4%. No state income tax.

Cost of Living: Movie ticket, $5; doctor appointment, routine, $28; plumber per hour, $40; baby-sitting per hour, $2.50 per child; dry cleaning, men's suit, $8–10; dinner for 4, local restaurant, $50–$80.

Community Infrastructure & Amenities:
Main Street
National Historic District
4-H
Bed-and-breakfast
Motion picture theater
Public library
Public parks: 11
Public swimming pool
Airport
Golf course, 18 holes
Emergency home shelter

Religious Denominations:

Anglican	Eastern Orthodox
Apostolic	Episcopal
Assemblies of God	Evangelical
Baptist	Four Square
Catholic	Lutheran
Christian	Lutheran (ELCA)
Church of Christ	Presbyterian
Church of Jesus Christ of	Quaker
Latter-Day Saints	Seventh Day Adventist
Church of the Nazarene	United Methodist
Community	

Newspaper: *Lander Journal*, 332 Main Street, Lander, WY 82520. 307-332-2323. Published twice a week. James Cocco, editor. 3-month subscription by mail, $16. *New York Times, USA Today, Casper Star Tribune, Riverton Ranger* also sold in town.

Annual Festivals and Events: February, International Pedigree Stage Stop Sled Dog Race; March, Wyoming State Winter Fair; Labor Day Weekend, Lander Jazz Festival; September, One Shot Antelope Hunt.

Further Information: Lander Chamber of Commerce, 160 N. First Street, Lander, WY 82520. 307-332-3892. 800-433-0662. landerchamber.org

Lebanon, NH 03766

Population: 12,768 (+5%)

Banks: 7, including 3 out-of-town banks.

Hospital: Dartmouth-Hitchcock Medical Center, 430 beds. Large population of physicians and other health care professionals in the area.

Location: 63 miles northeast of Concord, just east of the intersection of I-89 and I-91, on the Connecticut River boundary with Vermont.

Geography/Climate: Elevation 607 feet. Gently rolling to hilly river valley terrain. Invigorating continental climate. Long, snowy, sometimes very cold winters. Pleasant, sunny summers. Colorful falls. January temperature averages: low, 8; high, 30. July: low, 53; high, 81. Average annual rainfall, 45 inches; snowfall, 98 inches.

Five Largest Employers: Dartmouth-Hitchcock Medical Center, 4,366 employees; Timken Aerospace, 650; Thermal Dynamics, plasma welding and cutting equipment, 330; Lebanon School District, 315; City of Lebanon, 206.

High School: Lebanon High School enrolls 750 students in grades 9–12, graduates 97%, sends 75% to college/university. Composite SAT for 77% of eligible students taking test, 1034.

Housing: 3BR 2BA house in good condition sells for about $139,000, pays real estate tax of about $4,500. Most people heat with oil.

Telecommunications: Verizon provides DSL service. Adelphia provides broadband connection via cable.

Sales, Income Taxes: No retail sales tax, no state income tax in New Hampshire.

Cost of Living: Movie ticket, $7; doctor appointment, routine, $40; plumber per hour, $45; baby-sitting per hour, $10; dry cleaning, men's suit, $6; dinner for 4, local restaurant, $80.

Community Infrastructure & Amenities:
United Way
National Historic District
Bed-and-breakfast
Community recreational center
Motion picture theater
Public library
Public parks: 4, totaling 3,000 acres
Public swimming pool
Airport
Golf course, 9 holes
Emergency home shelter

Religious Denominations
Assemblies of God
Baptist
Catholic
Church of Jesus Christ of Latter-Day Saints
Congregational
Evangelical
Jehovah's Witnesses
Methodist
United Church of Christ
United Methodist
Synagogue in Hanover, 5 miles. Most other major denominations represented in nearby towns.

Newspaper: *Valley News.* 603-448-2711. Published daily. Gordon Frank, editor. 3-month subscription by mail, $38. *New York Times, Wall Street Journal, Manchester Union Leader* also sold in town.

Annual Festivals and Events: Home Life Show, Expo Trade Show. Various shows on the Green, downtown. Contact the Chamber for details.

Further Information: Greater Lebanon Chamber of Commerce, P.O. Box 97, Lebanon, NH 03766. 603-448-1203. lebanonchamber@lebanonchamber.com

Littleton, NH 03561

Population: 6,144 (+1%)
Banks: 8 banks in town, including 6 locally owned.
Hospital: Littleton Regional Hospital, 40 beds.

Location: On Interstate 93, halfway between Boston and Montreal, across the river 10 miles from St. Johnsbury, Vermont, in northern New Hampshire.

Geography/Climate: Rolling Connecticut River valley, nestled against the White Mountains at elevation 822 feet. 24 miles west of 6,288-foot Mount Washington, highest point in New Hampshire. Vigorous Northern New England climate with cold, snowy winters, though somewhat protected from nor'easters by the mountains. Average 53 inches of snow, 160 freezing days, 20 zero days. January lows average 8 degrees; highs, 26. Pleasant summers, low humidity. July lows, 60; highs, 82, but with 6 days at 90 or above. Average rainfall, 33 inches.

Five Largest Employers: Littleton Regional Hospital, 380 employees; Littleton Coin Company, collectibles, 325; Burndy Corporation, electrical connectors, 260; Supervisory Union No. 35 (Littleton), 141; Montgomery Wire, 110.

High School: Littleton High School enrolls 300 students in grades 9–12, graduates 85%+, sends 75% of graduates to college. Composite SAT for 75% of eligible students taking test, 519 verbal; math 520.

Housing: 3BR 2BA house sells in the range of $140,000 to $160,000, pays annual real-estate tax of $2,200. Most households heat with oil.

Telecommunications: Verizon provides DSL service. Adelphia provides broadband connection by cable.

Sales, Income Taxes: None.

Cost of Living: Movie ticket, $6; doctor appointment, routine, $45; plumber per hour, $40; baby-sitting per hour, $5; dry cleaning, men's suit, $7; dinner for 4, local restaurant, $52.

Community Infrastructure & Amenities:
United Way
Main Street
National Historic District
YMCA/YWCA
4-H
Bed-and-breakfast
Community recreational center
Motion picture theater
Public library
Public parks: 4, totaling 50 acres
Public swimming pool
Airport
Country club
Golf course
Emergency home shelter

Religious Denominations:
Assemblies of God
Baha'i
Baptist
Bible Christian
Catholic
Christian Science
Congregational
Episcopal
Evangelical
United Church of Christ
United Methodist

Newspaper: *The Courier*, 365 Union Street, Littleton, NH 03561. 603-444-3927. courier-littletonnh.com. Published weekly; Tim McCarthy, editor. 3-month subscription by mail, $14.50. *New York Times*, *Wall Street Journal*, state daily newspapers also sold in town.

Annual Festivals and Events: June, Trout Tournament; last Saturday September, Art Show; Thanksgiving Weekend, Christmas Parade & Craft Show.

Further Information: Littleton Area Chamber of Commerce, 120 Main Street, Littleton, NH 03561. (603) 444-0898. chamber@ncia.net, townoflittletonnh.org

Marshall, MN 56258

Population: 12,735 (+3.75%)
Banks: 8, including 6 branches.
Hospital: Weiner Memorial Medical Center, 49 beds.

Location: 150 miles southwest of Minneapolis, 88 miles northeast of Sioux Falls, South Dakota, in southwestern Minnesota.

Geography/Climate: Flat to gently rolling terrain. Demanding weather, with winter and summer extremes. January average low temperatures several degrees below zero. Seasonal snowfall, 35 inches, Without snow cover, frost penetrates 3 to 4 feet. Short but pleasant spring arrives mid-April. Torrid midsummers with 19 days into the 90s. Frequent thunderstorms, occasional tornadoes. Lovely falls. Average rainfall, 25 inches. Windy.

Five Largest Employers: Schwan's Sales Enterprises, 2,500 employees; Heartland Foods (turkeys), 500; HyVee Foods, 400; US Bancorp, 400; Weiner Memorial Medical Center, 385. Marshall is home of Southwest State University and the seat of Lyon County.

High School: Marshall High School enrolls 923 students in grades 9–12, graduates 99%, sends 69% to college/university. Composite ACT score for 49% of students in grades 11-12 taking test, 22.6.

Housing: 3BR 2BA house in good condition, $100,000–$125,000. Taxes, $1,200–$2,200. Town draws its water suppy from 12 wells within a 6-mile radius. Most households heat with electricity.

Telecommunications: Qwest Communications, Mcleod USA serve the area. DSL and T1 service available; also cable connection to Internet.

Sales, Income Taxes: 6.5% retail sales tax, food and clothing exempt. State income tax, scaled 5.35% to 7.85%.

Cost of living: Movie ticket, $6; doctor appointment, routine, $56; plumber per hour, $60; baby sitting, per hour, $3; dry cleaning, men's suit, $7.70; dinner for 4, local restaurant, $80.

Community Infrastructure & Amenities:
United Way
Community leadership training program
YMCA/YWCA
4-H
Bed-and-breakfast
Movie theater
Public library
Public swimming pool
Airport
Country club
Emergency home shelter

Religious Denominations:
Assemblies of God
Baptist
Catholic
Church of Christ
Church of Jesus Christ of Latter-Day Saints
Community
Episcopal
Evangelical
Full Gospel
Jehovah's Witnesses
Lutheran
Lutheran (ELCA)
Lutheran (Missouri)
Methodist
Presbyterian
United Methodist
Wesleyan

Newspaper: *Marshall Independent*, 507-537-1551. marshallindependent.com. Published 6 days a week. 3-month subscription by mail, $27. Russ Labat, editor. *Minneapolis Tribune* also sold in town.

Annual Festivals and Events: International Rolle Bolle Tournaments, Lyon County Duck Dayz, Festival of Kites, Pursuit of Excellence Marching Band Competition. Call for dates: 507-532-4484.

Further Information: Marshall Area Chamber of Commerce, P.O. Box 352B, Marshall, MN 56258. 507-532-4484. chamber@starpoint.net

Moses Lake, WA 98837

Population: 14,953 (+33%)
Banks: 12 banks, including 2 locally owned.
Hospital: Samaritan Healthcare, 50 beds.

Location: 176 miles east of Seattle, 109 miles west of Spokane, on Interstate 90 in east central Washington.

Geography/Climate: Flat, sagebrush desert where not irrigated, at 1,060-foot elevation. Average annual rainfall, 8 inches, peaking in fall; snowfall, 15 inches. January average temperature range: low, 19 degrees; high, 34. July low, 54 degrees; high, 87. Average 28 days below freezing; 28 days above 90. Can peak above 100. Low relative humidity. Rainless periods of a month to 6 weeks not uncommon in summer.

Five Largest Employers: Moses Lake School District, 629 employees; J.R. Simplot Company, 540; Basic American Foods/Sunspiced, potatoes, 370; Advanced Silicon Materials, 360; Inflation Systems, 320.

High School: Moses Lake High School enrolls about 2,000 students in grades 9–12, graduates 92%, sends 49% to college/university. Composite SAT for 58% of eligible students taking test, 1042. ACT, 22.8.

Housing: 3BR 2BA house sells for $95,000+. A house assessed at $100,000 pays $1,530 in real-estate tax. Most people heat with electricity.

Telecommunications: Grant County Public Utility District provides broadband connection at 100 Mbps.

Sales, Income Taxes: Retail sales tax, 7.8%, grocery food exempt. No state income tax.

Cost of Living: Movie ticket, $7.50; doctor appointment, routine, $62; plumber per hour, $50; baby-sitting per hour, $2.50–$6; dry cleaning, men's suit, $7; dinner for 4, local restaurant, $50.

Community Infrastructure & Amenities:
United Way
Community foundation (Assets $1.3 million)
Boys Club/Girls Club
4-H
Bed-and-breakfast
Motion picture theater
Public library
Public parks: 25, totaling 463 acres
Public swimming pool
Airport
Country club
Golf courses (2), 18 holes each
Emergency home shelter

Religious Denominations:

Assemblies of God	Friends
Baha'i	Interdenominational
Baptist	Jehovah's Witnesses
Catholic	Lutheran
Christian	Lutheran (ELCA)
Church of Christ	Lutheran (Missouri)
Church of God	Mennonite
Church of Jesus Christ of Latter-Day Saints	Methodist
Church of the Nazarene	Nondenominational
Community	Pentecostal
Disciples of Christ	Presbyterian USA
Episcopal	Seventh Day Adventist
Evangelical	United Methodist
Four Square	

Newspaper: *Columbia Basin Herald*, 813 W. Third Avenue, Moses Lake, WA 98837. 509-765-4561. Published Monday through Friday; Paul Burke, editor. 3-month subscription, $51.68. *New York Times, Wall Street Journal, Wenatchee World* also sold in town.

Annual Festivals and Events: Last weekend March, Spring Fair/Home Show and Junior Livestock Show; Memorial Day Weekend, Spring Festival; third week August, County Fair and Rodeo; mid-June through mid-October, Farmers Market and Craft Bazaar. Professional entertainment most Saturday evenings throughout the summer at McCosh Park Amphitheater.

Further Information: Moses Lake Area Chamber of Commerce, 324 S. Pioneer Way, Moses Lake, WA 98837. 509-765-7888. information@moses-lake.com

Natchitoches, LA 71457

Population: 17,865 (+2.5%)

Banks: 6, including two locally owned.

Hospital: Natchitoches Parish Hospital (affiliated with Christus Shumpert): 78 acute-care beds, 112 long-term care beds.

Location: 282 miles northwest of New Orleans, 73 miles southeast of Shreveport, in the Red River Valley of northwestern Louisiana.

Geography/Climate: "Two features characterize the climate throughout the Gulf South: high humidity and a brief but perfect spring and fall," writes Stanley Dry in *Gulf South: Louisiana*. April and May are pleasant. Summers are hot and humid, relieved only by frequent thunderstorms. The long fall season, from late September into early December, promotes outdoor activity. January temperatures range from 35 low to 57 high; July, 72 low to 94 high. Average 36 days at freezing or below; 90 days at 90 or above.

Five Largest Employers: Northwestern State University of Louisiana employs 2,953 people; Con Agra Poultry, 1,100; Natchitoches Parish School Board, 1,064; Alliance Compressors, 700; Natchitoches Parish Hospital, 453.

Northwestern State University enrolls about 6,300 students and is ranked among fourth tier Regional Universities by *U.S. News & World Report*.

High School: Natchitoches Central High School enrolls 1,350 students in grades 9–12, graduates 97%, sends 80% to college/university. Composite ACT for 80% of eligible students taking test, 19.3 (2000-2001).

Housing: 3BR 2BA house sells in the range of $110,000 to $140,000, pays real-estate taxes in the range of $500 to $700. Most people heat with natural gas.

Telecommunications: Bell South provides DSL service. Cox Communications provides broadband Internet connection via cable.

Sales, Income Taxes: Retail sales tax, 8%. State income tax, scaled 2% to 6%.

Cost of Living: Movie ticket, $6; doctor appointment, routine, $52; plumber per hour, $50; baby-sitting per hour, $5; dry cleaning, men's suit, $9; dinner for 4, local restaurant, $30–$65.

Community Infrastructure & Amenities:

United Way	Motion picture theater
Community leadership training program	Public library
	Public parks
Main Street	Public swimming pool
National Historic District	Airport
Boys Club/Girls Club	Country club
4-H	Golf course, 18 holes
Bed-and-breakfast	
Community recreational center	

Religious Denominations:

AME	Full Gospel
Apostolic	Independent
Assemblies of God	Interdenominational
Baptist	Jehovah's Witnesses
Catholic	Lutheran (Missouri)
Church of Christ	Methodist
Church of God	Nondenominational
Church of Jesus Christ of Latter-Day Saints	Pentecostal
Church of the Nazarene	Presbyterian
Community	Seventh Day Adventist
Disciples of Christ	United Church of Christ
Episcopal	United Methodist
Evangelical	Wesleyan

Newspaper: *Natchitoches Times*, 904 Highway 1 South, Natchitoches, LA 71457. 318-352-3618. Published Tuesday through Saturday; Carolyn Roy, editor. 3-month subscription, $43.75. *Wall Street Journal*, *USA Today*; Dallas, Houston, and New Orleans dailies also sold in town.

Annual Festivals and Events: January, Creole Heritage; February, Mardi Gras; April, Jazz/R&B Festival; June, Melrose Arts and Crafts Festival; July, Celebration on the Cane; October, Tour of Historic Homes and Plantation; November–December Festival of Lights, Christmas Festival. Natchitoches is where the movie *Steel Magnolias* was filmed.

Further Information: Natchitoches Convention & Visitors Bureau, 781 Front Street, Natchitoches, LA 71457. 800-259-1714. est1714@natchitoches.net

Nauvoo, IL 62354

Population: 1,063 (–0.5%)
Banks: 1.
Hospital: Fort Madison Community Hospital (14 miles), 50 beds. There are a physician and nurse practitioner in town.

Location: 235 miles southwest of Chicago, 30 miles southwest of Burlington, Iowa, hidden in a bend of the Mississippi River in western Illinois.

Geography/Climate: Rolling prairie at elevation 580 feet. Continental climate with a wide range of temperatures during the year—intensely hot and humid stretches in summer and bitterly cold periods in winter. January averages from the teens to upper 20s; July, from 65 to 85. Average 129 days below freezing, 14 days at 90 or above. Annual rainfall, 34 inches; snowfall, 29 inches.

Five Largest Employers: ConAgra Nauvoo Blue Cheese Factory, 85 employees; Kraus Properties, 84; Nauvoo-Colusa School District, 64; Nauvoo Family Inn & Suites, 55; Nauvoo Restoration, 36.

High School: Nauvoo-Colusa High School enrolls 175 students in grades 9–12, graduates 93%. Sends 80% to college/university. Composite ACT for 100% of eligible students taking test, 20.9.

Housing: 3BR 2BA house in good condition, $90,000. Real estate tax on such a house, about $1,000. Town water supply comes from the Mississippi River. Most people heat with natural gas.

Telecommunications: Citizens Communications provides DSL service.

Sales, Income Taxes: Retail sales tax, 6.25%. State income tax, 3%.

Cost of Living: Doctor appointment, routine, $56; plumber per hour, $40; baby-sitting per hour, $2; dry cleaning, men's suit, $8.55; dinner for 4, local restaurant, $60.

Community Infrastructure & Amenities:
National Historic District
4-H
Bed-and-breakfast
Community recreational center
Public library
Public parks: 4, totaling 159 acres. Additional 536 acres privately owned but open to public.
Golf course, 18 holes
Food pantry

Religious Denominations:
Baptist
Catholic
Church of Jesus Christ of Latter-Day Saints
Community of Christ (Reorganized Church of Jesus Christ of Latter-Day Saints)
Lutheran (ELCA)
Presbyterian USA
Restoration Branch of the Church of Jesus Christ
United Methodist

Newspaper: *Nauvoo New Independent*, 1245 Mulholland Street, Nauvoo, IL 62354. 217-453-6771. beautifulnauvoo.com. Published weekly. Jane Langford, editor. 3-month subscription, $15.

Annual Festivals and Events: In the early 1840s, Nauvoo was a thriving town of 12,000 Mormons under the spiritual leadership of Joseph Smith. But within a few years, most of the residents continued west, eventually settling in Utah. Nauvoo remains a center of the Mormon faith, however. In the spring of 2002, the reconstructed temple of the Church of Jesus Christ of Latter-Day Saints opened once again. Saturday before Easter, Biennial Passion Play; last weekend July–first weekend August, City of Joseph Pageant; Labor Day Weekend, Grape Festival; first weekend December, Holiday Walk; second Saturday December, Christmas Dinner in Old Nauvoo.

Further Information: Nauvoo Visitors Bureau, P.O. Box 500, Nauvoo, IL 62354. 877-NAUVOO-1

Page, AZ 86040

Population: 6,809 (+3%)
Banks: 3, one of which is locally owned.
Hospital: Page Hospital, 27 acute care beds.

Location: 132 miles north of Flagstaff, 10 miles south of the Utah line, on a mesa above Glen Canyon Dam with a view of Lake Powell-Wahweap Bay.

Geography/Climate: Red rock, plateau country. Dry, high desert at 4,300 feet. Sunshine on 88% of days. Total annual precipitation, 6.28 inches. Daily average temperature, December–January: low, 30; high, 45; July: low, 70; high, 97.

Five Largest Employers: Lake Powell Marinas, 780 employees; Page Schools, 600–650; Yamamoto Bits, 600–650; Navajo Generating Station, 480–500; U.S. Department of the Interior, 400–500.

High School: Page High School enrolls 1,175 students in grades 10–12, graduates 93%, sends 35% to college/university. Composite ACT for 48% of eligible students taking test, 21.

Housing: 3BR 2BA house sells in the range of $150,000 to $175,000, pays $500 to $600 real estate tax. Most people heat with electricity or LP gas.

Telecommunications: Qwest provides Internet connection at maximum 56 Kbps.

Sales, Income Taxes: Retail sales tax, 8.4%. State income tax scaled 2.87% to 5.04%.

Cost of Living: Movie ticket, $6; doctor appointment, routine, $25; plumber per hour, $45; baby-sitting per hour, $4; dinner for 4, local restaurant, $50.

Community Infrastructure & Amenities:
United Way
Community foundation (Assets $50,000)
Main Street
4-H
Bed-and-breakfast
Motion picture theater
Public library
Public parks: 4, totaling 10 acres
Airport
Country club
Golf course, 36 holes
Emergency home shelter

Religious Denominations:
Assemblies of God
Baptist
Catholic
Church of Christ
Church of God
Church of Jesus Christ of Latter-Day Saints
Church of the Nazarene
Episcopal
Faith Bible
Friends
Jehovah's Witnesses
Lutheran
Methodist

Newspaper: *Lake Powell Chronicle*, 3 Elm Street Mall, Page, AZ 86040. 928-645-8888. lakepowellchronicle.com. Published weekly; Sue Shinneman, editor. 3-month subscription, $19. *New York Times, Wall Street Journal, Arizona Daily Sun, Arizona Republic* also sold in town.

Annual Festivals and Events: March, A Taste of Page; June, Cowboy Days & Indian Nights Pow Wow; September, Rodeo; December, Festival of Lights Boat Parade.

Further Information: Page Lake Powell Chamber of Commerce, 644 N. Navajo, Suite B, Page, AZ 86040. 928-645-2741. pagelakepowellchamber.org

Pierre, SD 57501

Population: 13,876 (+7.5%)
Banks: 5, including 3 locally owned.
Hospital: St. Mary's Healthcare Center, 86 acute-care beds, 23 subacute.

Location: Dead center South Dakota on the banks of the Missouri River, 32 miles north of I-90, 209 miles south of Bismarck, 395 miles southwest of Minneapolis, 523 miles northeast of Denver.

Geography/Climate: Rolling grasslands at midcontinent, subject to severe summers with stretches of 100-degree plus, subzero days in December, January. Average temperature in July, 91; January, 18. Spring can begin as early as March but also much later and can be brief. Lots of sunshine, rare fog. Pleasant fall leading into hunting season. Weather suitable for flying all but 10 or so days a year.

Five Largest Employers: State of South Dakota, 2,200 employees in the capital and departments; St. Mary's Healthcare Center, 470; Pierre School District, 350; federal government agencies, 240; Dakotamart, 150.

High School: T. F. Riggs High School enrolls 920 students in grades 9–12, graduates 98%, sends 67% to college/university. Composite ACT for 84% of eligible students taking test, 23.4.

Housing: 3BR 2BA house sells in the range of $85,000 to $100,000, pays about $1,500 in real-estate tax. Most people heat with natural gas.

Telecommunications: Qwest provides DSL service. Midcontinent Cable provides broadband connection by cable.

Sales, Income Taxes: Retail sales tax, 6%. No state income tax.

Cost of Living: Movie ticket, $8; doctor appointment, routine, $36; plumber per hour, $45; babysitting per hour, $2; dry cleaning, men's suit, $7.25; dinner for 4, local restaurant, $40.

Community Infrastructure & Amenities:
United Way
Community foundation (Assets $37 million)
Community leadership training program
Main Street
National Historic District
YMCA/YWCA
Boys Club/Girls Club
4-H
Bed-and-breakfast
Motion picture theater
Public library
Public parks: 8, totaling 286 acres
Public swimming pool
Airport
Golf course, 18 holes

Religious Denominations:

Assemblies of God	Jehovah's Witnesses
Baha'i	Lutheran
Baptist	Lutheran (ELCA)
Catholic	Lutheran (Missouri)
Charismatic	Methodist
Christian	Nondenominational
Church of Christ	Pentecostal
Church of Jesus Christ of	Presbyterian USA
Latter-Day Saints	Seventh Day Adventist
Church of the Nazarene	United Church of Christ
Community	Wesleyan
Episcopal	
Evangelical	

Newspaper: *Pierre Capital Journal*, 333 W. Dakota Avenue, Pierre, SD 57501-0878. 605-224-7301. capjournal.com. Published daily; Terry Hipple, editor. 3-month subscription, $32.50. *New York Times*, *Wall Street Journal*, *USA Today*; and Rapid City, Sioux Falls, and Aberdeen dailies also sold in town.

Annual Festivals and Events: January through February, State Legislative Session; August, Riverfest; November, Goosefest.

Further Information: Pierre Area Chamber of Commerce, 800 W. Dakota Avenue, Pierre, SD 57501. 800-962-2034. contact@pierrechamber.com

St. Albans, VT 05478

Population: 7,673 (+4.6%)
Banks: 6, including one branch bank.
Hospital: Northwestern Medical Center, 70 beds.

Location: Northwestern corner of Vermont, just off the eastern shore of Lake Champlain. 30 miles north of Burlington, 62 miles south of Montreal.

Geography/Climate: Vigorous New England weather marked by long, cold winters averaging in the low 20s; pleasant, comparatively short summers averaging in the 70s but with a few days up to 90; cool falls. 79 inches of snow, 33 inches of rain on average. Varied, scenic landscape of lakeshore, rolling farmland, hills.

Five Largest Employers: U.S. Immigration & Naturalization Service, 1,100 employees; Northwestern Medical Center, 366; Mylan Laboratories, pharmaceuticals, 300; Fonda Group, paper containers, 238; Bellows Free Academy (high school), 188.

High School: Bellows Free Academy enrolls 1,042 students in grades 9–12, sends 70% to college/university. Composite SAT for 61% of eligible students taking test, 953.

Housing: 3BR 2BA house sells for about $120,000 and pays about $1,800 in real-estate tax. Most people heat with natural gas.

Telecommunications: Verizon provides DSL service. Adelphia provides broadband Internet connection by cable.

Sales, Income Taxes: Retail sales tax, 5%. State income tax, 24% of federal tax liability.

Cost of Living: Movie ticket, $6; doctor appointment, routine, $57; plumber per hour, $40–$50; baby-sitting per hour, $3; dry cleaning, men's suit, $9.75; dinner for 4, local restaurant, $40.

Community Infrastructure & Amenities:
United Way
Main Street
4-H
Community recreational center
Motion picture theater
Public library
Public parks: 3, totaling 15 acres
Public swimming pool
Emergency home shelter

Religious Denominations:
Assemblies of God
Baptist
Catholic
Church of the Nazarene
Congregational
Episcopal
Jehovah's Witnesses
Presbyterian
United Methodist

Newspaper: *St. Albans Messenger*, 281 N. Main Street, St. Albans, VT 05478. 802-524-9771. samessenger.com. Published daily except Sunday; Emerson Lyn, editor. 3-month subscription, $39. *New York Times*, *Wall Street Journal*, *Boston Globe* also sold in town.

Annual Festivals and Events: Last weekend in April, Vermont Maple Festival; Sunday closest to July 4, Bay Day—The Great Race, triathlon; weekend before Thanksgiving, Pumpkin Lighting; third weekend in December, Christmas in the Park.

Further Information: St. Albans Area Chamber of Commerce, 2 N. Main Street, St. Albans, VT 05478. 802-524-2444. stalbanschamber.com

Saranac Lake, NY 12983

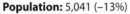

Population: 5,041 (−13%)
Banks: 5, including one locally owned.
Hospital: Adirondack Medical Center, 100 beds.

Location: 180 miles north of Albany, 50 miles southwest of Plattsburgh, 9 miles from Lake Placid, in Adirondack Park of northern New York State.

Geography/Climate: Elevation 1,600 feet, in mountainous, lake, and wooded terrain surrounded by the largest area of preserved wilderness east of the Mississippi River. Long, cold winters with average snowfall of 133 inches. Average temperatures: winter low, 5; high, 27; summer low, 50; high, 75. Average annual rainfall, 39 inches.

Largest Employers: Adirondack Medical Center, general hospital, 520 employees; Saranac Lake School District, 300; American Management Association logistical support center, 200; Trudeau Institute, medical research, 107.

High School: Saranac Lake High School enrolls 607 students in grades 9–12, graduates 99%, sends 80% to college/university. Composite SAT for 68% of eligible students taking test, 1067.

Housing: 3BR 2BA house sells for about $110,000, pays about $3,000 in real estate tax. Most people heat with oil.

Telecommunications: Verizon provides DSL service. Adelphia provides Internet connection via cable.

Sales, Income Taxes: Retail sales tax, 7%. State income tax scaled 4% to 6.85%.

Cost of Living: Doctor appointment, routine, $45; plumber per hour, $32; baby-sitting per hour, $3; dry cleaning, men's suit, $15; dinner for 4, local restaurant, $60.

Community Infrastructure & Amenities:
United Way
Community leadership training program
Main Street
National Historic District
4-H
Bed-and-breakfast
Community recreational center
Public library
Public parks: 15 parks, totaling 15 acres.
Public swimming pool
Airport
Golf course, 9 and 18 holes
Emergency home shelter

Religious Denominations:
Adirondack Alliance
Assemblies of God
Baptist
Catholic
Christian
Church of Jesus Christ of Latter-Day Saints
Church of the Nazarene
Episcopal
Jehovah's Witnesses
Lutheran
Methodist
Nondenominational
Pilgrim Holiness
Presbyterian
Seventh Day Adventist
United Church of Christ
United Methodist

Newspaper: *Adirondack Daily Enterprise*, 61 Broadway, Saranac Lake, NY 12983. 518-891-2600. Published daily except Sunday. Cathy Moore, editor. *New York Times, Wall Street Journal, Plattsburgh Press Republican* also sold in town.

Annual Festivals and Events: Two weeks in February, Winter Carnival; first full week August, Can-Am Rugby Tournament, 30-team tournament; first weekend after Labor Day, Adirondack Canoe Classic, 3-day race; September, Festival of the Lakes.

Further Information: Saranac Lake Area Chamber of Commerce, 30 Main Street, Saranac Lake, NY 12983. 518-891-1990. 800-347-1992. info@saranaclake.com

Scottsbluff, NE 69361

Population: 14,732 (+7.4%)
Banks: 6, including three locally owned.
Hospital: Regional West Medical Center, 279 beds.

Location: 452 miles west of Omaha, 200 miles northeast of Denver, 20 miles from the Wyoming border, in the Nebraska Panhandle.

Geography/Climate: High plains country at elevations surpassing 4,000 feet. Rocky Mountains to the west wring moisture out of weather systems from the Pacific Coast, giving Scottsbluff a sunny, dry climate much of the time. January average temperatures: low, 12; high, 38. July: low, 59; high, 90. Seasonally, 25 days below zero, 32 days above 90. Average annual precipitation, 15 inches; snowfall, 43 inches.

Five Largest Employers: Regional West Medical Center, 910 employees; Aurora Loan Services, 400; Sykes Intl., 400; Scottsbluff Public Schools, 370; Panhandle Coop, 300.

High School: Scottsbluff High School enrolls 963 students in grades 9–12, graduates 98%, sends 60% of graduates to college/university. Composite ACT for 69% of eligible students taking test, 21.7.

Housing: 3BR 2BA house costs about $85,000, pays about $1,500 in real-estate tax. Most people heat with natural gas.

Telecommunications: DSL available. Charter Communications provides broadband communication via cable.

Sales, Income Taxes: Retail sales tax, 6.5%. State income tax scaled 2.51% to 6.68%.

Cost of Living: Movie ticket, $6; doctor appointment, routine, $50; plumber per hour, $43; baby-sitting per hour, $3 (whole-day care, $16); dry cleaning, men's suit, $8; dinner for 4, local restaurant, $40.

Community Infrastructure & Amenities:

United Way
Community foundation
Community leadership training program
Main Street
National Historic District
YMCA/YWCA
4-H
Bed-and-breakfasts (3)
Community recreational center
Motion picture theater
Public library
Public parks, 17.
Public swimming pool
Airport
Country club
Golf course, 18 holes

Religious Denominations:

Assemblies of God
Baptist
Catholic
Christian
Church of Christ
Church of Jesus Christ of Latter-Day Saints
Church of the Nazarene
Disciples of Christ
Episcopal
Evangelical
Four Square
Independent
Interdenominational
Jehovah's Witnesses
Jewish Congregation
Lutheran
Lutheran (ELCA)
Lutheran (Missouri)
Methodist
Nondenominational
Pentecostal
Presbyterian
Seventh Day Adventist
Wesleyan

Newspaper: *Star Herald*, 1405 Broadway, Scottsbluff, NE 69363. 308-632-9000. starherald.com. Published daily; Joe Craig, editor. 3-month subscription, $35. *New York Times, Wall Street Journal, Denver Post/Rocky Mountain News, Omaha World Herald, USA Today* also sold in town.

Annual Festivals and Events: March–April, Spring Fling/Business Expo; Cinco de Mayo, events honoring Hispanic culture and heritage; June, West Nebraska All-Stars Football/Volleyball; first weekend June, Sugar Valley Rally, antique car rally sanctioned by GreatRace; second weekend July, Oregon Trail Days, honoring the pioneers.

Further Information: Scottsbluff/Gering United Chamber of Commerce, 1517 Broadway, Suite 104, Scottsbluff, NE 69361. 308-632-2133. scottsbluffgering.net

Seaford, DE 19973

Population: 6,699 (+18%)
Banks: 5, all branches of banks owned out of town.
Hospital: Nanticoke Memorial Hospital, 129 beds.

Location: 83 miles southeast of Baltimore, 200 miles southwest of New York City, 29 miles west of the Atlantic Ocean, on the Nanticoke River in central Delmarva Peninsula.

Geography/Climate: Flat coastal plain, 6 feet above sea level. Proximity to Chesapeake Bay and Atlantic Ocean protects the area from extreme variations of a continental climate. January averages: high, 41; low, 24. July averages: high, 85; low, 65. Average annual precipitation, 50 inches, including snowfall of 18 inches.

Five Largest Employers: DuPont nylon plant, 1,016 employees; Nanticoke Memorial Hospital, 930; Seaford School District, 480; Wal-Mart, 380; Methodist Manor House, 203.

High School: Seaford Senior High School enrolls 1,007 students in grades 9–12, graduates 90%, sends 71% to college/university and 5% to technical or trade school. Composite SAT I and II for 45% of eligible students taking test, 1188.

Housing: 3BR 2BA house sells for about $102,000, pays about $500 in real-estate tax. Most people heat with oil or electricity.

Telecommunications: Comcast provides broadband Internet connection via cable.

Sales, Income Taxes: No retail sales tax, State income tax scaled 2.2% to 5.95%.

Cost of Living: Movie ticket, $8; doctor appointment, routine, $65; plumber per hour, $45; baby-sitting per hour, $5; dry cleaning, men's suit, $7.75; dinner for 4, local restaurant, $45.

Community Infrastructure & Amenities:
United Way
Main Street
Boys Club/Girls Club
4-H
Bed-and-breakfast
Public library
Public parks
Public swimming pool
Country club
Golf course, 18 holes
Emergency home shelter

Religious Denominations:

Alliance	Jehovah's Witnesses
AME	Link Ministries
Baptist	Lutheran
Catholic	Maranatha
Christian	Nondenominational
Church of Christ	Pentecostal
Church of God	Presbyterian
Church of Jesus Christ of	Seventh Day Adventist
Latter-Day Saints	United Methodist
Church of the Nazarene	Wesleyan
Episcopal	
Full Gospel	

Newspaper: *Leader & State Register*, P.O. Box 1130, Seaford, DE 19973. 302-629-5505. newszap.com. Published weekly; Aaron Kellam, editorial coordinator. 3-month subscription, $8. *Seaford Star*, P.O. Box 1000, Seaford, DE 19973. 302-629-9788. seafordstar.com. Published weekly; Bryant Richardson, editor. 6-month subscription, $13.50. *New York Times*, *Wall Street Journal*, *USA Today*, regional dailies also sold in town.

Annual Festivals and Events: Nanticoke Riverfest, Southern Delaware Heritage Trail Bike Tour, Miss Seaford Pageant, Community Concert Series, Christmas Caroling in the Park. Call for dates.

Further Information: Greater Seaford Chamber of Commerce, P.O. Box 26, Seaford, DE 19973. 302-629-9690, 800-416-GSCC. www.seafordchamber.com

Somerset, KY 42502

Population: 11,352 (+0.5%)

Banks: 9, including two locally owned.

Hospital: Lake Cumberland Regional Hospital, 252 beds.

Location: 75 miles south of Lexington, 129 miles northwest of Knoxville, Tennessee, in south central Kentucky.

Geography/Climate: Rolling terrain, elevation 975 feet, on the Cumberland Plateau on the western edge of the Appalachian Mountains and the northeastern approach to Lake Cumberland, 8 miles south. Continental climate without the worst extremes. Weather averages: January temperatures, low 25, high 42; seasonal snowfall, 12 inches; 97 days at freezing or below, two subzero days. July temperatures, low 66, high 86; 16 days at 90 degrees or above. Precipitation, 47 inches. September, October generally dry, clear, and quite pleasant.

Five Largest Employers: Lake Cumberland Regional Hospital, 936 employees; Crane Company, plumbing fixtures, 325; Southern Belle Dairy, 275; Hartco Flooring 272; Ready-Mix Concrete, 225.

High School: Somerset High School enrolls 575 students in grades 9–12, graduates 90%+, sends about 74% to college/university. Composite ACT for 88% of eligible students taking test, 21.

Housing: 3BR 2BA house sells in a midrange of $92,000 to $98,000, pays about $990 in real estate tax. Most people heat with natural gas or electricity.

Telecommunications: Verizon offers DSL service. Charter Communications offers broadband connection to the Internet via cable.

Sales, Income Taxes: Retail sales tax, 6%, grocery food exempt. State income tax, scaled 2% to 6%.

Cost of Living: Movie ticket, $7; doctor appointment, routine, $40; plumber per hour, $25; baby-sitting-per hour, $5; dry cleaning, men's suit, $7; dinner for 4, local restaurant, $35.

Community Infrastructure & Amenities:

United Way	Motion picture theater
Community leadership training program	Public library
Main Street	Public parks
YMCA/YWCA	Public swimming pool
Boys Club/Girls Club	Airport
4-H	Country club
Bed-and-breakfast	Golf course, 18 holes
Community recreational center	Emergency home shelter

Religious Denominations:

AME	Disciples of Christ
Apostolic	Episcopal
Assemblies of God	Full Gospel
Baptist	Jehovah's Witnesses
Catholic	Lutheran
Christian	Lutheran (ELCA)
Church of Christ	Methodist
Church of God	Nondenominational
Church of Jesus Christ of Latter-Day Saints	Pentecostal
Church of the Nazarene	Presbyterian USA
	Seventh Day Adventist

Newspaper: *Commonwealth Journal*, P.O. Box 859, Somerset, KY 42502. 606-679-8191. somerset-kentucky.com. Published daily except Saturday; David Thornberry, editor. 3-month subscription by mail, $23.40. *Somerset-Pulaski News Journal*, P.O. Box 1565, Somerset, KY 42502. 606-678-0161. somerset@newsjournal.com. Published twice weekly; Stuart Arnold, editor. 6-month subscription, $18. *New York Times, Lexington Herald-Leader, Louisville Courier-Journal* also sold in town.

Annual Festivals and Events: September, Railroad Days; November, Antiques & Collectibles Show & Sale; every fourth Saturday, March to October, Mid-Summer Nites Cruise-In (antique car show).

Further Information: Somerset-Pulaski County Chamber of Commerce, 209 E. Mt. Vernon Street, Somerset, KY 42502. 606-679-7323. www.lakecumberland.org

Spearfish, SD 57783

Population: 12,125 (+14.7%)
Banks: 5, all branches of banks headquartered elsewhere.
Hospital: Lookout Memorial Hospital, 40 beds.

Location: 389 miles west of Sioux Falls, 375 miles northeast of Denver, 10 miles east of the Wyoming state line, in the High Plains of extreme west central South Dakota.

Geography/Climate: Situated between rolling prairie to the north and Black Hills National Forest to the south, a scenic drive to ski hills and Mt. Rushmore National Monument. Semiarid continental climate. January temperatures range from single-digits above zero to 32 degrees; July, from lower-60s to upper 80s. Annual average 169 days below freezing, 32 days above 90. Precipitation, 16 inches; snowfall, up to 45 inches.

Five Largest Employers: Banner Health Black Hills, 319 employees; Black Hills State University, 305; Spearfish School District, 254; Pope & Talbot, sawmill, 245; Wal-Mart, 196.

High School: Spearfish High School enrolls 758 students in grades 9–12, graduates 98%, sends 60% to college/university. Composite ACT for 78% of eligible students taking test, 21.1.

Housing: 3BR 2BA house sells for about $100,000. Real-estate taxes on such a house, $1,811. Most people heat with electricity.

Telecommunications: Qwest provides DSL service. Black Hills Fiber Com, MidContinent provide broadband Internet connection via cable.

Sales, Income Taxes: 7% retail sales tax. No state income tax.

Cost of Living: Movie ticket, $6.75; doctor appointment, routine, $50; plumber per hour, $45; baby-sitting per hour, $2; dry cleaning, men's suit, $7.50; dinner for 4, local restaurant, $60.

Community Infrastructure & Amenities:
Community foundation (Assets $500,000)
Community leadership training program
Main Street
National Historic District
4-H
Bed-and-breakfast
University/Community recreational center
Motion picture theater
Public library
Public parks: 9, totaling 84 acres
Airport
Country club
Golf course, 18 holes
Emergency home shelter

Religious Denominations:

Assemblies of God	Lutheran (ELCA)
Baptist	Lutheran (Missouri)
Catholic	Nondenominational
Church of Christ	Presbyterian
Church of the Nazarene	Seventh Day Adventist
Community	United Church of Christ
Episcopal	United Methodist
Independent	Wesleyan
Jehovah's Witnesses	
Lutheran	

Newspaper: *Black Hills Pioneer*, 315 Seaton Circle, Spearfish, SD 57783. 605-642-2761. bhpioneer.com. Published daily; Stewart Huntington, editor. 3-month subscription, $25.80.

Annual Festivals and Events: Third full weekend in July, Festival in the Park, arts and crafts; Last full weekend in September, HarvestFest, arts and crafts.

Further Information: Spearfish Area Chamber of Commerce, 106 W. Kansas, Spearfish, SD 57783. 605-642-2626. spearfish.sd.us

Spencer, IA 51301

Population: 11,317 (+2%)
Banks: 6, including 3 branch banks.
Hospital: Spencer Municipal Hospital, 99 beds.

Location: 188 miles northwest of Des Moines, 103 miles northeast of Sioux City, in rolling farmlands of northwestern Iowa.

Geography/Climate: Continental climate influenced by the interaction of large-scale weather systems moving across the northern plains. Cold winters, warm summers; normally ample rain, averaging 26 inches. Snowfall, 32 inches. January daily temperatures range from single digits above zero to upper 20s; July, mid-60s to mid-80s, with as many as 24 days at 90 degrees or above. Average annual humidity, 72%.

Five Largest Employers: Eaton Corporation, truck components, 500 employees; Spencer Municipal Hospital, 425; Iowa Lakes Community College, 240; Perry-Judd's Heartland Division, printer, 200; Maurer Manufacturing, farm equipment, 95.

High School: Spencer High School enrolls 734 students in grades 9–12, graduates 99%, sends about 50% of graduates to college/university. Composite ACT for 90% of eligible students taking test, 20–21.

Housing: 3BR 2BA house sells in the range of $50,000 to $100,000. Median real estate tax on that range, $900. Most people heat with natural gas.

Telecommunications: Spencer Municipal Utilities provides broadband cable connection to the Internet.

Sales, Income Taxes: Retail sales tax, 6%. State income tax scaled 0.36% to 8.98%.

Cost of Living: Movie ticket, $6; doctor appointment, routine, $40; plumber per hour, $100; baby-sitting per hour, $3; dry cleaning, men's suit, $15; dinner for 4, local restaurant, $25.

Community Infrastructure & Amenities:
United Way
Main Street
YMCA/YWCA
4-H
Bed-and-breakfast
Motion picture theater
Public library
Public parks: 5 parks, totaling 400 acres
Public swimming pool
Airport
Country club
Golf course, 18 holes
Emergency home shelter

Religious Denominations:
Assemblies of God
Baptist
Catholic
Church of Christ
Church of Jesus Christ of Latter-Day Saints
Church of the Nazarene
Disciples of Christ
Evangelical
Jehovah's Witnesses
Lutheran (ELCA)
Lutheran (Missouri)
Seventh Day Adventist
United Methodist
Wesleyan

Newspaper: *Spencer Daily Reporter*, 310 E. Milwaukee, Spencer, IA 51301. 712-262-6610. dailyreporter.com. Published Tuesday through Saturday; Ben Montgomery, editor. 6-month subscription, $35.

Annual Festivals and Events: February, Bridal Show; March, Home/Health Show; May, Beef Event & Country Street Dance; June, Flagfest; July, Farm/City Mixer; September, "World's Greatest County Fair"; October, Scarecrow Contest & Moonlight Madness; early December, Grand Meander & Tuba Christmas.

Further Information: Spencer Chamber of Commerce, 122 W. Fifth Street, Spencer, IA 51301. 712-262-5680. spencerchamber@smunet.net

Tifton, GA 31793

Population: 15,060 (+6%)
Banks: 7, including one locally owned.
Hospital: Tift Regional Medical Center, 191 beds.

Location: 180 miles southeast of Atlanta, 233 miles northwest of Orlando, on the I-75 expressway to Florida.

Geography/Climate: Flat to gently rolling coastal plains of south central Georgia accented by long-leaf pine, magnolia, live oak trees. Mild winters with only 10–12 nights low as 30 degrees. January averages: high, 60; low, 40. July averages: high, 90; low, 70. Average annual rainfall, 47 inches.

Five Largest Employers: Target Distribution Center, Tift County Board of Education, Tift Regional Medical Center, all employing 1,000+ people; Shaw Industries, 831; Tifton Aluminum, 490.

High School: Tift County High School enrolls 1,342 students in grades 10–12; graduates 79%; sends 25% of graduates to 4-year college, 34% to 2-year, 22% to technical school. Composite SAT for 65% of eligible students taking test, 975.

Housing: 3BR 2BA house sells from high $80s to low $100s. Most people heat with electricity.

Telecommunications: BellSouth provides DSL service.

Sales, Income Taxes: Retail sales tax, 7%. State income tax, scaled 1% to 6%.

Cost of Living: Movie ticket, $5; doctor appointment, routine, $50; plumber per hour, $60; baby-sitting per hour, $5; dry cleaning, men's suit, $5.50; dinner for 4, local restaurant, $25.

Community Infrastructure & Amenities:
United Way
Community leadership training program
Main Street
YMCA/YWCA
4-H
Bed-and-breakfast
Community recreational center
Motion picture theater
Public library
Public parks: 9, totaling 24 acres
Public swimming pool
Airport
Country club
Golf course, 18 holes
Emergency home shelter

Religious Denominations:

Apostolic	Full Gospel
Assemblies of God	Interdenominational
Baptist	Jehovah's Witnesses
Catholic	Lutheran
Charismatic	Methodist
Christian	Nondenominational
Church of Christ	Pentecostal
Church of God	Presbyterian
Church of Jesus Christ of	Seventh Day Adventist
Latter-Day Saints	United Methodist
Church of the Nazarene	
Episcopal	

Newspaper: *Tifton Gazette*, 211 N. Tift Avenue, Tifton, GA 31794. 229-382-4321. sgaonline.com. Published daily except Monday; Frank Sayles, editor. 3-month subscription, $26.90. *Wall Street Journal, Atlanta Constitution* also sold in town.

Annual Festivals and Events: First weekend in May, The Love Affair—Fine Arts Festival; late September, LaFiesta del Pueblo, Hispanic festival; first Saturday in December, Hometown Holiday Celebration.

Further Information: Tifton-Tift County Chamber of Commerce, P.O. Box 165, Tifton, GA 31793. 229-382-6200. tiftonchamber.org

Ukiah, CA 95482

Population: 15,497 (+3%)
Banks: 19, including 8 branch banks.
Hospital: Ukiah Valley Medical Center, 111 beds.

Location: 120 miles north of San Francisco, 30 miles inland from the Pacific Ocean, on U.S. 101.

Geography/Climate: Fertile, deep valley of the Russian River within the Coast Ranges, surrounded by vineyards, orchards, and oaks on the foothills. Rainfall averages 45 inches, mainly in the December-February period. Winter temperatures seldom below mid-20s. Hot, dry summer days into the mid-90s, cooled by afternoon sea breeze to the 60s–70s.

Five Largest Employers: County of Mendocino, 1,308 employees; Ukiah Unified School District, 809; Ukiah Valley Medical Center, 570; Fetzer Vineyards, 500; Mendocino College, 500.

High School: Ukiah High School enrolls 2,050 students in grades 9–12, graduates 98%, sends 76% to college/university. Composite SAT, 1123.

Housing: 3BR 2BA house sells for about $200,000, pays about $2,000 in real-estate taxes. Most people heat with natural gas.

Telecommunications: Pacific Bell provides DSL service.

Sales, Income Taxes: Retail sales tax, 7%. State income tax scaled 1% to 9.3%.

Cost of Living: Movie ticket, $7; doctor appointment, routine, $30; plumber per hour, $66; baby-sitting per hour, $2.50; dry cleaning, men's suit, $7; dinner for 4, local restaurant, $60.

Community Infrastructure & Amenities:
United Way
Community foundation
Community leadership training program
Main Street
Boys Club/Girls Club
4-H
Bed-and-breakfast
Community recreational center
Motion picture theater
Public library
Public parks: 5
Public swimming pool
Airport
Golf course, 18 holes
Emergency home shelter (winter only)

Religious Denominations:
Assemblies of God
Baptist
Catholic
Christian
Church of Christ
Church of Jesus Christ of Latter-Day Saints
Church of the Nazarene
Episcopal
Evangelical
Jehovah's Witnesses
Lutheran
Lutheran (Missouri)
Methodist
Pentecostal
Presbyterian
Seventh Day Adventist
United Methodist

Newspaper: *Ukiah Daily Journal*, 590 S. School Street, Ukiah, CA 95482. 707-468-3500. ukiahdailyjournal.com. Published daily except Saturday; Kevin McConnell, editor. 3-month subscription, $30. *New York Times, Wall Street Journal, San Francisco Chronicle, Santa Rosa Press Democrat* also sold in town.

Annual Festivals and Events: Taste of Downtown, Cinco de Mayo, Comedy Alley, Fabulous Flashback Car Show, Hometown Christmas, Sundays in the Park (concerts), Tuesday Night Market, Farmers' Market. Check the Web site for dates and times.

Further Information: City of Ukiah, 300 Seminary Avenue, Ukiah, CA 95482. 707-463-6200. www.cityofukiah.com

Valentine, NE 69201

Population: 2,820 (–0.3%)
Banks: 4, including 3 branch banks.
Hospital: Cherry County Hospital, 38 beds.

Location: 298 miles northwest of Omaha, 131 miles north of North Platte, 9 miles south of the South Dakota state line, by the Sandhills of far north central Nebraska.

Geography/Climate: Demanding midcontinental climate, with subzero winters and near-100-degree summers. Cold air masses from Canada move in rapidly, often dropping temperatures 20 to 30 degrees in fall and winter. One or two heavy snowstorms likely with as many as 30 days below zero. Rainfall averages 24 inches a year; thunderstorms common during June and July. Seasonally, 29 days at 90 degrees or above.

Largest Employers: City of Valentine, 150 employees; Henderson's IGA, grocery store, 125; Alco Discount Store, 50; Texaco Travel Center, 30.

High School: Valentine Rural High School enrolls 270 students in grades 9-12, graduates 99%, sends 30% of graduates to college/university. Composite ACT for 50% of eligible students taking test, 22.1.

Housing: 3BR 2BA house sells for $85,000 to $90,000, pays about $1,400 in real estate tax. Most people heat with electricity.

Telecommunications: Qwest provides digital connection at 56 Kbps.

Sales, Income Taxes: Retail sales tax, 5%, but does not apply to grocery food. State income tax, 2.51% to 6.68%.

Cost of Living: Movie ticket, $6; doctor appointment, routine, $60; plumber per hour, $30–$60; baby-sitting per hour, $2.25; dry cleaning, men's suit, $7.75; dinner for 4, local restaurant, $30–$65.

Community Infrastructure & Amenities:
Community foundation (Sandhills Area Foundation)
Main Street
4-H
Bed-and-breakfast
Motion picture theater
Public library
Public parks: 2
Public swimming pool
Airport
Golf course, 9 holes

Religious Denominations:
Assemblies of God
Baptist
Berean
Catholic
Church of Jesus Christ of Latter-Day Saints
Episcopal
Evangelical
Lutheran
Lutheran (ELCA)
Lutheran (Missouri)
Methodist
Presbyterian USA
Seventh Day Adventist
United Methodist

Newspaper: *Midland News*, 146 W. 2nd Street, Valentine, NE 69201. 402-376-2833. Published weekly, Laura Eastman, editor. 1-year subscription by mail, $30. *New York Times*, *Wall Street Journal*, *Omaha World Herald* also sold in town.

Annual Festivals and Events: Ice Fishing Tournament; Valentine's Day, Valentine Coronation & Masquerade Ball; Nebraska High School Rodeo Finals; Cattlemen's Ball; Cherry County Fair & Rodeo; Bison Roundup-Fort Niobrara; 1st weekend October, Old West Days and Nebraska Cowboy Poetry Gathering; Pumpkin Patch Craft Show. Call Chamber for dates.

Further Information: Valentine Chamber of Commerce, P.O. Box 201, Valentine, NE 69201. 402-376-2969, 800-658-4024. www.heartcity.com

Vernal, UT 84078

Population: 7,714 (+16%)
Banks: 4, including one locally owned.
Hospital: Ashley Valley Medical Center, 39 beds.

Location: 171 miles east of Salt Lake City, 320 miles west of Denver, on the central portion of the Outlaw Trail, in northeastern Utah.

Geography/Climate: Semi-arid high country, elevation 5,331 feet, ringed by Diamond Mountain, Blue Mountain, Green River Gorge. Wide seasonal changes in weather tempered by mountain ranges. Annual rainfall, 8 inches; snowfall, 25 inches. January high temperatures average 31; low, 5. July high, 90; low, 50. Low humidity, sunny.

Five Largest Employers: Uintah School District, 900 employees; Ute Indian Tribe, tribal government, 500; Wal-Mart, 400; Uintah County, 280; Ashley Valley Medical Center, 200.

High School: Uintah High School enrolls 1,325 students in grades 10–12, sends about 30% of graduates to college/university.

Housing: 3BR 2BA house sells in a midrange of $81,500 to $95,000. Real estate tax on such a house, $350. Most people heat with natural gas.

Telecommunications: DSL service available.

Sales, Income Taxes: Retail sales tax, 6.75%. State income tax, 2.3% to 7%.

Cost of Living: Movie ticket, $6; doctor appointment, routine, $40; plumber per hour, $60; baby-sitting per hour, $2.50; dry cleaning, men's suit, $10; dinner for 4, local restaurant, $40.

Community Infrastructure & Amenities:
Main Street
4-H
Bed-and-breakfast
Motion picture theater
Public library
Public parks: 5
Public swimming pool
Airport
Country club
Golf course, 18 holes

Religious Denominations:
Assemblies of God
Baptist
Catholic
Christian
Church of Christ
Church of God
Church of Jesus Christ of Latter-Day Saints
Community
Episcopal
Independent
Jehovah's Witnesses
Lutheran (Missouri)
Nondenominational
Seventh Day Adventist
United Church of Christ

Newspaper: *Vernal Express*, 54 N. Vernal Avenue, Vernal, UT 84078. 435-789-3555. vernal.com. Published weekly; Steve Wallis, editor. 3-month subscription, $11.50. *Salt Lake Tribune, Deseret News, Denver Post, USA Today* also sold in town.

Annual Festivals and Events: February, Water Conference; March, Health Fair; July, Dinosaur Roundup Rodeo; September, Business Symposium; November, Trees for Charity; December, Lighting of Dinosaur Gardens.

Further Information: Vernal Area Chamber of Commerce, 134 W. Main, Vernal, UT 84078. 435-789-1352. vchamber@easilink.com, vernalcity.org

Wahpeton, ND 58075

Population: 8,586 (–6%)
Banks: 8, including one locally owned.
Hospital: St. Francis Medical Center, 47 beds.

Location: 200 miles northwest of Minneapolis-St. Paul, 270 miles south of Winnipeg, 50 miles south of Fargo, in extreme southeastern North Dakota.

Geography/Climate: Origin of the Red River, the largest north-flowing river in the United States, part of the Hudson Bay drainage area. Fertile river valley surrounded by flat, open terrain. Rugged winters. Dakota winters turn unremarkable 36-inch average annual snowfall into mountainous snow-drifts. January temperatures average 14 degrees high, 5-below low, with plunges to 25 below zero. Pleasant, dry summers: July highs average 83, with a few days into the mid-90s; lows average 58. Average rainfall, 21 inches.

Five Largest Employers: Imation, video cassettes, floppy disks, 664 employees; Primewood, Inc., particleboard cabinets, agricultural belting, 490; North Dakota State College of Science, 327; Minn-Dak Farmers Cooperative, 243; Cargill, Inc., 145.

High School: Wahpeton Senior High School enrolls 558 students in grades 9–12, graduates 99%, sends 90% of graduates to college/university. Composite ACT for 80% of students taking test, 22.6.

Housing: 3BR 2BA house sells in the range of $50,800 to $99,200. Median real estate tax for a house that price, $1,700. Most people heat with natural gas.

Telecommunications: Qwest and 702 Communications provide DSL service.

Sales, Income Taxes: Retail sales tax, 6.5%. State income tax, 14% of federal tax.

Cost of Living: Movie ticket, $6; doctor appointment, routine, $58; plumber per hour, $47; baby-sitting per hour, $1.80; dry cleaning, men's suit, $6.25; dinner for 4, local restaurant, $40–$50.

Community Infrastructure & Amenities:
United Way
Boys Club/Girls Club
4-H
Motion picture theater
Public library
Public parks: 6, totaling 132 acres
Public swimming pool
Airport
Country club
Golf course, 18 holes

Religious Denominations:
Assemblies of God
Baptist
Catholic
Christian
Church of God
Church of Jesus Christ of Latter-Day Saints
Episcopal
Jehovah's Witnesses
Lutheran
Lutheran (ELCA)
Lutheran (Missouri)
Methodist
Pentecostal
Seventh Day Adventist
United Church of Christ
United Methodist

Newspaper: *Daily News*, P.O. Box 760, Wahpeton, ND 58074. 701-642-8585. wahpetondailynews.com. Published daily except Saturday and Monday; Jim Hornbeck, editor. 3-month subscription, $30. *Fargo Forum*, *Minneapolis Star-Tribune*, *USA Today* also sold in town.

Annual Festivals and Events: Carousel Days, Crazy Dakota Daze, Employer/Employee Community Picnic, Business After Hours. Check Web site for dates and times.

Further Information: Economic Development Department, 1900 N. 4th Street, Wahpeton, ND 58075. 701-642-8559. wahpeton.com

Washington, IA 52353

Population: 7,047 (–0.4%)

Banks: 4, including three locally owned.

Hospital: Washington County Hospital & Clinics, 40 beds.

Location: 110 miles southeast of Des Moines, 235 miles west of Chicago, in southeastern Iowa.

Geography/Climate: Rolling agricultural prairie. Continental climate with severely cold winters and hot, humid summers. Averages: days freezing or below, 136; zero or below, 16; 90 or above, 22; snowfall, 30 inches; rainfall, 36 inches; thunderstorm days, 47. Sunny days, 100; partly sunny, 100.

Five Largest Employers: Washington Community School District, 300 employees; Norwood, printer, 293; Washington County Hospital & Clinics, 250; Modine Manufacturing, heat-transfer products, 190; Fansteel Washington, wire forms and fasteners, 190.

High School: Washington High School enrolls 395 students in grades 10–12, graduates 97%, sends 90% to college/university. Composite ACT for 75% of eligible students taking test, 21.6.

Housing: 3BR 2BA house sells in the range of $80,000 to $120,000. Real-estate taxes for that range, $1,500 to $2,500. Most people heat with natural gas.

Telecommunications: Iowa Telecom provides DSL service.

Sales, Income Taxes: Retail sales tax, 5%, grocery food exempt. State income tax, scaled 0.36% to 8.98%.

Cost of Living: Movie ticket, $5; doctor appointment, routine, $42; plumber per hour, $36; baby-sitting per hour, $2.50–$3; dry cleaning, men's suit, $9.50; dinner for 4, local restaurant, $42.

Community Infrastructure & Amenities:
Community foundation (Assets $100,000)
Community leadership training program
YMCA/YWCA
4-H
Bed-and-breakfast
Motion picture theater
Public library
Public parks: 5, totaling 70 acres
Public swimming pool
Airport
Country club
Golf course, 9 holes
Emergency home shelter

Religious Denominations:
Assemblies of God
Baptist
Catholic
Christian
Church of Christ
Church of God
Church of Jesus Christ of Latter-Day Saints
Church of the Nazarene
Disciples of Christ
Jehovah's Witnesses
Lutheran (ELCA)
Mennonite
Methodist
Presbyterian USA
Seventh Day Adventist
United Methodist

Newspaper: *Washington Evening Journal*, 111 N. Marion Avenue, Washington, IA 52353. 319-653-2191. news@washjrnl.com. Published Monday through Friday; Darwin Sherman, editor. 3-month subscription, $25.75. *New York Times, Wall Street Journal, USA Today, Des Moines Register* also sold in town.

Annual Festivals and Events: First week in May, Gallery Walk, local and regional artists; first Sunday in June, Flight Breakfast, fly-in breakfast and plane show; second Sunday in June, Central Park Car & Truck Show; third week of July, Washington County Fair; first Saturday after Labor Day, Craft Festival; first full weekend in December, Candlelight Tour of Homes.

Further Information: Washington Chamber of Commerce, 212 N. Iowa Avenue, Washington, IA 52353. 319-653-3272. washcofc@lisco.com

West Plains, MO 65775

Population: 10,866 (+18%)
Banks: 8, including 5 branches of banks owned elsewhere.
Hospital: Ozarks Medical Center, 98 beds.

Location: 201 miles southwest of St. Louis, 280 miles southeast of Kansas City, 15 miles north of the Arkansas state line, in south central Missouri.

Geography/Climate: Ozark country. Rugged, low landscape of hardwood forests and spring-fed streams. Mild climate, relatively free of extremes. January lows average 32; highs, 44. Occasional ice, sleet. 8 inches of snow in December–March period. Total annual precipitation, 43 inches. July low temperatures average 78; highs, 90.

Five Largest Employers: Ozarks Medical Center, 1,046 employees; Marathon Electric, fractional horsepower electric motors, 599; Systems & Electronics, Inc., 560; Bruce Hardwood Floors, 430; West Plains R-7 Schools, 389.

High School: West Plains High School enrolls 1,237 students in grades 9–12, graduates 95%, sends 54% to college/university. Composite ACT for 56% of eligible students taking test, 21.2.

Housing: 3BR 2BA house sells in the range of $55,000 to $75,000, pays $350 to $450 in real-estate tax.

Telecommunications: Verizon provides Internet connection at 56 Kbps.

Sales, Income Taxes: Retail sales tax, 6.475%. State income tax, scaled 1.5% to 6%.

Cost of Living: Movie ticket, $5.50; doctor appointment, routine, $35; plumber per hour, $30; baby-sitting per hour, $5 (weekly, $75 to $95); dry cleaning, men's suit, $7.40; dinner for 4, local restaurant, $40.

Community Infrastructure & Amenities:
United Way
Community foundation
Main Street
4-H
Bed-and-breakfast
Community recreational center
Motion picture theater
Public library
Public parks: 14, totaling 180 acres
Public swimming pool
Airport
Country club
Golf course, 18 holes
Emergency home shelter

Religious Denominations:
Assemblies of God
Baptist
Catholic
Christian
Church of Christ
Church of God
Church of Jesus Christ of Latter-Day Saints
Episcopal
Jehovah's Witnesses
Methodist
Pentecostal

Newspaper: *West Plains Daily Quill*, P.O. Box 110, West Plains, MO 65775. 417-256-9191. westplainsquill.com. Published daily, Frank L. Martin III, editor. 3-month subscription, $11.71. *Wall Street Journal*, *USA Today*, *Springfield News-Leader* also sold in town.

Annual Festivals and Events: Memorial Day Weekend, Show-Me 100, late-model stock car races; last weekend in June, Skyfire, 4th of July fireworks; June, HOBA Bluegrass Festival; August, Howell County Fair; November, Christmas Parade.

Further Information: Greater West Plains Area Chamber of Commerce, 401 Jefferson Avenue, West Plains, MO 65775. 417-256-4433. info@w.p.chamber.com

Yreka, CA 96097

Population: 7,290 (+5%)

Banks: 7, including 4 branches of banks headquartered elsewhere.

Hospital: Fairchild Medical Center, 30 beds.

Location: 291 miles north of San Francisco, 28 miles south of the Oregon state line, on Interstate 5 at the top of California.

Geography/Climate: North end of Shasta Valley at 2,595-foot elevation, surrounded by Klamath National Forest, 16 miles northwest of 14,162-foot Mt. Shasta. Four seasons. Natives report an "interesting" winter, with 20 inches of snow; nice spring, warm summer, colorful fall. January average temperatures range from 24 to 44; July, 52 to 92. May hit 100 degrees midsummer but cools off at night. Fall starts in late October, onset of the rainy season. Average year-round humidity at noon, 55%.

Five Largest Employers: Government agencies, including Siskiyou County, U.S. Forest Service, school districts, 1,600+; Fairchild Medical Center, 280; Nor-Cal Products, 273; Rays/Price Less Grocery, 173.

High School: Yreka High School enrolls 825 students in grades 9–12, graduates 97%, sends 60% of graduates to college/university. Composite SAT for 60% of eligible students taking test: verbal 502, math 502.

Housing: 3BR 2BA house priced at about $150,000 midmarket, taxed at $1 per $100 appraised/taxable value.

Telecommunications: PacBell provides Internet connection at 56 Kbps.

Sales, Income Taxes: Retail sales tax, 7%. State income tax, scaled 1% to 9.3%.

Cost of Living: Movie ticket, $6; doctor appointment, routine, $60; plumber per hour, $45–$55; baby-sitting per day (day care), $10; dry cleaning, men's suit, $9; dinner for 4, local restaurant, $50.

Community Infrastructure & Amenities:
United Way
National Historic District
YMCA/YWCA
4-H
Motion picture theater
Public library
Public parks: 7, totaling 675 acres
Public swimming pool
Airport
Golf course, 9 holes
Emergency home shelter

Religious Denominations:

Assemblies of God	Four Square
Baha'i	Interdenominational
Baptist	Jehovah's Witnesses
Catholic	Lutheran
Christian	Lutheran (ELCA)
Church of Christ	Methodist
Church of God	Nondenominational
Church of Jesus Christ of	Pentecostal
Latter-Day Saints	Presbyterian
Church of the Nazarene	Presbyterian USA
Community	Religious Science
Eastern Orthodox	Seventh Day Adventist
Episcopal	United Methodist
Evangelical	

Newspaper: *Siskiyou Daily News*, 309 S. Broadway, Yreka, CA 96097. 530-842-5777. siskiyoudaily.com. Published Monday through Friday; Bruce Jones, editor. 3-month subscription, $31.50. *New York Times*; *Wall Street Journal*; and San Francisco, Sacramento, Medford dailies also sold in town.

Annual Festivals and Events: July, Concerts in the Park, Humbug Hurry-up (dirt bike contest); first full week of August, Siskiyou Golden Fair; September, Siskiyou Century Cycling (31-, 64-, 103-mile ride); Thanksgiving weekend, Holiday Parade.

Further Information: Yreka Chamber of Commerce, 117 W. Miner, Yreka, CA 96097. 530-842-1649. yrekachamber.com

Chapter 7:
Figuring the Cost

Budgeting for Your New Lifestyle in a Small Town

You can live for less in a small town.

Okay, that's a sweeping generalization and perhaps suspect at first sight. But after you run all the numbers, I think you'll find it's true. This chapter is your little tutorial on comparing your current cost of living to what you can find in a small-town setting. Most of the cost items I discuss are very familiar to anyone who pays household bills on a regular basis. Let me alert you, however, that at the end of the chapter I drift into Alan Greenspan mode and talk about major forces in small-town life that offset certain urban imperatives. If that sounds like voodoo economics, it probably is.

But back to reality. The cost of living for a household is composed of many line items like housing, food, transportation, and health care. Those are the biggies. You will quickly add some others, like entertainment, vaca-

tions, hobbies, and charitable contributions. Not to mention clothing, utilities, and—oh, yes—retirement. (Sorry this chapter is beginning on such a depressing note, budgetwise.) Figure 7-1 on page 187 works as both a checklist of the components in your present cost of living and a comparison table with the estimated costs in the small town of your dreams. You may want to photocopy the form so that you can use it a number of times for documenting cost scenarios in various places.

What are you likely to find in this comparison? Later in the chapter I discuss some specific cost differences between cities and small towns, but here are some general observations concerning that large group of items called utilities:

- **Costs that stay the same.** Most utility costs in a small town will be in line with costs prevailing in the general region, irrespective of whether it's urban or rural. So if you're staying in the same geographic area, you'll probably pay the same rate for electricity, natural gas, gasoline, heating oil, cable TV, and telephone. The cost of transportation to your far-out small town could boost the cost of heating oil and gasoline, however. On the other side of the coin, if you're moving from an oil-heating region like the Northeast to a hydro-electric region like the Northwest, your home heating-cooling costs in the new place could be much less. Investigate!

- **Costs that look the same but are actually much higher.** Make sure that you compare the cost of service to the extent of service. This is particularly true concerning telephone service. Even if the basic monthly charge is the same in a small town as in a city, you may be getting much less for your money in the small town. Telephone service to the hinterlands is a lot better today than it was five years ago, but many rural areas still lack high-speed phone lines, like DSL and T-1 connections. Pushing computer data through a 56 Kbps connection will try your patience. And you may find that certain popular ISPs—Internet service providers—don't have a local, toll-free number for you to connect to in the small town of your plans. Those toll charges add up quickly when you're online!

Real Estate—Cashing in Your Metro-Area Equity

This is how the real estate equation worked for the Crampton family when we moved in 1990 from the Chicago metro area to the small town of Greencastle, in west central Indiana. Houses were selling fast when we put our 1960s-vintage ranch-style house on the market in Flossmoor, Illinois, a suburb thirty

miles south of the Loop. Our three-bedroom, two-bath house encompassed 1,600 square feet and sold for $160,000. Our new home in Greencastle was a ninety-year-old, two-story frame house half a block from the campus of DePauw University. It had four bedrooms and one and a half baths, measured about 2,600 square feet, and we bought it for $84,000. That transaction, plus what I have learned from others who have made the city-to-small-town shift, is the basis of Crampton's law:

Moving from city to small town, you get twice the house for half the cost.

No, the numbers don't work out precisely in my case, and they may not be right on the money in your case, either. But the "law" describes a generally very favorable situation when you take your city-suburb real estate proceeds into the country: You'll have money left over, possibly quite a bit of money, which you can use for other nice things.

Real estate taxes will be less, too. Citing our experience again, when we moved from suburb to small town in 1990, we said good-bye to an annual tax bill of $3,600 and warmly greeted a new bill of $636. That's right—in our new small-town home, the tax bill was one-sixth what we had been paying in the city suburbs. (Fast forward: eleven years later, our real estate tax bill has risen to $930—still a bargain.) But remember, you get what you pay for. In the Chicago suburb we had a fabulous park-and-recreation program, including indoor tennis courts and indoor ice-skating rink; a high school that had National Merit Scholars and sent graduates to Ivy League schools; and first-rate municipal services. In comparison, the small Indiana town is downscale by several notches—decent parks and schools and town services but nothing to brag about the way they do in affluent suburbs.

Paying the Tax Man

After you calculate the difference in real estate tax between city-suburb and small town (and rub your hands with glee), you'll want to take a look at several other taxes that apply to the small town you are investigating:

- Retail sales tax
- State income tax
- License taxes

License taxes may seem unimportant: "I don't fish or hunt, and I'm not in business, so what kind of licenses do I need?" you're thinking. But I'm thinking about car, truck, motor home, and recreational trailer licenses—for example, the tag you buy for the trailer that you haul your bass boat on. In the state where you now live, these common annual license fees may be incidental, like fifty bucks a year. But in the state you're moving to, license tags may amount to real money. At my home base in Indiana, the total cost this year to license three cars, none of them fancy and all over two years old, is $479. (Maybe this is the flip side of low real-estate taxes; what do you think?)

At each town listed in Chapter 6, there's a data line for retail sales tax and state income tax. To make a thorough inquiry, however, I suggest logging onto the Internet and digging out all the local details. Here are three Web sites to try:

www.bakershore.com/bsatable.htm
www.vertexinc.com/cybrary
www.taxadmin.org

The last site listed above leads you to the Federation of Tax Administrators. Figure 7-2 on the next page shows you a table of state income taxes prepared by the FTA for tax year 2001. For updates, you'll want to check out the Web site.

For details about local town and county sales taxes, you can use the *bakershore* Web reference, for example. Navigating through that site, I went hunting for Brewton, Alabama, one of the towns listed in this book. And what I found was the detailed report shown in Figure 7-3. When you total up sales taxes, you have to be careful to include both the local and state portions. In the case of Brewton, the local sales tax on most items is 3 percent, but the state portion—given in fine print at the bottom of the report—is 4 percent. Total, 7 percent, or one of the higher retail sales tax rates in the nation. The true burden of this tax in any locale depends, however, on what's exempt. In many places, grocery food, prescription medicine, and clothing are exempt, for example.

Which raises the question: Should you shop for a town based on the state and local tax rates? If you're weary of paying state income tax, for example, should you narrow your search to states where there is *no* state income tax or one that is applied on only a limited basis? For your information, as of 2002, those states are Alaska, Florida, Nevada, New Hampshire, South Dakota, Tennessee, Texas, Washington, and Wyoming. Lots of nice small towns in those states!

My answer is, tax rates should have some influence on your selection of a small town as your new home base. But they're just one of many factors. If you're using taxes as your main motive, I suggest moving to a nice island in the Bahamas.

STATE INDIVIDUAL INCOME TAXES
(Tax rates for tax year 2001—as of January 1, 2001)

State	Tax Rates Low	Tax Rates High	# of Brackets	Income Brackets Low	Income Brackets High	Personal Exemption Single	Personal Exemption Married	Personal Exemption Child.	Federal Tax Ded.
ALABAMA	2.0	5.0	3	500	3,000	1,500	3,000	300	*
ALASKA	No State Income Tax								
ARIZONA	2.87	5.04	5	10,000	150,000	2,100	4,200	2,300	
ARKANSAS	1.0	7.0	6	2,999	25,000	20	40	20	
CALIFORNIA	1.0	9.3	6	5,454	35,792	72	142)	227	
COLORADO	4.63		1	—Flat rate—		—None—			
CONNECTICUT	3.0	4.5	2	10,000	10,000	12,000	24,000	0	
DELAWARE	2.2	5.95	7	5,000	60,000	110	220	110	
FLORIDA	No State Income Tax								
GEORGIA	1.0	6.0	6	750	7,000	2,700	5,400	2,700	
HAWAII	1.5	8.5	8	2,000	40,000	1,040	2,080	1,040	
IDAHO	2.0	8.2	8	1,000	20,000	2,900	5,800	2,900	
ILLINOIS	3.0		1	—Flat rate—		2,000	4,000	2,000	
INDIANA	3.4		1	—Flat rate—		1,000	2,000	1,000	
IOWA	0.36	8.98	9	1,162	52,290	40	80	40	*
KANSAS	3.5	6.45	3	15,000	30,000	2,250	4,500	2,250	
KENTUCKY	2.0	6.0	5	3,000	8,000	20	40	20	
LOUISIANA	2.0	6.0	3	10,000	50,000	4,500	9,000	1,000	*
MAINE	2.0	8	4	4,150	16,500	2,850	5,700	2,850	
MARYLAND	2.0	4.8	4	1,000	3,000	2,100	4,200	2,100	
MASSACHUSSETS	5.6		1	—Flat rate—		4,400	8,800	1,000	
MICHIGAN	4.2		1	—Flat rate—		2,800	5,600	2,800	
MINNESOTA	5.35	7.85	3	17,570	57,710	2,900	5,800	2,900	
MISSISSIPPI	3.0	5.0	3	5,000	10,000	6,000	12,000	1,500	
MISSOURI	1.5	6.0	10	1,000	9,000	2,100	4,200	2,100	*
MONTANA	2.0	11.0	10	2,100	73,000	1,610	3,220	1,610	*
NEBRASKA	0.51	6.68	4	2,400	26,500	91	182	91	
NEVADA	No State Income Tax								
NEW HAMPSHIRE	State Income Tax is Limited to Dividends and Interest Income Only								
NEW JERSEY	1.4	6.37	6	20,000	75,000	1,000	2,000	1,500	
NEW MEXICO	1.7	8.2	7	5,500	65,000	2,900	5,800	2,900	
NEW YORK	4.0	6.8	5	8,000	20,000	0	0	1,000	
N. CAROLINA	6.0	7.75	3	12,750	60,000	2,500	5,000	2,500	
N. DAKOTA	2.67	12.0	8	3,000	50,000	2,900	5,800	2,900	*
OHIO	0.691	6.980	9	5,000	200,000	1,050	2,100	1,050	
OKLAHOMA	0.5	6.75	8	1,000	10,000	1,000	2,000	1,000	*
OREGON	5.0	9.0	3	2,350	5,850	132	264	132	*
PENNSYLVANIA	2.8		1	—Flat rate—		—None—			
RHODE ISLAND	25.5% Federal tax liability								
S. CAROLINA	2.5	7.0	6	2,310	11,550	2,900	5,800	2,900	
S. DAKOTA	No State Income Tax								

| State | Tax Rates | | # of | Income Brackets | | Personal Exemption | | | Federal Tax |
	Low	High	Brackets	Low	High	Single	Married	Child.	Ded.
TENNESSEE	State Income Tax is Limited to Dividends and Interest Income Only.								
TEXAS	No State Income Tax								
UTAH	2.30	7.0	6	750	3,750	2,175	4,350	2,175	*
VERMONT	24.0% Federal tax liability (x)								
VIRGINIA	2.0	5.75	4	3,000	17,000	800	1,600	800	
WASHINGTON	No State Income Tax								
W. VIRGINIA	3.0	6.5	5	10,000	60,000	2,000	4,000	2,000	
WISCONSIN	4.6	6.75	4	1,500	112,500	700	1,400	400	
WYOMING	No State Income Tax								
DISTRICT OF COLUMBIA	5.0	9.0	3	10,000	30,000	1,370	2,740	1,370	

Figure 7-2: Use this table to compare state income taxes between your present home state and your possible future home state. *Source: Federation of Tax Administrators*

Figure 7-3: Sales tax details for the town of Brewton, Alabama. The Internet will lead you quickly to local tax information.

BREWTON
Locality Code: 9306
County Location: ESCAMBIA COUNTY

Current Tax Rates as of the 1st of January 2002

Tax Type	Rate Type	Rate	Active Date	Action	PJ	Administrator
CONSUMERS USE	AUTO	1.000%	10-01-1995	AC	Y	ALATX
CONSUMERS USE	FARM	1.000%	10-01-1995	AC	Y	ALATX
CONSUMERS USE	GENERAL	3.000%	01-01-1997	RC	Y	ALATX
CONSUMERS USE	MFG. MACHINE	1.000%	10-01-1995	AC	Y	ALATX
LODGINGS	GENERAL	2.000%	10-01-1995	AC	Y	ALATX
RENTAL TAX	AUTO	1.000%	03-01-1999	NT	Y	ALATX
RENTAL TAX	GENERAL	3.000%	03-01-1999	NT	Y	ALATX
RENTAL TAX	LINEN	3.000%	03-01-1999	NT	Y	ALATX
SALES TAX	AUTO	1.000%	10-01-1995	AC	Y	ALATX
SALES TAX	FARM	1.000%	10-01-1995	AC	Y	ALATX
SALES TAX	GENERAL	3.000%	01-01-1997	RC	Y	ALATX
SALES TAX	MFG. MACHINE	1.000%	10-01-1995	AC	Y	ALATX
SALES TAX	VENDING	3.000%	01-01-1997	RC	Y	ALATX
SALES TAX	W/D FEE	$2.000	10-01-1995	AC	Y	ALATX
SELLERS USE	AUTO	1.000%	10-01-1995	AC	Y	ALATX
SELLERS USE	FARM	1.000%	10-01-1995	AC	Y	ALATX
SELLERS USE	GENERAL	3.000%	01-01-1997	RC	Y	ALATX
SELLERS USE	MFG. MACHINE	1.000%	10-01-1995	AC	Y	ALATX

Guidelines for Estimating Your Everyday Costs

Transportation

The cost of getting around is generally higher in a small town than in a suburb or city. Why is that? There are three main reasons:

1. No mass transit.
2. Everyone of driving age requires a car.
3. When you go someplace out of town, it's at least 100 miles roundtrip.

Mass transit. Once upon a time, every small town in America was linked to every other small town either by a bus route or the railroad. When I was a teenager I rode the trolley—clickety-clack, six miles down the track—to visit my girlfriend in the next town. Ah . . . the romance of railroading! Today the old right-of-way has been converted into a bike-hike trail. That's okay in sunlight but doesn't get you very far at night. You may be lucky enough to move to a small town that's a stop on the Amtrak system. But there aren't many in this book—twelve by our count (in alphabetical order: Alpine, Texas; Amherst, Massachusetts; Brattleboro, Vermont; Brewton, Alabama; Bryan, Ohio; Crawfordsville, Indiana; Ellensburg, Washington; Glenwood Springs, Colorado; Hermann, Missouri; Holdrege, Nebraska; Litchfield, Connecticut; Red Wing, Minnesota; St. Albans, Vermont). Amtrak does stop reasonably close to a number of other small towns, however. Go to www.amtrak.com for details.

So much for rail service. How about taxis? Can you hail a cab by raising your arm on Main Street in Bisbee or Walnut Street in Bryan? Not likely. Many towns do have a taxi service, but no taxis cruise for fares in small towns. Buses? A few towns sponsor special runs, like from the old folks home to Wal-Mart, or occasional day-long trips to distant malls. But that's about it.

One car for every licensed driver. The good news about cars in Small Town USA, is that insurance generally costs less per household than in a metro area. The reasons are vandalism and car theft: There's less of it in a small town. (Don't expect much of a break on insurance for young drivers, however. Teens are teens.) The bad news is that you may need to add a car or two to the household fleet so that everyone has his/her own means of transportation. Are you ready to add another car payment to the monthly budget?

You may at first think the reason you are expanding the household fleet of vehicles is that Great American Rite of Passage, otherwise known as teenagers getting their first driver's license. But newly licensed drivers have the same imperatives wherever they live, whether it's a city, a suburb, or a small town. No, the real reason you will need more sets of wheels in a small town is the combination of two other factors, one of which I have already mentioned—lack of mass transportation. The other factor is the number of people per household who need a means of getting to work every day. In many city and suburban settings, you can take a bus or a train to work, and millions of people do. In a small town, your only choice is a car.

When the Cramptons moved to rural Indiana, we immediately had to buy another vehicle (we chose a shiny black pickup truck) so that two of us could get to work, in opposite directions, every workday. Previously, one of us had taken a commuter train to work, the way that people do in Chicago, New York, Boston, San Francisco, Atlanta, and numerous other urban centers. Yes, we had to acquire still another car when our son got his license. But we would have done that in the suburbs, too.

Everyplace out of town is 100 miles roundtrip. That's an exaggeration, of course. Some places are 90. But my point is, if you want to keep your leased vehicle under 12,000 miles a year, good luck! None of the small towns listed in this book is less than 40 miles from a metropolitan center (the place you go to shop, see a movie or a game, eat at a fancy restaurant). Some are much farther out, such as Silver City, New Mexico, which is 200 miles east of Tucson; or St. Albans, Vermont, 62 miles south of Montreal.

My spouse and I think we're reasonably close to an urban area—92 miles roundtrip to downtown Indianapolis. But still that's a lot of gasoline, a lot of time on the road, a lot of wear and tear on vehicles over time. It's a trade-off you should be aware of, part of the cost of selecting a small town as your new base of operations.

Services

Services generally cost less in small towns—you can find examples of selected costs (movie ticket, visit to the doctor, plumber per hour, dry cleaning, baby-sitting, restaurant meal) at any of the towns listed in Chapter 6. Need an attorney in a small town? The hourly bill may be one-third or less than the city scale, possibly $100. A visit to the hairdresser? Sixty dollars including tip in a small town versus $90+ in a city. The main reason for these small-town bargains is the comparatively lower cost of labor, office space, and overhead in a less-competitive, country market.

Food and Drink

Groceries cost no less in a small town than in the city, possibly more because of transportation. The produce department, meat department, and deli probably will offer a more limited selection than in a city or suburb because there is less demand. Eating out at a well-regarded, locally owned restaurant may cost 25% to 40% less than in a comparable city-suburban establishment, primarily because of the reduced cost of space and labor. At the two top establishments in my hometown, for example, dinner entrees run $11 to $14 on average.

Why Money Goes Farther in a Small Town

You have to live in a small town for several years before you begin to appreciate the main point of this chapter, that money stretches farther in a small town. Earlier I detailed some of the real money savings (and some of the genuinely increased costs) that you will see in the household budget. For example, housing and services are generally less, transportation is generally more. Those items show up right away in monthly cash flow. But after a few years, if you sense that your budget is under less pressure, the explanation may be that you no longer feel obligated to

- Keep up with the Joneses
- Keep up with fashion
- Run off to the mall whenever you're blue

Taking them in reverse order, getting a mall fix is a lot harder when you live in a small town. The nearest mall may be at least sixty-five miles away. It takes some planning to get there, probably more planning than you have in mind when you fall into a blue funk that only a shopping expedition can cure.

The second item on the list—keeping up with fashion—is connected to the mall item, of course. Less mall cruising, less exposure to changing styles, whether you're looking at clothing, furniture, or home appliances. But style and fashion just seem to matter less in a small town. My theory on this is simple: How you look is less important than who you are, and because practically everyone in a small town knows who you are (or at least it seems that way), superficial things like fashion grow less important over time. Everyone can see right through the exterior ornaments to the real you. Or, as Wanda Urbanska and Frank Levering report in *Moving to a Small Town*, "You can't be a good small-town lawyer and think that just because you wear a jacket and tie, you're something special. You have to convey an attitude that says, 'I've got to wear this uniform because it's what's expected of me.' You have to be a person first, one who just happens to be practicing law."

I don't mean to suggest that small-towners are style un-conscious. They know what's hot and what's not, but they don't mind hanging on to last year's fashions for another season or two. Nobody's going to notice, and the budget lasts longer.

That leaves the up-with-the-Joneses matter. Keeping up with your neighbors has minor fashion-style twists, though I'm thinking more about the big-ticket or long-term items, like adding a gallery wing to the house because everyone on the block is doing it, or painting the whole place every few years whether it needs it or not, or keeping your four-ton, jet-black SUV in showroom condition, rain or shine. I think you will find there is much less pressure to conform in ways like that in a small town. Why? What rules about earthly possessions are suspended when you move out of a sophisticated urban area into the country?

The answer is not that some miraculous change in human nature occurs in small towns, where there is just as much pride, greed, and envy as anyplace else. What's different is simply scale: A small town is not big enough to support large, exclusive enclaves of people who share the same economic class, whether it's upper class or lower class. So people of various income levels tend to mix it up better in a small town than in a suburb, for example. Small towns are pretty good melting pots that way. Drive through any town and you'll see what I mean—large, well-maintained houses on the same block as smaller, neglected places, representing probably nothing more than the ebb and flow of good fortune or spare time, or both, and altogether fairly insignificant. Rich man, poor man—small towns remind you that community resources count more than individual wealth.

Comparing Costs

Use this form to compare the cost of living where you now reside to the estimated cost in a selected small town. I suggest using monthly costs because you probably can recite them from memory (writing those checks every month).

	$ Present	$ Small Town
Mortgage/rent	_____	_____
Taxes	_____	_____
Maintenance	_____	_____
Garage	_____	_____
Utilities:		
Water/sewer	_____	_____
Garbage collection	_____	_____
Electricity	_____	_____
Gas/oil (heat)	_____	_____
Telephone	_____	_____
Cable TV/Satellite	_____	_____
Internet	_____	_____
Cars	_____	_____
Other transportation	_____	_____
Food	_____	_____
Health (MD, DDS, Rx)	_____	_____
Insurance	_____	_____
Savings	_____	_____
Other	_____	_____
	_____	_____
	_____	_____
TOTALS	_____	_____

Chapter 8:

Finding a Place to Live in a Small Town

Understanding the Small-Town Market

That Saturday in June when the Crampton family arrived for the first time in Greencastle, Indiana, we were on a mission. We had contracted to sell our house in the Chicago suburbs and needed to find a new place to live in our chosen small town, and do it all in a day, if possible. Such a timetable may sound ridiculously swift. How can you possibly check out dozens of listings, weigh the pros and cons of various neighborhoods, compare prices of similar properties, talk it over in a high family council, etc., etc., all in one day?

The answer is simple: That day that we arrived in our new hometown in west central Indiana, there were exactly four houses on the market. Four houses—count 'em. Two of the candidates we checked off without even venturing inside. I forget exactly what we didn't like about them, but they must have had zero curb appeal. I should explain

that we were looking for an old house, a place with some character, so to speak. If it needed a little TLC, that was okay. We had renovated two previous dwelling places and rather liked the challenge. But we were not interested in a spiffy new house in a subdivision—that would be entirely too *suburban* for our taste. After all, we were leaving suburbia and seeking something new.

(I've got to be careful to speak only for myself on this matter of boldly going forth into the backcountry. My spouse thought we were headed for the abyss. Our then preteen son didn't like the idea, either. Suburbia was all he had ever known, and it was very comfortable. I think they both came to appreciate the character of the town we had moved to and the old house that became our new home, but only after they had made new connections and we had put our personal stamp on our dwelling place. Our daughter, who had just graduated from college and was beginning her career in Chicago, initially thought we had abandoned her by moving 165 miles south. But we managed to close that gap. In fact, she wound up marrying a wonderful guy whose career took them to an Indiana town only twenty-eight miles from our new homestead.)

The first house we looked at in Greencastle simply oozed character. It was a two-story brick building with a wide front porch. It sat several steps up from the street (not just any street but Washington Street—the main street—just down the block from the funeral home, so you get an idea of the neighborhood: *très* chic). And this house had a past! Built sometime before the Civil War, the house had been occupied by various leading citizens over the years. Someone told us it was a stop on the Underground Railroad, but we had our doubts—those places seem to be as numerous as the houses where Washington slept.

House No. 1 was impressive inside, too. High ceilings. Wide plank floors. Solid brick interior walls. Grand-scale wooden trim. Lots of space. But it had drawbacks, including a nineteenth-century kitchen so small you had to step outside to dry the dishes. Those massive interior brick walls also boxed in the kitchen like a small fortress. The house had stately old hot water radiators, my favorite kind of heat. But there were no ducts for air-conditioning, and Indiana does become humid in the summertime.

That left House No. 2, take it or leave it. After a fairly quick walk-through, we decided to take it. This was a two-story, box-shaped frame house, painted tan, with green shutters—a bit offbeat from the traditional and quite attractive. We later learned that this house was called a "Pattern House," and we guessed the name meant that a local resident needed a house and got the pattern from some standard source of those things, handed it to a carpenter, and said, "Build this." The house was built in 1908 and had about 2,700 square feet of living space, formally arranged: Living room with fireplace, dining room, kitchen, and powder room on the first floor; four bedrooms and a bathroom on the second floor. Cellar walls built partly of stone and partly of concrete, and an ancient cast-iron furnace as big as a cyclotron. Originally it was fueled by coal—you could see where the coal bunker had been—but it had been converted to gas many years before.

We bought the house and moved in five weeks later. It's pictured in Figure 8-1.

Our experience is not uncommon: If you are looking for an older house in the heart of a small town, you may not find much of a selection. Unlike many suburbs, where "For Sale" signs sprout like dandelions, the housing stock does not turn over as rapidly in a small town. People put down deep roots. Some spend their whole lives in the same house: An elderly lady on our block actually was born in the house where she lives and appears content to die there as well.

With limited housing on the market, you may have to adopt a bolder tactic: Cruise the town, find a house you like, knock on the front door, and make an offer. We know two families in Greencastle that did this, and it worked. Real estate people in other towns confirm that this direct approach does happen, though they would prefer that it not.

Figure 8-1: The house the author bought in Greencastle, Indiana. It cost $84,000 in 1990 and had a market value of about $180,000 in 2001.

Starting Your Search Online

The Internet has created a national showplace for the small-town housing market, and that's revolutionary. Without leaving the comfort of your city condo, you can take a look at houses for sale in many faraway places and—who knows?—maybe get on the phone to learn more, go for a visit, and make your move. Small-town brokers who are smart enough to create an attractive and easy-to-navigate Web site are receiving many initial inquiries because of their initiatives. Though it's gratifying when you can download a screenful of tempting properties at astounding bargain prices, your success rate, if it's like mine, may not be better than 50 percent.

One weekend morning I jotted down the names of three towns in various parts of the country, places I know because they are listed in this book but otherwise just random: Bardstown, Kentucky; St. Albans, Vermont; and Ukiah, California. I could not find any real estate sites in Bardstown or St. Albans, but Ukiah yielded a beauty—North Country Real Estate, mendohomes.com. You may want to take a look, for a taste of California.

Making a Deal: What Can You Buy for about $150,000?

Housing is a bargain in small towns compared to metropolitan areas, as I assert in several places in this book. Now for some proof, almost all of it right on the money—you recognize that "$150,000" is a plus-or-minus number stretching loosely in both directions. With a handful of exceptions, if you arrive with that sort of purchasing power, you should be able to find a rather nice place to live.

The examples that follow all are based on conversations with real estate salespeople in early 2002, so you may want to crank in some corrections if you have procrastinated on your move to small-town America or if national economic developments have changed housing costs to a marked degree. The five towns selected for presentation here represent several different kinds of markets, from upscale old money to down-home middle class—enough variety to give you a pretty good sense of the center of the marketplace.

Madison, Georgia (pop. 3,636)

Madison can just about set its own price. That's rare in small towns, but Madison, Georgia, is a rare place. Founded in 1809 and named for President James Madison, the small community sixty miles east of Atlanta became the home of prosperous plantation owners who built elegant mansions in the shade of live oaks and lived in a style befitting their wealth. A guide to Georgia published in 1845 described Madison as "The most cultured and aristocratic town on the stagecoach route from Charlestown to New Orleans."

In 1861, Madison's young men went off to fight for the Confederacy. In 1864, the home they left to defend appeared threatened as Union troops, fresh from burning Atlanta, marched eastward to decommission still other parts of Georgia. The way the story is told around Madison today, as troops under the command of General Henry Slocum neared the outskirts of the genteel town, a prominent local resident with Northern sympathies (he was against Secession, at least) assembled a delegation of equally earnest Madisonians to plead that the town be spared. It was spared, more or less, and became known in later years as the town that General Sherman refused to burn. Presumably, Charlestonians still had a nice place to stop on the way to New Orleans, and vice versa.

As the live oak trees matured along Main Street, Madison became even more alluring. In recent years, closeness to Atlanta (about an hour away) has jacked up both outside interest and the cost of living. "Madison is the exception to the small-town rule," says Glynn Gill, a real estate salesperson."You can live in other towns for less money. But the reason we have become pricey is we get so many people here who can live anyplace they choose." Some of them may have read the review in *Travel Holiday* magazine in 2001, declaring Madison "the No. 1 small town in America." All that attention has not hurt real estate values. Most of the houses on Main Street have been restored, and when they come on the market—not often—they command prices that would please an old plantation owner's heart.

But within walking distance of downtown you can find some very nice properties at prices competitive with, say, the metropolitan Atlanta market, Gill says. For example, a home of recent vintage in the historic district with master bedroom suite, office/nursery adjoining, two bedrooms and bath upstairs, hardwood floors, screened porch, large kitchen and breakfast room, was on the market in early 2002 at $239,000.

Some new houses described as historic reproductions are priced even more competitively. For example, a two-story frame building with open kitchen with sitting area, hardwood floors, three bedrooms, two and a half baths, and porches all around was listed at $182,500.

Figure 8-2: A historic reproduction house, on the market in 2002 for $182,500 in Madison, Georgia.

Alpine, Texas (pop. 6,750)

You can't get much farther away from an urban area than Alpine, Texas. The nearest big city is El Paso, and that's a lonely four-hour drive to the northwest. Alpine is so far from civilization that your car radio spins across the AM and FM bands without finding anything strong enough to land on. But if Alpine is remote, it's worth every bit of the journey. This is the high country of West Texas—a stunning landscape of sunburnt ranch lands, the air so dry it crackles and the light so pure it's close to divine. Some people say the quality of light is even better than in New Mexico.

Of course, being far out is part of the appeal of Alpine. But once you arrive, you may be a surprised to find not only cowboys in pickup trucks but college professors in SUVs. There's a small campus of the state university system in town—a popular place for high school teachers to pursue graduate credit in summer school. Alpine has the small scale of a homey, friendly place, and it's growing at a healthy, sustainable pace: population up 13 percent since 1990. Ken Clouse, a real estate broker in town, says his town has always been interesting to Texans from metroplexes like Houston, San Antonio, and Dallas–Fort Worth. And the odd outlander from the Midwest or California has come poking around from time to time. But after the terrorist attacks on New York and Washington in September 2001, Clouse began to see an unprecedented level of interest in the Alpine area from residents of the Northeast. The initial contacts came in through the Internet site of DeVillier Real Estate (cowboysncadillacs.com).

"We've done two separate deals for people from Boston," Clouse recalled. One of the Bostonians bought an existing house and the other built a new place. Both had sold high in the urban Northeast market and bought low in West Texas. "For example," Clouse said, "one man sold for $450,000 up there and built a brand-new house here for $150,000."

In the Alpine market, $150,000 buys quite a bit of house. One listing at the DeVillier agency in early 2002 was a new three-bedroom, two-and-a-half bath, two-story house totaling 1,600 square feet with a wraparound porch and an attractive hillside setting. The house itself was on the market at $112,500. If you wanted to buy the adjacent rental property—an older, one-bedroom home with private yard—you could wrap up the whole deal for $167,500.

Grinnell, Iowa (pop. 9,105)

Grinnell, Iowa, is the quintessential college town. The famous small college in this central Iowa community consistently ranks near the top of the list among private liberal arts colleges in the United States. Grinnell College, with an enrollment of 1,300 students and a faculty-staff complement of 659 people, is a very significant part not only of local cultural life but also the local economy. When you add in the professionalism and payrolls at other sizable local employers (for example, Grinnell Mutual Reinsurance Company, 631 employees; and Grinnell Regional Medical Center, 300 employees), you understand why

the housing market is sometimes tight in Grinnell.

"We always have a low supply of houses on the market and a high demand," says Karen Ashby, owner of First of Grinnell GMAC real estate agency. Although by comparison to East Coast or West Coast prices Grinnell is very reasonably priced, compared to the Midwestern small-town market, it's "a pricey market," she says. People move to Grinnell because of job transfers. Some move in because they prefer to live in a small town and commute to a city for work. Ashby recalls one double-income household where one spouse commutes daily to Des Moines, about sixty miles west; the other commutes to Iowa City, about sixty miles east.

Many house hunters begin looking at the Grinnell marketplace on the Internet, Ashby says. When we talked, her agency's Web site listings included a two-story, vinyl-sided house on a corner lot, close to an elementary school and a high school, and a public park including the municipal swimming pool—a nice location on the northwest side of town (see Figure 8-3). Built in 1968, the house has five bedrooms, two baths, formal dining room, family room, a finished full basement, and an attached two-car garage. Total square feet, 2,100. Offering price, $159,900. Taxes, $2,152.

Figure 8-3: Close to everything and yours for $159,900 in Grinnell, Iowa.

Kosciusko, Mississippi (pop. 7,372)

First, you have to learn to pronounce the name of this town the way natives do. Try this: kozzy ESS ko. I imagine that General Thaddeus Kosciusko, for whom the town is named, would only say "God bless you!" if he heard his name spoken that way. The general was a Pole (as in "from Poland,") who served on General George Washington's staff during the American Revolution. So far as historians know, General Kosciusko never visited north central Mississippi, but the town thought enough of his service to discard its original name, Red Bud Springs, and become a living monument to an early national hero.

No sleepy southern town, Kosciusko has hustle. It is a county seat and commercial center about seventy miles up the Natchez Trace from the state capital, Jackson. A sizable number of local residents commute to jobs in Jackson. Some go even farther, flying offshore to oil rigs in the Gulf of Mexico—two weeks pumping crude, one week back home in the hill country, enjoying the good life in a friendly small town.

People work hard in Kosciusko but they also have fun. The day I talked with Larry Caraway, owner of Kosciusko Realty, there was a lot of serious food preparation going on in advance of the First Baptist Church Wild Game Dinner, an annual feast featuring roast deer, alligator, fish, possum, squirrel, beaver, moose, elk, and other wild critters brought 7down by local hunters. "Strictly a men thing, women are not invited, and we get a lot of flack over that," Caraway says. The women do think well enough of the macho event to provide dessert, however.

"We start cutting up the meat at 6 A.M.," Caraway reports. " We fix it and cook it here in huge smokers." By the time they all sit down in the Baptist Church hall there will be a hungry crowd of perhaps 600 men from all over the state, loads to eat, and an after-dinner speaker of national renown. "We usually have the dinner right after the deer season closes," Caraway says. "Everybody looks forward to it—and people from other churches attend. It's a tremendous outreach for our church and gets a lot of people into that (church) environment who normally would not come to church."

Caraway moved to Kosciusko seven years ago from Jackson and commuted to the state capital for several years before concentrating on his local real estate business. Newcomers arrive in town for a variety of reasons, he says. Some have jobs locally, like the construction specialists at work on two new power plants being built in the area. But many continue to work elsewhere, like the airline employee from Mobile who viewed Kosciusko as an escape from the faster pace of a metropolitan area.

Kosciusko has an elegant old courthouse and a prosperous-looking downtown square. The newest building downtown is the operations center and executive office of Merchants & Farmers Bank, a NASDAQ-listed, locally owned banking institution with branches stretching across nearly half the state and assets of more than a billion dollars.

The town has a variety of neighborhoods and a good stock of larger, well-maintained, older homes. One place that was listed by Kosciusko Realty in early 2002 is a 121-year-old house just a few blocks off the square. It has four bedrooms, two and a half baths, 11-foot ceilings, hardwood floors, a large front porch, and—set on two city lots—plenty of breathing room. This 2,414-square-foot house was listed at $118,000. Caraway figured the real estate taxes would be about $1,100 a year.

Chapter 9:

Getting a Job— Or Bringing It with You

Reinventing Yourself

The sign outside a roadside business near my home town shows how resourceful you sometimes have to be in putting together a livelihood in a small town. It announces the enterprise like this:

**Stained Glass
& Crafts**

·

**Bait &
Tackle**

I don't know the people who own this place but I assume it's a single corporate enterprise with two operating divisions—the worm bucket and the stained-glass table. Whatever, this is one of the more unusual "ampersand" businesses in town but a familiar way to make 1 + 1 = an income. You have to think outside the box in a small-town market. There may not be enough customers to keep you going in your first love—fashioning windows for gothic cathedrals, for example—so

you have to add a cash cow, like night crawlers. Some other business combinations in town are only slightly less bizarre: birdfeed & auto parts; cowboy clothes & formal attire; video store & tanning salon; hardware & package shipping. So far as I know, none of the barbershops in town does surgery. But the beauty parlors are always open to new ideas. The phone book ad for one salon says, "Beauty Salon &." Now *that's* catchy, and I suspect that every woman knows exactly what the unstated other side of the business amounts to.

It's handy to talk about retailing, because the lessons are so obvious. Niche specialties can be tough to establish in a small town if you have to rely entirely on local trade. Of course, if your business plan is to have both a local presence and sell over the Internet, that's different. (And if bricks-and-clicks is your plan, you'll want to check the town very carefully to make sure that it's wired for high-speed communication like DSL—digital subscriber line—and that FedEx and UPS offer their fastest service to and from your location.)

Besides doing what you *have* to do to make a living in your adopted small town, moving there can give you an opportunity to do what you *want* to do, perhaps the chance of a lifetime to reinvent who you are, so far as you are defined by your work. Why is that? Because you arrive without any particular ID. You're an unknown quantity, a blank slate. So if you've been a professional something-or-other for a number of years and want to become a retailer or a restaurateur, for example, nothing can stop you except insufficient start-up capital, good advice, or determination. Yes, you do have some of this freedom in the city, but the social-cultural pressure to remain in your niche may discourage you from trying. By comparison, most small towns are in constant need of new ventures—and new venturers—to remain vital. Small towners tend to judge you on what you can do today, not on what you may have done yesterday. So, carpe diem!

Looking for Work Before You Move

Later in this chapter I talk about moving your present job to your new home in a small town. But for now, assume you are looking for employment in the new place and want to make an orderly search. Here's a plan:

- **Subscribe to the local newspaper.** Use the Internet to find the name and address of the local newspaper. Begin by typing in the name and state, "Marshall Minnesota," for example. This will lead you to a number of listings for the community, generally including the local newspaper. (Take a look at the town listings in Chapter 6 and you'll see newspaper details.) A three-month or six-month subscription by mail won't cost much and you will begin to get a sense of the employment prospects. You may be underwhelmed by the job ads—this is not like settling down with the employment section of the *L.A. Times* or the *Chicago Tribune*. There may be only a handful of positions advertised, and most of them unskilled and low pay. Aside from the help-wanted ads, however, the news columns may suggest possibilities for employment if you're willing to pursue them. I'm thinking, for example, about news stories of local people retiring from their occupation in town, or the arrival of a new business, or the expansion of a local institution like a school or a government agency. It's unrealistic to think that you can land a job by reading the newspaper from hundreds of miles distant, but your knowledge of current comings and goings gleaned from the newspaper may provide leads when you arrive in town and begin getting acquainted.

- **Log on.** In selected fields—health services and government services, in particular—you may be able to find live leads to job vacancies plus realistic possibilities of making a serious initial contact by telephone. Small town hospitals and nursing homes seem to always need professionals. For example, Figure 9-1 is a recent Internet posting by the Ripon Medical Center, in Ripon, Wisconsin, which was seeking part-time RNs, LPNs, and a surgical technician at the time.

EMPLOYMENT OPPORTUNITIES

Position	Department	Shift(s)	FTE
Registered Nurse	OB	3-11 pm & every other weekend	.7
Registered Nurse	Med/Surg	12 hr night shift; every other weekend	.9
Registered Nurse	Surgery	Days; call 1 night/week & 1 weekend/month	.5
LPN	Med/Surg	Nights	.8
LPN	Med/Surg	Days/PMs	.7
Surgical Tech	Surgery	One day per week; call one weekend per month	.2

For further information, please contact:

Nichole Weir - (920) 748-9164
Human Resources

or email nicholeweir@riponmedicalcenter.com

Figure 9-1: An Internet job posting from Ripon, Wisconsin.

Another tactic via the Internet is to identify companies that have plants or offices in the town you're interested in. Often you can find a handy list of such companies somewhere on the chamber of commerce or industrial development commission Web site—look for links to those organizations on the town's home page (which sometimes is the chamber's home page). With a company identified by name, the next step is to see if you can find a corporate Web site and job postings. You may get lucky and find a company Web site at the top of the first town page you open. That's what you see in Figures 9-2 and 9-3—Minnesota Corn Processors at the top of the Web site matches for "Marshall Minnesota," and a portion of job listings at the time (Production Supervisor in Training, Area Manager Utilities, Entry Level Positions).

Web Site Matches 1 - 20 of 21 | **Next 1 >**

1. **Minnesota Corn Processors** - established as a farmer-owned cooperative. Manufactures corn syrup, starches, ethanol, and corn co-products.
http://www.mcp.net
More sites about: **Minnesota > Marshall > Agriculture**

2. **Marshall School** - independent coeducational college-preparatory school.
http://www.marshallschool.org/
More sites about: **Minnesota > Duluth > Private High Schools**

3. **John Marshall High School**
http://www.rochester.k12.mn.us/john-marshall/
More sites about: **Minnesota > Rochester > John Marshall High School**

4. **Robert Marshall Company** - representing switch, elastomer keypad, electric motor, electromechanical component manufacturing companies.
http://www.rmarshall.com
More sites about: **Minnesota > Minneapolis > Electronics > Board Level Components**

Figure 9-2: A Yahoo! search for "Marshall Minnesota" yields a company link—and job prospect—at the top of the list.

- Production Supervisor in Training
- Area Manager Utilities

You can also apply by sending an e-mail message to Human-Resources@mcp.net Include your cover letter in the body of the message, and attach your resume as either a MS Word document (.doc) or as ASCII text. Be sure to include the position you are applying for in the cover letter.

To apply by mail, send your resumé to:

Minnesota Corn Processors
Attn: Human Resources
901 N Hwy 59
Marshall, MN 56258

Figure 9-3: Brief job descriptions and application details at the Minnesota Corn Processors plant in Marshall, Minnesota, a town listed in this book.

Small towns that are doing interesting things in economic development (meaning *job creation*) are frequently in the spotlight at national organizations that study and support these efforts. Visiting the following organizations on the World Wide Web may reveal the name of small towns with interesting job prospects. Generally, you can reach a Web site by simply typing the organization's name into a search engine.

- Aspen Institute Community Strategies Group
- Center for the New West
- Community Development Society
- EconData.net
- Heartland Center for Leadership Development
- Illinois Institute for Rural Affairs
- Laboratory for Community and Economic Development
- National Main Street Center
- Rocky Mountain Institute
- Southern Rural Development Center
- TVA Rural Studies

- **Get a local telephone book.** Small-town phone books are wonderfully *small*. The phone book for my town measures 6 by 9 inches and weighs only 5 ounces—and all the phone numbers begin with the same three digits! You can really get your hands around a universe that size. But the first problem is getting a phone book from afar, and that is not so easy. You must know the name of the telephone company that serves the area, then call the company business office and ask how to order a directory. Sometimes there's a direct number. For example: Southwestern Bell, 800-792-2665 (800-SWB-BOOK); Verizon, 800-888-8448. The advantage of having a local phone book is obvious: You can check to see if any relatives live in town! (But if you have to use the phone book for that purpose, they probably are not *close* relatives.) More to the point, the classified business portion of the directory shows you not only business establishments but also social services and professionals— churches, clubs, mental health services, private schools; attorneys, doctors, den-

tists, acupuncturists, etc. Browsing the Yellow Pages can give you a quick look at the local business-professional establishment as well as cultural-recreational facilities, like public parks, country clubs, and bowling alleys.

- **Check your college alumni directory.** Perchance a graduate of your alma mater lives in the town of your dreams. What a wonderful excuse to call and introduce yourself, and the old alum will be so relieved to know you're not asking for a donation! After the pleasantries, prepare to settle down for a long chat: Small-towners love to talk about where they live.

Looking for Work After You Arrive

If your advance research on the community has produced the names of employers that look interesting, presumably you have already initiated some contact with them by mail or telephone, introducing yourself and setting the stage for a personal meeting when you are in town. I'm assuming you know how to proceed in that direction. But if you arrive in town without any job prospects and need to find employment, try one or more of these approaches to the marketplace:

- **Introduce yourself to the director of economic development.** The town may not have such a person. But if it does, and he or she is good, you can learn a great deal in a short time about what's happening on the local business scene.

- **Introduce yourself to the mayor.** Some towns have periodic social events to greet and welcome new arrivals. Don't wait for an invitation. Go say hello to the town's chief executive. You'll learn the names of businesspeople, and the mayor will mention your name to others in the local establishment.

- **Stop by the chamber of commerce office.** You can learn the regular meeting times of business and civic organizations such as Rotary, Kiwanis, and Lions. You may even be invited as a guest.

- **Knock on doors.** See a business that looks interesting? Walk in and speak to the owner or manager. You can do that with much more success in a small town than in a city because there are fewer gatekeepers to deny access, and fewer tall fences, locked doors, and callous receptionists.

- **Volunteer.** Small towns need a constant supply of volunteers. That's how much of the essential work of a community gets done. Look for opportunities in the economic development office, town hall, the courthouse, the hospital, or nonprofit organizations like Habitat for Humanity. Good way to make new friends.

- **Join a church.** You don't have to be a church member to find satisfying employment in a small town, but it can't hurt. Churches in small towns often are more visibly active in serving human needs than churches in cities, simply because the church organization often substitutes for government or nonprofit agencies in

supplying emergency care to small-town residents in need—I don't mean you in your job quest but people who have been burnt out of their homes, for example, or otherwise suffered bad luck. The church is an anchor, a source of new friendships.

Moving Your Profession

If you're self-employed and can manage your business via the Internet, telephone, and overnight delivery, you can work from just about anywhere, including the small town of your dreams. What occupations qualify? Here are some that come to mind at once:

- Stockbrokers and financial analysts
- Marketing and public relations consultants
- Business management consultants
- Environmental consultants
- Political consultants
- Writers and editors
- Software writers
- Researchers
- Designers

There must be many others. The key, of course, is whether you can really build and maintain a business long distance, with infrequent one-on-one contact with your clients. And there's another factor: Even if your business model does operate efficiently via Internet and FedEx, will *you* operate efficiently without the stimulation of colleagues? That's the trade-off when you move your self-employment from the city and to the country—fewer spur-of-the-moment lunch dates with fellow professionals.

But assuming that you can be productive

and happy operating from some remote Shangri-la, what do you need to check before moving your enterprise to a small town? Here's my short list:

- **Broadband communications.** I've said this elsewhere and it bears repeating: Check the speed of data communications lines available to residences in the small town. Small towns are decidedly unequal on this point. If the telephone company provides DSL service, great. If the cable TV company provides a broadband connection, double great. But if neither service is available in town, don't even think about telecommuting there.

- **Overnight delivery.** If your potential location is on the "Second Day" delivery list, you may want to reconsider.

- **Licensing.** If you operate your business from your home and the business is invisible from the street, no worries. That's the case with virtually all telecommuting and consulting—it blends into the neighborhood and should raise no questions with local authorities about business licensing. The legal form of your business may raise a tax flag, however. If you are incorporated in the state, that fact will sooner or later come to the attention of the local tax office and you could get a bill for your business assets.

- **Professional talent when you need it.** Check the phone book for CPAs, attorneys, and systems specialists. Go talk with a loan officer at a local bank. Ask around about the availability of part-timers for keyboarding, mailing preparation, etc.

Scott Cloud
Commuter

It takes Scott Cloud about six hours to commute one way to work from his home in Northfield, Minnesota. But considering that work is 400 miles away, at O'Hare airport in Chicago, that's pretty good time. Scott is a pilot for United Airlines, flying 757s and 767s out of Chicago to both coasts and sometimes Alaska. Beginning a typical work week, Scott says good-bye to the family—wife Linda, daughter Kaitlin, fourteen, and son Ben, eleven—and drives forty miles up I-35 to Minneapolis–St. Paul International Airport, where he hitches a ride on a United flight to O'Hare. Within a couple of hours he's at the controls of a jetliner high over the nation somewhere. Four days later, after crisscrossing the country a few times, he's back at O'Hare, his weekly stint over, and he heads home to small-town Minnesota.

Airline flight crews can live just about anywhere, it seems, so long as there's a sizable airport nearby. And it's not uncommon, Scott says, for pilots to live in small towns, including the small towns where they grew up. That's how it is for the Cloud family. Linda Cloud was born in Northfield and Scott moved to a farm just outside of town when he was in eighth grade. He graduated from St. Olaf, one of the two colleges in Northfield; trained as a Navy pilot at Pensacola, Florida; was stationed at San Diego for a few years; and while waiting for a job opportunity with the airlines, piloted a Cessna Citation on drug interdiction runs for the U.S. Customs Service in Central and South America.

United Airlines hired Scott in 1995, based him in Los Angeles and San Francisco, and the Cloud family settled down in San Diego—which was fine at the time, he says. But the tug of the old home territory was strong—family ties. Linda's parents and one brother live on a farm just north of Northfield, and her other brother lives half an hour away. Scott's brother, who also flies for United, lives just down the street in Northfield, and his sister lives on a farm south of town. Having an extended family nearby is reassuring when you are away for days at a stretch on your job, Scott says.

For the Cloud kids, Northfield was a totally new experience. Suddenly, their routines became both simpler and more complex. Scott explains: "We felt the sense of community was missing in San Diego. For example, Ben would play basketball with one group of kids, then baseball with a totally different group of kids, roller hockey with a different group, and go to church and school with still *another* group of kids." And in Northfield? "All those five groups—they're the same kids. There's much more continuity. I think the friendships grow stronger because kids are continually involved with each other."

And on Main Street, the merchants know who you are, too. One weekday afternoon, Ben Cloud needed to replace his hockey stick before practice but he didn't have any money. His dad recounted the transaction.

"What's your name?" the shopkeeper asked.

"Ben Cloud," he said.

"Scott or Steve?" the shopkeeper inquired further, sorting it out between the two Cloud brothers living in town.

"Scott," said Ben.

"Just tell your dad to come see me," the shopkeeper said, establishing a line of credit for his young customer.

"You don't have to worry about your kids downtown in a small town," Scott Cloud says. "And the kids also know that if they're messing around the word gets back. There's a sense of accountability in a small town because everybody knows everybody. In a big city you can road rage if you feel like it. You don't care about how you act because you think, 'I'm never going to see those people again.' In this town, I think people go out of their way to be kinder. If you're a screwball, it'll get around."

Amy Gage
Telecommuter,
Magazine Editor,
Soccer Mom

Amy Gage moved to Northfield, Minnesota, in 1993 to become editor of the local newspaper, the twice-weekly *Northfield News*. What could be more small-town than small-town newspaper editor? In fact, Amy had grown up in another Minnesota small town, Mankato, so she had the pedigree. But she also had twenty years of experience as a journalist in the Twin Cities, raising the question, Can a small-town girl who has found happiness in the big city make her peace with a small town again? Well, yes and no.

The problem with sitting in the editor's chair in an upscale small town is paying the rent. "It's very hard to earn a living in this town if you don't work for one of the colleges," Amy says, referring to Carleton and St. Olaf. "The year I was editor here my husband had to work outside of the home"—he was an at-home dad. "We couldn't make it. I took a 35 percent pay cut to come here."

But they knew they wanted to stay in Northfield, among other reasons so that their young sons could attend the local public schools, regarded as among the best in the state. "It's a very highly educated community and there is great interest in the schools. Every bond issue passes by large margins," Amy says.

To get back on the city-scale wage track but enjoy small-town benefits, she worked out a deal with a Minneapolis employer to telecommute a portion of the time—six or seven days a month. "I am a senior editor at *Minneapolis-St. Paul Magazine* and I do some work for their sister publication, *Twin Cities Business Monthly*," she explains. Previously a columnist at *St. Paul Pioneer-Press*, Amy is in demand as a speaker.

So the small town–big city connection works okay? Amy says it does, in spite of the commute, which she barely tolerates. "Northfield really is a nice place to live. I can honestly tell you there is no other small town in Minnesota I would live in, and that's because of the colleges. I don't think I ever venture out from home and not see someone I know, someone I recognize, someone I can say hello to. I'm a soccer mom here, literally. As a woman I feel safer here than I did in the Cities. I will walk my dog before sunrise and frankly not give it a second thought—though I don't know how smart that is!"

"I think our proximity to the Cities allows many of us to have in some ways the best of both worlds. We can earn the city income and—" she hesitates, and laughs, "and pay city prices here."

Deborah and John
One Job in Town, One Job Out of Town

Born and reared in Wylie, a small town near Dallas, Deborah West went to college at Southern Methodist University and the University of Texas, lived overseas for awhile, and finally settled on Fredericksburg, Texas, as home. Over a period of about four years, she and her husband have put together an employment package that suits their needs—one job in town, one job out of town. He manages a landscaping business in Fredericksburg, she teaches Pilates, the physical exercise program, at a studio in Austin, commuting seventy-five miles three days a week.

That all sounds very well worked out, possibly in advance. But the truth is, neither Deborah nor John had jobs in place when they moved to the small Texas town in the Hill Country. What they did have was faith in their ability to make things work, economically. They bought a tiny, brightly painted, vintage-1902 house half a block off Fredericksburg's main street, and they both got jobs in the local retail establishment. That's easy to do in Fredericksburg, which is known throughout Texas for its antique stores, galleries, boutiques, restaurants, and otherwise very nice quality of life for a small town. The place is a weekend mecca for hundreds of people from Houston to Dallas to San Antonio and beyond. As one measure of the town's hospitality (not to mention revenue by tourism), Fredericksburg and environs has more than 300 bed-and-breakfast establishments welcoming visitors.

Working in retail is a good way to break into the local job market, Deborah says. Volunteering your service to local community organizations is another good way to begin making contacts and friendships. Personality helps. "We're pretty outgoing," she says. "We have acquired a group of friends here that are all transplants, as well—artists, architects, stone sculptors."

And don't forget determination. "We really jumped through hoops to be able to stay in Fredericksburg—major hoops," Deborah says. They turned their cute little house into a weekend guesthouse and moved temporarily back to Austin so that Deborah could study to become a certified Pilates instructor. "Eventually I will open a studio here in town, but I really like the city, too," she says, "and I actually enjoy going in three days a week to Austin."

Chapter 10:
What Makes a Small Town Tick

Sorting out Clichés

Hollywood has produced many durable impressions about life in Small Town, USA. In the movies, the power center of a clichéd small town is somewhere along Main Street, somewhere between the shoot-em-up saloon full of smoke and whiskey and a pack of outlaws planning to rob the bank; and the bank itself, where the honest and caring manager contends with powers of darkness, usually from out of town, to preserve the accounts of his trusting local customers—sort of like Jimmy Stewart in *It's a Wonderful Life*. The county courthouse is another handy stage for revealing the character and characters of a fictional, everyman's small town.

But the people who make things happen in a real small town probably are not in the saloon or the bank or the courthouse very much. They are in the neighborhoods, schools, and business district, for the most part ordinary people leading ordinary lives.

What makes them exceptional is the way they respond to the community's needs, frequently as volunteers. The opportunity to step forward and provide leadership is perpetual in a small town, because needs are continuous and resources generally in short supply—except for human capital. Some of the people who make a small town tick have enriched the place simply by choosing to move there and helping to preserve the population base, in effect, voting with their feet for the small-town life, and by their presence alone making the place better. Others have familiar roles and responsibilities—the mayor, the newspaper editor, the bankers and business leaders. In this chapter, we meet a few people like that, who tell their stories in their own words.

The Editor

Editing the newspaper is one of the more personally demanding jobs in a small town.

If you do your job well, meaning that you present the whole, unvarnished story of daily life in the community, you're bound to make some people mad as hell at you almost every day you publish. And these are not just nameless, faceless subscribers out in the precincts; these are your neighbors, people you pass on the street or encounter in the supermarket or at church or at the Friday night high school basketball game. If, as editor, you expect to remain in the community for any length of time, you have to find a way to manage the constant tension between doing your job honestly, fairly, and completely, and preserving friendships.

For example, Frank L. Martin, III, editor of *The Daily Quill*, in West Plains, Missouri. Martin was one of several national recipients in November 2000 of the George Award, presented by *George* magazine, which flourished briefly before the untimely death of its founder, John F. Kennedy, Jr. Martin was recognized as "The Bravest Newsman," with the subhead: "Deep in the Ozark Wilderness, Where Extreme Politics Mix With Ever Present Violence, This Journalist Howls Against Bigotry and Racism. A Lot of People Would Like to Silence Him." Several years before he received the George Award, Martin offered insights into his community.

Frank L. Martin III, editor and publisher, *Daily Quill*, West Plains, Missouri

What makes this town different, what gives it, I think, the unique character, is fostered by the fact that early settlers were very poor refugees from other parts of the world, principally Tennessee and Kentucky, who didn't have the wherewithal or the ambition to go further west to good, tillable land. Our agriculture here is limited to livestock because we have almost no topsoil—a red clay soil full of rocks, on which you can't grow anything but grass.

The early settlers moved here from Appalachia only because the spaces were more open. They were very provincial, some would say backward. It was kind of an outlaw area. Jesse James has relatives in the area. Ma Barker's gang used to have a rest area here.

The way it affects life now: We have the same pioneer spirit, the same mind-your-own-business kind of tolerance. But since the '60s a lot of people have moved to the area both to retire and get back to the land, New Age people. The town has taken the best of the ideas that are brought in and managed to embrace them and work them into the culture rather than having them dilute the culture. So, you get the best of the old spirit and best of the new ideas.

A couple of years ago I went to a university-sponsored discussion of the uniqueness of this part of the country. As a group we listed the best and worst traits of the typical Ozark native. Number One on the list of best was the fierce feeling of independence that natives have inherited as a tradition. When we got around to discussing the worst it was the same item: resistance to change. The result is we have something between a fairly stable economy and planned progress. I don't mean mindless Babbittism but a well-reasoned approach to planned growth.

This is one of the few communities I know of its size which retains its youth. As a percentage, you find a lot more young people graduating, working away professionally, and coming back. We have a very interesting group of people in the 40–50 age group who have had diverse experiences but have chosen to come back here and raise their families.

The Mayor

Small towns never seem to have enough money, and for many residents, that's just fine. "Live within your means," they tell elected officials, echoing a bit of rural philosophy. "Make do with what you've got—use it up, wear it out!" they declare in Yankee territory. You hear the same sentiments in Dixie and the rural West. But a funny thing can happen on the way to parsimony in a small town: Someone suggests that a reasonable investment of money (No new taxes!) leveraged by a major investment of ingenuity and voluntary community service (Volunteers are lining up already!) can spell the difference between a ho-hum, second-rate place and a town we can really be proud of.

In the best small towns, ideas like that bubble up all the time. Just ahead in this section, Diane Harrop recalls how things happened in Douglas, Wyoming, when she was mayor. Harrop now consults with community groups in small towns, helping them to identify solutions to local problems. A recent example in Douglas: One group of residents who are interested in establishing a Boys and Girls Club have been frustrated by the lack of a suitable location in town. Another group of residents who want to convert an old, outdoor ice skating rink into an indoor rink have been frustrated because they can't raise enough money.

"Putting the two together made sense to me on a number of levels," Harrop said. "So I pitched the idea to both groups as well as some key local opinion leaders. Everyone has been able to see multiple advantages, and grantors are now taking another look at funding this capital project because of the new collaborative elements involved. The hockey parents are willing to become the initial volunteer base for the B&G Club and see this as an opportunity to draw more kids into their skating programs."

Diane Harrop, former mayor, Douglas, Wyoming

During my term we embarked on several projects that continued to bloom even after I left office. In the past few years, we've completely redone the historic retail street of town. A lot of money went into things you'll never see, like getting rid of old coal chutes. We put in new sidewalks, textured at the corners—it looks like flagstone but it's concrete. We installed ornamental lightposts. It's maybe the most improved street in southeast Wyoming, and served as a visible focal point for a whole community effort during our state's Centennial Year. We also constructed a new entrance to the State Fairgrounds and a railroad interpretive museum—a locomotive and several wonderful old train cars which also house the Douglas Chamber of Commerce.

We are the home of the Jackalope, as you may know. The Jackalope statue used to be in the highway median. Now it is downtown in Centennial Jackalope Square, with picnic tables, nice plants and trees, restrooms. I've noticed for the first time that tourists and out-of-state hunters are spending time walking around downtown. That's the whole idea we had in fixing up the downtown—to make it more inviting and accessible to citizens and visitors alike.

I think Douglas is doing well. I see a return to optimism, and I think that's vital. There was a kind of refusal to look ahead, to take a leap of faith on behalf of ourselves. That happens in small towns—"If it ain't broke, don't fix it." In larger places, people know they have to keep moving or they will fall behind. In small towns, people fool themselves into thinking they can keep things just the same, and that isn't valid. There is no standing still.

I grew up in larger places. I went to college in Lawrence, Kansas. I lived in Boulder and taught outside of Kansas City. In none of those places was I ever really tempted to get involved to change things for the better. I felt swallowed up, simply because the world was so big. I've come to learn in this small place that I have a lot of abilities, that I have a lot to give.

Moms, Dads, Kids

No matter where they live, all kids sooner or later complain, "There's nothing to *do!*" Small-town kids may complain more often because, in fact, there are many fewer options for entertainment, amusement, or sport in a small town compared to a city. There may be only one movie theater, if that; one bowling alley, if that; one "Strip" to cruise with your gang; one strip mall, maybe, on the edge of town, but no mall as in Mall of America. Boring, boring, boring, the kids say. Of course, they could use their imagination and create their own entertainment, though many parents grow uneasy with

impromptu arrangements, especially when teenagers are involved.

At about that point in the conversation, someone may say, "We need a recreational center—a place where kids can have fun with their friends, a place that's handy and safe and inexpensive, maybe even designed by the kids and run by them. A place that kids really like and where parents will know they'll be okay."

Such a place must be on every small town's wish list. A small number of towns— they must be the envy of many others—have found a way to fund and establish a big-name recreational center like a YMCA/YWCA or a Boys and Girls Club. But it's never easy. To plant the idea of a youth center and nurture it through the shaky early stages, a town needs initially a small number of people with the wherewithal and the persistence to stick with the plan and watch it blossom into a program that's popular with kids and well attended. That's how it happened in Brattleboro, Vermont, where a group of parents saw an opportunity to transform an old downtown nightclub into a weekend dance hall and gathering place for teenagers.

Nancy Hagstrom, former president of the teen center in Brattleboro, Vermont

The teens needed a place of their own where they could feel good about themselves and learn they could get high on a good time without chemical assistance. The Teen Center answered that need and provided a fun place to be for over 600 teens every weekend and became a popular hangout during the week. But as the years went by, the popularity of the weekend dances began to wane while the need for after-school pro-

grams became more evident. The Teen Center responded with the introduction of several structured after-school programs to include photography and guitar instruction, SAT classes and tutoring, and peer group mediation as well as alcohol and substance abuse prevention programs. The teens even set up their own hot line.

Then Brattleboro began having problems with skateboarders whizzing through parking lots and down sidewalks. So we built a skate park inside the other half of the mammoth albatross of a building we had acquired. It remains a popular hangout for a lot of enthusiastic athletes.

Our biggest struggle was with finances. Many of the kids we served could not afford to pay for the use of the center or its programs, and we didn't ask them to. The building is huge and expensive to heat, the mortgage was always lurking even though the banks were supportive, the roof leaked, quality staffing was costly. Although we continued to receive grants and help from the Thomas Thompson Trust—and Brattleboro continued to give and give and then give some more, as it always does—we struggled.

The answer came with our charter as a Boys and Girls Club of America. Today the Teen Center has a different name and serves a broader age group. The weekend dances are back and again host hundreds of teens. We have a large study room equipped with computers. After-school programs serve more than 150 kids during the week and include leadership training, photography, skateboarding, the JCPenney Power Hour program, movies, and a variety of other programs created and developed by the fascinating partnership of kids and adults who want to share their time and talents.

Ice Hockey Dad

Scott Cloud, a United Airlines pilot who lives in Northfield, Minnesota, grew up playing ice hockey, as many Minnesota kids do, and his son is following in Dad's footsteps. Ben Cloud plays in the Peewee League—180 or so kids in sixth and seventh grade. Along with kids in the older leagues, they keep the city-owned Northfield Ice Arena humming with games through the winter.

Scott serves on the Hockey Association Board as coordinator of coaches, meaning that he recruits fifteen or sixteen volunteer dads required each season, makes sure they're all certified as ice hockey coaches, and organizes tryouts. All of which sounds like a well-oiled winter recreational machine in a comfortable small town near the Twin Cities—which it is, but the credit goes primarily to the hard work and persistence of town residents and only secondarily to town government.

Scott Cloud recounts how the indoor ice arena came into being. "It was 1976 and I was playing eighth–ninth grade hockey," he said. "About eleven of us guys were really into hockey. We didn't have a high school team at that time and the parents kept pushing for one." But the school district said it had higher priorities.

Enter: private initiative. So that kids could play high school ice hockey, two dads—one a professor at St. Olaf College, in town, and the other a local businessmen—used their own funds to build Northfield's first indoor ice-skating arena. The city later acquired the arena—the place where young Ben Cloud plays hockey today.

The Real Estate Man

Real estate sales people are the unofficial welcoming committee in most small towns. Vested interests aside, the best of them can offer newcomers a pretty good, quick look at a community—and some idea of the price you'll pay to become part of it.

Cap deRochemont, president, C.R. deRochemont Real Estate, Rockland, Maine

Although greater in area than all the other New England states combined, Maine itself is probably a small town. You have an opportunity to really know your fellow townsman for good or bad. There are fewer phonies in small towns than in large cities because it's pretty hard to fool someone where you are well known.

Volunteering your service over and over and over again, that's the price of admission to live in a small town. I think I'm pretty standard. I have served as president of the hospital, president of Rotary, president of the chamber of commerce—again, not because of any unique talents on my part. The burden of responsibility of each of these positions is shared with a rather limited force of people. You're not one in a million. You're one in seventy-nine hundred. Your opportunity for service gives you a chance to be part of the community, not just a spectator.

I served on the board of directors of Camden National Bank for twenty years, a bank that has been recognized as one of the strongest and best-run banks in Maine.

I am living in the same house that has been in the family for 131 years. I live in a typical two-and-a-half story wooden home, converted about 71 years ago from a barn to a residence, with an office on the first floor. For me, this is "world headquarters."

Entrepreneurs

It's cause for celebration when a new business arrives in a small town. The ribbon-cutting is front-page news. The mayor and assorted dignitaries talk about the new enterprise as a significant addition to the local economy, and they thank the entrepreneurs for their vote of confidence in the community. And every word they say is true. In a city setting, the establishment of a new business may be practically invisible; in a small town, it's a measurable change in jobs, tax revenue, community vitality.

Entrepreneurs come to town by various routes. Some are long trails through family history.

Justin Rashid, founder and owner, American Spoon Foods, Petoskey, Michigan

I grew up in Detroit and summered here from an early age, twelve miles east of Petoskey in a lost, forgotten lumber town called Wildwood. It's there I really bonded with this landscape and part of the country. I think if you talk to a lot of people you'd see that pattern. They started to come here to their parents' cottage—and spent the rest of their lives trying to figure out a way to get back.

I moved back sixteen years ago and opened a little roadside produce market. It did very well in the summer and bombed in the winter. One of my customers moved to New York to become a dancer. At the River Cafe, underneath the Brooklyn Bridge, she met Larry Forgione, who was making his reputation as the quintessential American chef. She introduced Larry to me. I started sending him some wild mushrooms and fruits. We both shared the fascination with wild foods. And we started this company, the finest fruit products in the world using Michigan fruits, especially cherries—one of the first companies to demonstrate you could make wonderful gourmet products from domestic produce.

We're a decent-sized company for a small town. We employ about sixty-five people and have four company-owned and two licensed stores and an American Spoon Gelato Café. We mail about 300,000 catalogs a year. Our stuff is sold in Williams-Sonoma, Marshall Field's, fine food stores all over the country. One hundred people go out and pick morel mushrooms for us. Morels that grow in the Midwest are much richer than the ones they get in the Northeast. We sell them for $21 a dried ounce. It takes about twelve ounces of fresh to make one dried ounce.

I grew up in the inner city of Detroit. I dreamed as a kid of living in a town like Petoskey, a real old-fashioned downtown, built on a human scale, intimate, with a little jewel of a city park, perched on a hill overlooking Lake Michigan. The one thing I miss about cities is not just the racial diversity but the cultural diversity that goes along with that of necessity. I grew up with a lot of black people. Petoskey is white—it's very white, except for a number of Ottawa Indians. I grew up in an Arabic family, half

Arabic, on the other side Irish/German. I miss ethnic food and the way we got together in extended families.

Petoskey is a very Christian town and that makes it very conservative. I sometimes wish it wasn't so. But on the other hand, the people here have a real sense of community. Very often in the city, because of diversity you have a lot of conflict. Though I don't know people from as many different ethnic groups, I do know people in all social strata, from all kinds of occupations I would never know if I were living in a city. I like that. People in the city associate with their own. They don't have a clear sense of where they fit into the picture. Small towns are comprehensible communities. My sons and daughter know people in every position. They have a better sense of the architecture of the local society.

My wife and I met at a repertory theater in downtown Detroit. We moved to New York. She was in off-Broadway, commercials, soap operas. I joined the Great Jones Repertory Company, ended up doing Agamemnon *in the Vivian Beaumont Theater, toured abroad. It's a good thing I wasn't more talented or I'd still be in New York or Los Angeles. I lasted three years in New York, then ran screaming to the country.*

My wife and I first got involved in local politics because of our concern about the impacts a proposed bypass could have on the rural character of our community and the prime farmland surrounding our town. She went on to serve on the planning commission and City Council and has been mayor for two years—not something she could have imagined when we moved here. She's won handily in both elections and is really devoted to the job. One of her main interests is working with officials in

Petoskey and surrounding townships to find ways to preserve open space for future generations.

Peter E. Viemeister, author, antiques dealer, activist, in Bedford, Virginia

I had been president of Grumman Data Systems Corporation, then ultimately vice president of Grumman Corporation. I left there when I was fifty, which was 1979. I've gotten into volunteer things in Bedford—chairman of the City/County Museum, officer of the local health foundation.

And I have a small antique book shop and an office in the back, where I write, slowly. I wrote The Historical Diary of Bedford, Virginia, USA. I also wrote Beale Treasure: History of a Mystery. That subject has been on a number of TV channels. My book A History of Aviation: They Were There is 350 pages and 300 photos. Peaks of Otter—Life and Times is about Virginia's most famous mountains--they happen to be in this county. Living in beautiful Bedford, I do business with the nation and the world through my Internet Web site: peterv.com.

The folks here are Democrats and Republicans, but they both believe in family. There tends to be a strong commitment to local churches, probably less than there was fifty years ago but stronger than in urban locations.

I notice that the smaller the town, the more likely it is that you know the other people moving around. You do not have that anonymity that allows you to be rude, hostile, aggressive, pushy. You're kind of on your good behavior. One of the most important goals all towns should have is to recapture the benefits of smallness. That's true not just in communities but in business and industry and government. In smallness you have folks accepting more responsibility for themselves and the outcome of what they do. If that concept could be nurtured in public school and on news programs and woven into TV entertainment, we could go a long way toward being more productive and competitive internationally.

Ultimately it comes back to the economic health of our society and the well-being of people, rooted in manners and basic values and ethics. The only place we hear about that any more is in church.

Postscript: Peter Viemeister selected Bedford, Virginia, as his home town after a methodical search of places based on criteria he believed important:

- Taxes per capita—"I didn't care what kind of taxes they were. If they spend it they've got to collect it one way or another."
- Climate—Not too different from what he was used to in Long Island. But no tornadoes and rare frequency of earthquakes.
- School truancy rate—instead of crime rate.
- Percentage of households that own their homes—"an indication of self-reliance."
- Access to higher education—"on the rationale that culture generally swirls around centers of education."

Chapter 11:

Paying Your Dues: What a Small Town Expects of You

Rules for New Arrivals

In their book *Moving to a Small Town*, Wanda Urbanska and Frank Levering list ten ways to endear yourself to the locals when you move to a small town. Their suggestions are sound advice if you are serious about small-town life. But the list, adapted here, also serves as a reality check on your expectations:

1. Patronize local merchants—do your shopping in town.
2. Never say things are "quaint"—you may sound patronizing.
3. Find common ground with people.
4. Always donate to worthy organizations asking for help.
5. Join clubs and volunteer.
6. Look for opportunities to compliment people.
7. Socialize with local residents.
8. Join a church.
9. Join a country club.
10. Deal with gossip—you can hardly avoid it.

If you are challenged by the thought of joining anything and prefer to call the shots as you see them, those ten commandments may be too heavy a cross to bear. Maybe you should reconsider the advantages of city life. But if you are willing to open up a bit and share your charming inner self with a number of new acquaintances, maybe you should make the effort in a small town. Most of the Urbanska-Levering reminders need no explanation and simply amount to making connections with the local economy and social infrastructure.

Courtesy and tact are particularly important when you are new in town because the locals are sizing you up just as much as you are looking them over. The warning not to call things "quaint" means to avoid pasting that label on a part of town that you view as a charming, old-fashioned feature but which may actually be a source of some embarrassment to local residents who wish they could afford something better. Unpaved streets, for example.

The last item on the list—gossip—may seem odd. Why is gossip a factor in a small town? You may consider it totally unimportant. In fact, your style may be to ignore gossip: Who cares? That attitude is common in cities, where you are one person among hundreds of thousands, and everyone minds his own business. But when you move to a small town, you become one among perhaps several thousand total; but more to the point, one among only a few hundred when you reduce the community of local interest to people who pay close attention to new arrivals in town, and to you in particular.

Naturally, the first question everyone wants to ask is, "Why did you move here?" And oldtimers who do not have a ready answer may invent one, based on fragmentary information about you—or no information at all. Idle speculation is a game everyone can play in a small town. If gossip annoys you, ignore the grapevine. But you'll miss out on a lot of the fun of living in a small town, where the chat group was invented.

Paying Your Dues in Madison, Georgia

Jerry and Margaret Caldwell had lived in Atlanta for thirty-five years, including those exciting years beginning in the 1960s when the Georgia capital was emerging not only as the metropolitan hub of the South but an urban center with star billing nationally and abroad. "It was a wonderful time in Atlanta," said Jerry, a retired IBM executive. In the late 1990s, with the children grown and off on their own, the Caldwells began thinking about another setting for the new period in their lives. "I thought the quality of life might be even better in a small town—maybe a little more convenience, maybe a little less traffic," Jerry said.

Because their kids all had settled in the Atlanta area, there was a good reason for the Caldwells to remain in north central Georgia, too. But where? You might expect the former national marketing director for a prestigious corporation to have a Big Blue exploratory plan to find the perfect small town. Not exactly. Somewhere the Caldwells had heard about Madison from somebody; planning was not like a NASA launch. "We just drove over," said Jerry, recalling his first look at Madison, a charming town with roots in the cotton culture of the early 1800s, a place where plantation owners had built large homes, where live oak trees shade pleasant streets, the town that General Sherman refused to burn on his march to the sea. Many antebellum homes remain. Some are private residences, some are museums.

That was some of the charm for the Caldwells. But the stronger attraction was the people of Madison and the ease of making friendships. "The more people we met here, the more we liked it," Jerry said. Was it hard to make acquaintances? Not at all—just do the usual things like have lunch in a local restaurant, attend a church, drop by a real estate office, and take the initiative. "If you're here you're going to meet people," he said. Almost immediately, the Caldwells found they had a circle of contacts in a pretty little community of about 3,600 people that was absolutely set apart from the nearby metropolis but close enough for easy access. They moved to Madison.

In Atlanta, if you want to be 100 percent anonymous you can be. You can disappear in the crowd, attracting no attention and receiving no assignments. But in Madison, Georgia, as in most small towns, it's very hard to remain anonymous if you have any sense of what's happening in town and how your talents, whatever they are, might serve a need. "You get the feeling, if everything is going to get done, I need to lend a hand," Jerry said.

In two years, he became a member of the governing board of his church, First United Methodist Church, with responsibility for visitation and outreach; the board of the Morgan County Republican Party; and the board of the Madison-Morgan Cultural Center, a converted school building that draws crowds of locals and visitors to a lively continuing program in the visual and performing arts. He also volunteers with Madison in May, an annual 5K race benefiting the local Habitat for Humanity organization.

Is Jerry Caldwell's experience exceptional? Probably. Is he the sort of person—capable, good natured, willing to lend a hand—that many small towns would love to welcome as a new resident? Most certainly.

"Jerry sounds very much like my parents when they arrived here forty years ago," said Preston Small, who grew up in Madison and runs a media production company there, producing programs for radio and TV. He remembers Madison when it was still primarily the hub of a farming community, and everybody came to town on Saturday night, crowding into the central square, and the stores stayed open late, some 'til midnight.

If Madison is a little jewel of a place today, the credit goes to town residents—volunteers and advocates like Preston's parents—who had a vision of the future, people who cared enough to fight to get simple things done, like getting the electric and phone lines buried in downtown Madison, so the clutter of utility poles could be removed, and completely renovating the city park on South Main Street. And planting trees: "Big trees don't grow overnight, and neither do the dogwoods you see down there," Preston said.

His parents had moved to Madison from Charleston, South Carolina, with two things in mind: a small-town environment for their children and a livelihood in the radio business. The Smalls bought the radio station in town, named it WYTH, 1250 AM, and gave it a slogan, "WYTH You in Mind."

Back then, before radio stations sold out to distant corporate owners and surrendered programming decisions to the satellite uplink, when you were custodian of the broadcast voice in a small community, you were automatically in the thick of things. Both for commercial reasons and civic pride, you were deeply involved in community affairs. "In my family we've always volunteered—it's been part of the family code," Preston said. "Because we owned the radio station we were peripherally involved in darn near everything that happened."

One big thing that happened was the arrival of the Interstate highway, I-20. It bypassed Madison several miles south, not surprising considering all the space that big roads need, and not all that far, residents reassured themselves, to preserve a good connection and keep Madison viable on the east-west axis. People did begin to wonder how the new interchange would affect the historic center of town: Would downtown merchants look for greater fortune out on the new highway and leave a graveyard of empty storefronts at the center of town? Such a highway-driven pattern of events is so familiar in small-town history—the Death of Downtown—that it should have become a ballad years ago. Though Madison appeared to be in no immediate danger of such a fate, the significance of I-20 was not lost on community leaders.

So when road planners announced their next big project—to build a bypass around Madison for the town's north-south axis, U.S. 441—local residents immediately sounded a general alarm. They saw how devastating the reduction of traffic through town could be on retailers who depended on a daily flow of paying customers. Step One, Preston said, was for Madison residents, both official and volunteer, to bear down on the state-federal bureaucracy and at least delay any action on the 441 matter—buying time for Madison to take Step Two: recreating the historic town center.

Gradually, as one then another retailer moved to new locations on the highway, some downtown storefronts became professional offices—insurance, real estate, law—and the place began to acquire a totally new look. Stroll around the square today and you see what foresight and determination can produce in the center of a small town: tree-shaded brick sidewalks, gas lamps, gift shops and art galleries, restaurants, and a collection of antique stores that draws visitors from afar.

Anchoring this marvelous array of consumer delights are a few solid institutions: Morgan County Courthouse, circa 1905; the post office; and two banks, including locally owned Bank of Madison, the largest in town.

Meanwhile, along Main Street and adjacent avenues in the heart of town, the Plantation-era mansions passed to the next generation or to new owners, including new arrivals in town, who lovingly restored and preserved the old homes. By good fortune and by design, Madison was becoming very interest-ing to day-trippers out of Atlanta, Athens, Charleston, and other parts of the Southeast. A tourism committee came into being, then a "CVB"—a convention and tourism bureau.

Madison knew exactly what it was doing, said Preston Small: "We're a town that has tourism as opposed to a tourism town. There's a subtle difference." Defining further: "A tourism town tends to be more by design like a Gatlinburg or a Cherokee. There's nothing wrong with that. It's a conscious decision." Madison would rather be known for a number of things besides a pleasant afternoon of antiques shopping.

And Madison doesn't want to be in anyone's pocket. "We have been very fortunate never to have been a one-corporation town," said Marguerite Copelan, director of the Madison CVB. "We have been very balanced, looking for those middle companies that employ 50 to 100 people, that bring in some manager people and (hire) some production and maintenance people." Such a blend places a balanced demand on the Madison economy and avoids overdependence on one megacorporation: "If it goes away, you're just really stuck," the CVB director said.

On the other hand, some recent arrivals in town soon feel stuck in a lifestyle that was not what they had imagined. "Small-town life is not for everyone," Preston said. "There are not as many activities; you are not as anonymous; there's no movie theater."

"And no bowling alley," Marguerite interjected.

"They *thought* they might like to talk to their neighbor going down the street, or to see people they know in the bank, when they find out they like that anonymity a little more than they thought they did," Preston said.

"Or they thought they'd love to be the big fish in the little pond, and they found out the little pond has its own way of doing things," Marguerite said. "Even though the community could accept you, it wasn't looking for a savior—somebody to fix everything. Some people have come and stayed five or six years and moved on."

"In my case," said newcomer Jerry Caldwell, "it's been better than I thought it would be—community, friends, and a sense of fitting in. But I'm not like everyone."

"I think Madison will grow," Jerry continued. "There are going to be too many people like me who are going to see the advantages of a small-town community and decide, if I don't *have* to be in Atlanta, I'm going to get out. Madison is a better place to raise my family and have a sense of community."

Marguerite, the CVB director, thought some new arrivals might even try to commute to jobs in Atlanta, as a small number of Madison residents already do, gritting their teeth for the hour-and-a-half drive during rush hour. But she prefers telecommuters: "Once they spend all that time driving to and from Atlanta, they don't have any time left for local service. To me, that's the death of a community—when you become a commuter community."

For one thing, you miss a lot of fun, said Jerry. He and his wife were doing some interior painting, applying a coat he described as "bright red, almost garish" in a corner of the living room. Hmm—strong statement, they thought. Maybe the furnishings and woodwork would tone the color down.

"That was four o'clock on a Sunday afternoon," Jerry said. "Margaret was shopping in Madison at nine o'clock the next morning and the owner said to her, 'Have y'all done something really wild at your house?'" News travels fast in a small town—and by mysterious means.

Preston Small understands the small-town appeal of knowing people and being known. He has had a number of opportunities to move his media enterprises elsewhere but has chosen to remain in Madison. "It's a great place to come back to," he said. "We used to blow the horn when we hit the county line—and we still do that sometimes."

Finding Your Niche

You can live a quiet, reclusive life in a small town, but that's no fun. A far more satisfying strategy is to find a way to contribute your services to the community. If the town does not notice your arrival and draft you at once, take the initiative, remembering that a small town with good prospects—the kind of place you are looking for—welcomes and depends on a steady influx of contributing members. The best towns are a paradox in that respect: They have the right to be smug about their success and to guard it jealously, slamming the door on newcomers. But they do exactly the opposite, making it easy for new residents to share their special talents, making everyone's life a bit better.

If you arrive in town with school-age kids, or if you have always been active in your church, or if you have an occupation that gives you visibility, you can count on hearing very shortly from someone in town offering you an opportunity for volunteer service. When that happens, consider it a blessing. Say yes.

Index

396.76 Crampton, Norm
CRA Making your move to one of
     America's best
     small towns

DATE DUE

JUN 03 03			
JUN 04 03			
OCT 07 03			